COVER UP

The Watergate in All of Us

Harry S. Dent

Here's Life Publishers

To my wife, Betty
And my children:
    Harry and Nancy Dent
    Dolly, Don and Blake Montgomery
    Ginny, Alton, Joshua, Jonathan and Harrison Brant
    Jack and Tracie Dent

For being used of God to love me and teach me.

Published by
HERE'S LIFE PUBLISHERS, INC.
P. O. Box 1576
San Bernardino, California 92402

HLP Product No. 951301

Library of Congress Cataloging-in-Publication Data
Dent, Harry S., 1930-
    Cover up: the Watergate in all of us.

    1. Water gate Affair, 1972-1974.   2. Man
(Christian theology)   I. Title.
E860.D46   1986   261.7'0973   86-9880
ISBN 0-89840-140-2

Except where otherwise indicated, all Scripture quotations in this book are taken from The Transformer, The New King James Version, © 1985 by Thomas Nelson, Inc., Nashville, Tennessee.

FOR MORE INFORMATION, WRITE:

L.I.F.E. — P.O. Box A399, Sydney South 2000, Australia
Campus Crusade for Christ of Canada — Box 300, Vancouver, B.C. V6C 2X3, Canada
Campus Crusade for Christ — 103 Friar Street, Reading RG1 1EP, Berkshire, England
Lay Institute for Evangelism — P.O. Box 8786, Auckland 3, New Zealand
Great Commission Movement of Nigeria — P.O. Box 500, Jos, Plateau State Nigeria, West Africa
Life Ministry — P.O. Box/Bus 91015, Auckland Park 2006, Republic of South Africa
Campus Crusade for Christ International — Arrowhead Springs, San Bernardino, CA 92414, U.S.A.

Live as free men, but do not use your freedom as a cover-up for evil; live as servants of God (1 Peter 2:16, NIV).

We have spoken freely to you, Corinthians, and opened wide our hearts to you. We are not withholding our affection from you, but you are withholding yours from us. As a fair exchange — I speak as to my children — open wide your hearts also (2 Corinthians 6:11-13, NIV).

CONTENTS

FOREWORD

Cover Up: The Watergate in All of Us eloquently and cogently addresses and answers the most critical questions facing all of mankind. Who am I? What is my mission in the world? Where am I in my relationships, my priorities, my values? What do I believe? Who do I believe? What is it that prods me — like the apostle Paul — to do what I know I should not do and not to do what I know I should do? (Romans 7:15)

My friend Harry Dent has written a fascinating and comprehensive message from a heart opened wide by the power and working of the Holy Spirit of God. The backdrop for answering these vital questions is the biggest political scandal in American history. The author lays the characters and events of Watergate — including his own life — alongside the teachings of the Holy Scriptures from Genesis to The Revelation. He concludes that we are all really Watergaters hiding in varying degrees from God and our fellow-man.

It was his own Watergate experience that prompted Harry to begin a search for the real truth, the real answers to these haunting questions. His former life epitomizes the church leader who means well but does not know well and thus does not do well in the light of God's eternal purpose for man.

Amazingly, the change in the life of another Nixon White House special counsel, Chuck Colson, struck the spark that lit the lamp of this fellow special counsel who eventually became an outstanding lay speaker, teacher, and writer for the glory of God and the good of man.

It was only when Harry Dent came face to face with the sin in his own soul that he really began to focus on what the writer of Hebrews calls that "so great a salvation." This is how Harry discovered the answers to these vital questions.

The key he found was an open heart submitted to God's truth and His purpose for Harry's life. He has poured this open heart full of God's truths onto these pages for all of us, inside and outside the church, to ponder. His passion today is to be a modern-day Ezekiel, a watchman for Jesus Christ. His cry is the same as that of the apostle Paul to the church at Corinth:

> We have spoken freely to you, Corinthians, and opened wide our hearts to you...open wide your hearts also.
>
> (2 Corinthians 6:11-13, NIV)

This book is a strong call to self-examination, commitment, service and transparency. I commend to you the teachings and the open heart of this author. And I challenge you to open wide your own hearts as you study through what could be one of the greatest challenges to your life, whatever your relationship to God may be.

Richard C. Halverson
Chaplain
United States Senate
May, 1986

PREFACE

Why another book on Watergate? And how in the world can one of the biggest political scandals in American history fit into, of all books, the Holy Bible? There are several answers.

First, the real genesis (or beginning) of the fall of the Administration of the thirty-seventh President of the United States of America has never been fully revealed, especially from its spiritual perspective.

Second, the basic misdeeds of Watergate are recorded first in the Bible in Genesis, chapter three, and were committed by the world's original father and mother, Adam and Eve. I call this the first "Watergate."

Third, the Bible is a book that reports on many "Watergates," from the beginning of man in Genesis to the last New Testament books written, and it forecasts many more, such as those in your life and mine.

Fourth, had the people involved in Watergate understood and been committed to the teachings of the Bible, it is very unlikely that there would have been a Watergate scandal.

Fifth, the Bible teaches not only how to perceive and handle potential Watergates, but also how to deal with them after they occur and how to profit from their lessons.

Therefore, the thesis of this book is that all of mankind needs to know the Holy Bible and live by its tenets not only to get to Heaven, and not only to help others get to Heaven, but also to be prepared to meet and cope with the Watergates of life. Any Watergate in our lives is a sudden confrontation with an event or experience which contains the potential — imagined or real — for destruction of our personal honor, worth, safety or well-being, or that of our family. Such an event could be death, illness, disability, bankruptcy, poverty, or the loss of love, security or status.

Are you prepared to meet and cope with the Watergates of your life?

If the Bible is true — and with this writer that is a given — then most of the people in this world will be unprepared to meet the Watergates in their lives. Also, every person will face accountability at that ultimate Watergate: the day when judgment is passed on what we believed and what we did with our beliefs, and our lives, on earth.

This book has been written to prepare people to meet the Watergates of their lives and the ultimate Watergate of Judgment

Day. Scriptural records of actual and, in some cases, symbolic life experiences of biblical characters and events are visual aids given for our benefit. Their purpose is to demonstrate to us the moral lessons from both the misdeeds and good deeds of the past. The principal problem in history is man. According to that famous writer, George Bernard Shaw, "The only thing we learn from history is that men never learn from history."[1]

I am not sure that we have learned much from the history lessons available to us in Watergate. There has been little real change in political, corporate, social or individual behavior in our nation. While the Congress has passed some laws to prevent Watergates in the future, there is a cry now to repeal some of those laws. In many cases they either are working too well and thus becoming too restrictive, or they are prompting more ingenious means of circumvention.

This book presents another approach to Watergate preventives and antidotes. This "new" approach is as old as the New Testament. The purpose of the events and teachings in the New Testament — from the Gospel of Matthew to the book of Revelation — is to show a new way for man to live in righteousness, with right conduct and behavior so he can have peaceful fellowship and harmony with his creator and his fellowman. Creating more laws will not accomplish that. What is required is the re-creation of people with changed, new hearts (wills) to issue voluntarily into right conduct, right relationships and right decision-making. The biblical approach teaches us to behave and to do right because we love God as He loves us — unconditionally. Jesus Christ called this *the law of love.*

> But when the Pharisees heard that He had silenced the Sadducees, they gathered together. Then one of them, a lawyer, asked Him a question, testing Him, and saying, "Teacher, which is the great commandment in the law?"
>
> Jesus said to him, " 'You shall love the Lord your God with all your heart, with all your soul, and with all your mind.' This is the first and great commandment. And the second is like it: 'You shall love your neighbor as yourself.' On these two commandments hang all the Law and the Prophets" (Matthew 22:34-40).

The premise of this book is: Our beliefs determine our attitudes, and our attitudes determine our actions and thus our conduct and course in life. Let me take you on an exciting journey, a vital quest in search of truth which I personally traveled as a consequence of my own Watergate.

It has been years since the covert break-in at the Watergate condominium-office complex was uncovered. Since 1972, much water has flowed past Watergate on the beautiful Potomac River that separates the capital city and the bedroom communities on the Virginia side of the District of Columbia.

The name Watergate was intended to be a pleasing and prestigious name for a Roman Catholic investment in Washington, D.C., next door to the John F. Kennedy Center for the Performing Arts. It comes right out of Scripture and the Holy Land. In the book of Nehemiah we find the name "water gate" used in chapters three and eight. Interestingly, Nehemiah was himself a political leader, the governor of Judea. He rebuilt the walls of Jerusalem, repairing and rebuilding also all of the gates into the city, of which the "water gate" was one. Ironically, a spiritual revival took place in front of the water gate of the city in Nehemiah's time. One of the purposes of this book is to explore whether a spiritual revival has come out of our 1972 Watergate.

Also, it is my prayer that our Lord will use this book to cause you honestly to re-examine your life, your values, your purpose and your understanding of truth — no matter who you are or where you are spiritually. As Socrates said centuries ago, "The unexamined life is not worth living."

I thank God that He, by many means, has "waked and shaked" me to re-examine my life under His divine guidance.

CHAPTER I

MAN'S WATERGATES IN LIFE

Though the mills of God grind slowly, yet they grind exceeding small;
Though with patience stands He watching, with exactness grinds He all.

Henry Wadsworth Longfellow[1]

The year 1969 is one I will never forget; a dream had become a reality. The thirty-seventh President of the United States of America was inaugurated on January 20 and I was there as a member of his team. My job as special counsel to the President was made to order: the President's coordinator for political liaison to the Republican Party across the country. Politics was my first love and the lord of my life.

Each member of the Nixon White House staff could sense the awesome power and responsibility of loyal service to the man whom our Chief of Staff, H.R. (Bob) Haldeman, said was "the most important man in the world." We owed to President Richard Nixon our total fealty. We were the only members of the Nixon Administration who answered only to the President. "Don't worry about your communications to the President," Haldeman told us. "Be specific and brief; leave nothing to his imagination. You'll be covered by Executive Privilege."

Then the crew-cut and stern Haldeman tacked on this command: "If any of you cannot give the President your full loyalty, there's the door! You can go back to where you came from! Any questions?" No one moved for the door or raised any questions. Harry Dent was not about to return to St. Matthews, South Carolina. Just as this was the President's moment, this was also my moment. Power was a big part of the White House experience and I was to relish it for four years. But there were also profile, prestige and the privilege of being teamed with all the President's men and the President himself in saving our country, our freedoms and the world from the forces of collectivism and dictatorship at home and abroad. To me this was a crusade that could help my personal cause as well, and that of my family. We were involved in what our leader called "a cause bigger than ourselves." Eight years of President Nixon could make the difference between peace and freedom on the one hand and war and servitude on the other. We considered him to be the best-prepared political leader ever to take the reins of the United States government with all of the powers vested therein as the foremost nation of the world.

At the end of 1968, my wife, Betty, was crushed emotionally when she learned by accident that I had accepted the job with the President-elect without consulting her or the children. I promised her that I would stay just one year. I would commute to Washington and not disturb the family, since three of our four children were in high school. Nor would we sell our new home. I just had to have this White House experience, even if only for one year. I knew there would be nothing quite like it.

Six years later, on December 11, 1974, I stood before a Watergate judge in the United States District Court for the District of Columbia, facing what appeared to be the end of my journey to the top of the world. The courtroom was packed with news reporters ready to write the political obituary of another Nixon man heading to jail and disgrace. Betty and our daughter Dolly were there also, fearing the worst.

My only consolation that morning was that the charge against me was a minor technicality that actually had nothing to do with Watergate. But the public, and the history books, would never comprehend this distinction — after all, it was the Special Watergate Prosecution Force that was bringing the charge.

Some of the highest officials in government already had been found guilty of conspiracy, obstruction of justice, and perjury. The President had resigned. Watergate casualties already included such people as Attorney General John Mitchell, Attorney General Richard Kleindienst, Commerce Secretary Maurice Stans, White House Chief of Staff Bob Haldeman, Chief Domestic Adviser John Ehrlichman, Special Counsel Charles Colson, Special Assistant Jeb Magruder, Counsel John Dean, and Special Counsel Egil Krogh. Now Harry Dent's name would be added to the Watergate trash heap.

What had happened? How had all of our good intentions, great visions and hard work come to this despicable end? Who could have imagined such a tangled mess? It even included the resignation of Vice President Spiro T. Agnew in another, non-Watergate-related, crime.

It wasn't until several years later, in 1978 when I came face to face with the real Harry Dent, that I began to find answers and began to understand the real problem of Watergate. I was by then immersed in a study of the Holy Bible, searching for the truth about both God and man. Was Jesus really God? Is man just stupid or does man have a basic character fault?

At the time I didn't understand why I had been led to the beginning of the Bible to seek these answers. But there they were, right up front in Genesis, the book of beginnings. Genesis reported that there was more than one person in the Godhead of creation and that a Messiah was promised to destroy man's nemesis, the one who introduced into the world man's basic problem — sin. What was man's sin? The breaking of the law and the efforts to cover up the law-breaking.

What was the basis of man's determination to flout God's authority? Man's pride. His selfishness. It was man's decision to be unlike God in righteousness but "like God" — as the serpent had suggested he could be — in power. The Lord began focusing my vision now so that the more I studied God's Handbook for Life, the more God's perspective became my perspective and the more I could perceive the real genesis of Watergate. It was with us as it was with Adam and Eve in the Garden of Eden. Man had taken a high view of himself and a low view of God.

Maybe this is what happened to all of us in the Nixon Watergate tragedy. Jeb Magruder had said, "I lost my moral compass." Was it a moral compass or God's compass? Had we lost God's direction and plan for His created human beings?

The correlatives between what happened to man in Genesis 3 and in the Nixon Watergate are most enlightening for study. The parallels of Adam and Eve in the Garden of Eden, the Nixon White House, and the life-wrenching experiences that take place in every family and life, contain some rich teaching for everyone.

In the late spring of 1972, the Administration of President Richard M. Nixon was well into its campaign for four more years. The campaign slogan was "Nixon now — more than ever." The 1968 campaign slogan, "Nixon's the one," would come back to haunt the 1972 re-election campaign after the fateful day, June 17, 1972, when Washington, D.C., police arrested four Cubans and one American burglarizing the offices of the Democratic National Committee at the Watergate condominium and office complex on the Potomac River. The joke of the day became: "Nixon's the one!"

Burglary is not an uncommon crime. But there turned out to be an unusual twist to this breaking of the law in the nation's capital city. These burglars were connected to the Committee to Re-elect the President.

The Nixon White House sought to handle what we called a "PR" problem, but it appeared that every time a decision button was pushed the computer spat out not only the wrong answer but the diametrically opposite course of action than should have been implemented.

The scene turned into a circus. Democrats, the news media and all the assorted "enemies" of Richard Nixon seemed to enjoy mauling the Nixonites. The arena was national television, with its klieg lights, covering the United States Senate's Watergate hearings. The audience was the up to 100 million people who gawked at TV sets in barber and beauty shops and in their homes and their offices. Following the United States Senate hearings came various court trials in the capital city and more television coverage. Later, the United States House of Representatives would have its day, in the summer of 1974, as it held hearings on impeaching the President. Loyal Nixonites were seen on television and in the criminal courts pointing their fingers at one another and even at the most untouchable of all, the President of the United States of America. Nixon became intensely absorbed with his own survival and the fates of his closest friends in the Administration, John Mitchell, Bob Haldeman and John Ehrlichman. Nixon has a keen intellect, a strong sense of reality about why people do what they do, and he had a determined drive to win and to win big. I believe he had the best interest of the security and well-being of his country at the core of his heart.

Yet at the bottom of Nixon's weaknesses was his deep sense of personal insecurity and a passionate obsession with his "enemies." The insecurity problem gave birth to the enemies problem and to another difficulty — Nixon's supererogatory impulse. This "supererogatory impulse or compulsion to try too hard, to overdo," helped to pave the way for the Watergate disaster. It was telegraphed down the line from the President to Haldeman and out to the rest of the Nixon White House and throughout the Administration. The message was clear: Turn on every available resource. We were commanded to win at all costs and to be totally loyal.

Added to these key factors in the fall of the Nixon White House — the insecurity, the enemies obsession and the supererogatory impulse — was the tunnel vision at the top of our staff.

In the campaign of 1972, we on the staff knew we had a

strong man with a strong program and a strong, fighting heart. The President had handicaps, but we saw those as being a Democratic Congress and a news media stacked with reporters who still harbored a grudge against Nixon for his unveiling of Alger Hiss as the Communist and perjurer we knew him to be. What our leader needed, we felt, was not just another squeaker victory in 1972 but a mighty mandate to change the nation's domestic policies. The turn-around would come through getting control of the old Franklin D. Roosevelt bureaucracy. Then, the Nixon team would seal this mandate with a new majority under the leadership of John B. Connally (then our Democratic Treasury Secretary). We would give the country eight years of Nixon and eight years of Connally in command of the United States Government.

No one believed in this vision and dream more than I. The only limitations for me were my old Boy Scout training and commitment to the code of honor. Although I was willing to push the edges of that code of honor for this great cause, I did not want to lose my honor and, as Commerce Secretary Maurice Stans later stated, "my good name." My grandfather, W.P. Prickett, had impressed on me the biblical injunction that a "good name is rather to be chosen than great riches..." (Proverbs 22:1, KJV). And my old Scoutmaster and Methodist lay minister, the late L.R. Kirk, had convinced me that the Boy Scout honor and laws were never to be ignored, especially by an Eagle Scout. Also, I felt God was watching me, although at the time I did not really understand this. I would ask God generally to forgive "my sins of omission and commission," but without full confession or real repentance.

Our Nixon team meant well, but our Nixon team was not prepared to face and handle Watergate. The only way seemed to be with blue smoke and mirrors. This was the way the advance-man mentality had worked: Use illusion to cover up the reality. That's the way it works in our personal Watergates also.

Advance men were daring young men who made things happen on presidential or election campaign travels. They were much like side-show barkers. Since the public wanted a show, they would get one on site and on the television news. Make things appear to be what they are not. The aim was to produce huge crowds with wildly cheering people praising and idolizing the leader, creating an illusion that the leader had more power, more praise, more prestige than he actually had, in order to advance his ends. The cuter the tricks employed in driving the crowds into a frenzy, the more the advance men win favor from on high. It's all a matter of good "public relations" and of helping one another up the ladder of success.

What the Nixon White House image and illusion makers saw in the Watergate break-in was a "PR" problem that had to be contained and repaired. How easy it had been to fix the problems in the election campaigns. The blue smoke and mirrors were even more available now that the levers of power were at hand. And the Federal Bureau of Investigation and the Central Intelligence Agency had been handling such matters for years *under cover.* If the FBI director could use covert activities in the name of internal security, and the CIA director could do likewise in the name of national security, why couldn't the White House do the same in the names of both internal and national security? After all, previous Administrations had engaged in wiretaps and "black bag" jobs (breaking and entering), so a cover-up, fix-it operation here would meet the precedents already set.

At the Pierre Hotel in late 1968, FBI Director J. Edgar Hoover had confided to President-elect Nixon information about political use of the FBI for wiretapping purposes against Nixon and others. The tapping of Dr. Martin Luther King by then Attorney General Robert Kennedy had become common knowledge all over Washington. J. Edgar Hoover's aide, William Sullivan, wrote, "To my memory the two administrations which used the FBI most for political purposes were Mr. Roosevelt's and Mr. Johnson's."[2] Covert operations in the government were becoming more and more prevalent, even for some political purposes.

The measure used by the Nixon Watergate people is the one we often employ in our own lives. We go by the standards set by man rather than those set by God. Almost everyone else doing something does not justify you or me in doing it too. The Bible teaches that God holds each of us accountable to His standards, not to ours. Jesus rebuked the apostle Peter for this fault.

> But He turned and said to Peter, "Get behind Me, Satan! You are an offense to Me, for you are not mindful of the things of God, but the things of men" (Matthew 16:23).

The first step in the Watergate debacle was the determination to set up a political intelligence-gathering operation by the Committee to Re-elect the President. The Watergate books establish that plans for funding this operation were approved on March 31,1972, at Key Biscayne, Florida, the President's vacation compound near Miami. Twice previously John Mitchell had disapproved what came to be called the Liddy espionage plan. In his book, *An American Life*, Jeb Magruder, Mitchell's campaign deputy, reports that Mitchell approved the plan on third consideration "only reluctantly." Magruder tabbed it "another of what I called his throwaway decisions, made under pressure to please the White House."[3] Mitchell still denies he ever approved the Watergate break-in.

Magruder gave three reasons for approval of the disastrous Liddy plan.

1. Gordon Liddy had asked for a much more expensive and wilder plan involving an "elaborate call girl/kidnapping/mugging/ sabotage/wiretapping scheme...he asked for the whole loaf when he was quite content to settle for half or even a quarter."

2. "Mitchell was operating under tremendous pressure." The former Attorney General was in the midst of an investigation in which a question was raised (but never acted on) about his having committed perjury. And, "Mitchell was affected by the terrible strain imposed on him by his wife."

3. "Finally, Liddy's plan was approved because of the climate of fear and suspicion that had grown up in the White House, an atmosphere that started with the President himself and reached us through Haldeman and Colson and others, one that came to affect all our thinking, so that decisions that now seem insane seemed at the time to be rational. It was all but impossible not to get caught up in the 'enemies' mentality." Magruder added, "We wanted to win the election and we wanted to win it big."[3]

The man in charge of the Liddy plan was George Gordon Liddy. He was a former FBI agent who never got over the fantasies of cloak-and-dagger operations. The dust cover on his book, *Will*, in which he tells almost everything about the Liddy plan and Watergate break-in, says "G. Gordon Liddy is different." This is quite an understatement. Read *Will*, and you will see what an unusual character this Gordon Liddy is. By the way, I believe that he is telling the truth.

In February, 1973, President Nixon told me — and evidently many others — that John Mitchell's wife, Martha, was in effect the cause of Watergate because she had so distracted Mitchell with her emotional, drinking and talking-to-reporters problems. I believe that a particular key to what happened to ignite the fuse that resulted in Watergate was the horrible misjudgment in bringing Gordon Liddy into the campaign and putting him in command of political espionage and "black bag" jobs. In their books on Watergate, each Nixon man reveals horror stories about Gordon Liddy. Even more is unveiled by Liddy himself in his book, *Will, the Autobiography of G. Gordon Liddy*.[4]

I would extend this bad judgment to the selections of E. Howard Hunt and James W. McCord, Jr. All three of these were under-cover operatives — Liddy and McCord for the Federal Bureau of Investigation and McCord and Hunt for the Central Intelligence Agency.

For all his daring, Gordon Liddy was an amateur as a James Bond-type covert operator. The break-in at the psychiatric office of Dr. Lewis Fielding in Beverly Hills, California, on September 3, 1971, yielded no fruit for the White House. It was turned against the White House because of the braggadocio of Gordon Liddy and Howard Hunt on their return from their attempt to embarrass another Nixon enemy, Dr. Daniel Ellsberg. This was the man who informed the news media of the "Pentagon Papers," secret Vietnam War decisions under Presidents John Kennedy and Lyndon Johnson. Nixon and Dr. Henry Kissinger believed the revelation of this national security information by Kissinger's former associate was harmful to their conduct of the Vietnam War and their efforts to resolve the unpopular and costly conflict peacefully.

Flying back to Washington, Liddy and his fellow break-in cohort, Howard Hunt, displayed to airline cabin attendants pictures of the two of them with disguises outside the office of Dr. Fielding. They bragged to the young ladies about their black bag exploit. Later, these two ladies identified Liddy and Hunt to the Watergate investigators. As a result of this ill-handled break-in, several people went to jail — Charles Colson, John Ehrlichman, Egil Krogh, and Liddy and Hunt, among others. Then, the Watergate break-ins in May and June, 1972, also failed and sent even more people to jail and forced the President from office.

Why did the Watergate burglars break into Democratic Party headquarters, and how were they apprehended by the District of Columbia police? First, the Liddy burglar team twice broke into the offices of Democratic Chairman Larry O'Brien at the Watergate complex. The first entry was on May 28, 1972. Liddy quotes Magruder as asking him: "How about putting a bug in O'Brien's office?" He says Magruder then emphasized: "Get in there as soon as you can, Gordon. It's important."[5]

Why O'Brien? That's a long story with many possible answers.

O'Brien was the most articulate Democratic spokesman against Republican personalities and causes. Also, he had been on a heavy retainer fee from the mysterious billionaire Howard Hughes. Hughes gave money to both political sides. The Watergate investigations revealed that he had given $100,000 in cash to Nixon via Bebe Rebozo. Did O'Brien know this because of his representation of Hughes? And would not O'Brien be embarrassed by publication of his retainer from Hughes? Nixon believed he had been defeated in the 1960 and 1962 elections because the Democrats had made much of a Hughes loan to Nixon's brother Donald.

Now he was deeply concerned that the revelation and exploitation of the new Hughes cash gift could doom his presidency.

According to a 1985 book, *Citizen Highes,* it was this paranoia by Nixon and his obsession with the O'Brien retainer that indeed ignited the Watergate break-in and scandal. Using thousands of secret Hughes papers, interviews and government documents, author Michael Drosnin claims to have provided the answer to the Watergate riddle:

> New information diclosed in this book now makes it clear that Nixon inspired the break-in in a desperate attempt to cover up the Hughes connection.[6]

The first entry proved to be a failure. The O'Brien bug did not work. The other tap, on the phone of an O'Brien subordinate, did work. It produced primarily romantic gossip.

So, on June 9, according to Liddy, Magruder told him to make another entry into O'Brien's office. This time they were to fix the non-working phone tap.[7] Also, Liddy says that he was told that the burglars were to photograph the files in O'Brien's desk. Liddy writes: "The purpose of the second Watergate break-in was to find out what O'Brien had of derogatory nature about us, not for us to get something on him or the Democrats."[8]

In the course of the break-in, Liddy made and permitted to be made several mistakes. The first entry door was taped in such a way that the tape over the lock could be seen. It was discovered by a guard and removed. Then, James McCord again taped the door the wrong way after Liddy decided the guard would not be smart enough to figure out the break-in. After the entry, McCord did not remove the tape. So the guard found the tape again. He wasn't as dumb as Liddy! He called the police. In his book, Liddy called this series of miscues "fatal."[9]

The blunders continued while the burglars were in O'Brien's office filming his desk files. The lookout across the street at the

Howard Johnson Motel warned by radio that there were flashlights on the eighth floor. Liddy was not concerned.[10] Another radio transmission did not disturb Liddy and Hunt. Then, a third transmission asked, "Hey, any of our guys wearing hippy clothes?"

"It was only then that Hunt and I realized that something was very wrong," Liddy reports in his book.

Another transmission ended with the exasperated cry, "It looks like...guns! They've got guns. It's trouble!"

Finally there came the first and final transmission from the entry team. "A whispered voice said, simply and calmly: 'They got us.'" And, with that, the first curtain began to fall on the Nixon Administration. It took more than two years for the final curtain to drop. But it did, on August 9, 1974, when, for the first time in American history a President resigned. A month later Nixon accepted a pardon for conspiring to cover up and thus obstructing justice in the case of the ill-fated burglary of June 17, 1972.

No one, not the entry team, the espionage leaders, the CREEP (Committee to Re-elect the President) officials who had approved covert operations, the White House staff or even the President himself, was prepared for the Watergate of his life. They had planned how to win but not how to lose.

In the White House the acceptable synonym for cover-up was "containment." I wonder what Adam and Eve would have called their cover-up? Possibly the fig-leaf syndrome. That's what they used to cover up their "Watergate." They had been tempted to disobey God. Selfishly, they tasted fruit from the forbidden tree for it "was good for food...it was pleasant to the eyes, and a tree desirable to make one wise" (Genesis 3:6). But they suddenly realized they were in trouble; they had transgressed the law of God, and their cover-up was immediate and automatic, just as Jeb Magruder described the one in Nixon's Watergate. They thought of nothing else but to cover their shame and guilt which was shown by their realization of their nakedness. Now they had crossed from the line of obedience to the will of God to that of disobedience. They could now be "like God" as the tempter had assured them. But, oh, if they could just back up and reject the advice of Satan, as they should have in the beginning. Instead they followed him further, compounding the first crime. There next came perjury, stonewalling, conspiracy, obstruction of justice, blaming others, etc. Then came the judgment of God. When this happened they were pushed out of the garden of paradise into the world of work and death.

The story of Watergate is a replay, thousands of years later, of the Garden of Eden. But, as in the garden, the creator has opened up a way for present day "Watergaters" to get back into a right relationship with Him. The Bible has a precious term for this: God's grace. This means that God loves His creatures so much that He will welcome the errant lawbreakers back into His fold. We have the only secure hiding place available — "with Christ in God" (Colossians 3:3).

Charles Colson provides the essence of this teaching:

> Watergate's lessons ought to remind us of who we are — and who He is. And that should not make us cynics, but should drive us into the arms of the living God. If so, Watergate anniversaries should always be occasions to sing anew the words of the Psalmist: "It is better to take refuge in the Lord than to trust in princes."[11]

There is a way back to God. Jesus Christ describes the way back: "Narrow is the gate and difficult is the way which leads to life" (Matthew 7:14).

Follow me as we discover the purpose of God's highest creation — man and woman — our nature as human beings, the problem with our nature and the great provision God has set before us to remedy this problem. We will find the answer in the old and new lives of many characters of biblical fame and Watergate infamy.

CHAPTER II

MAN'S AUTOBIOGRAPHY IN GENESIS 3

There I was, chairman of the White House prayer breakfast group, as lost as Satan and didn't realize it.

Harry S. Dent

There are 1,178 chapters in the Bible, many of which are great chapters of truth and penetrating reality. The late Dr. G. Campbell Morgan of Westminster Chapel in London, along with a Bible study class, chose 49 of them and Dr. Morgan wrote about them in his book, *Great Chapters of the Bible.* One of the chapters he wrote about was Genesis 3.

I have chosen to write this book around Genesis 3 because this is the most important chapter in the Bible for me. Through it God spoke to me most meaningfully in my life. I was on a spiritual journey seeking the meaning of all I had experienced and learned in this world and had begun my own personal study of the Bible with Genesis, chapter 1. In this narrative on the creation of the world and the first man and woman, I perceived God's purpose for man and thus man's meaning in this life. Then in Genesis 3, I came face to face with the real Harry Dent. It was as if God grabbed me by my collar, pulled me into the study, and showed me how these great truths about the nature and problems of man applied to my own life. At age forty-eight, I came to realize beyond any reasonable doubt (the standard of proof required for conviction in a criminal case) that attorney Harry Dent was guilty of the original sin against God. Reasonable doubt disappeared when I began reading books and commentaries explaining the teachings of Genesis 3 in down-to-earth terms, with illustrations and examples that I could understand and accept.

The first book I examined was A.W. Tozer's *The Pursuit of God.* On page 11, Dr. Tozer hit me with a very simple but profound truth. He wrote, "We pursue God because...He has first put an urge within us that spurs us to the pursuit. 'No man can come to me,' said our Lord, 'except the Father which hath sent me draw him'."[1] Clearly the Father had forged in me an insatiable hunger for truth. And He directed my quest to the Holy Bible.

Dr. Tozer's writings showed me that the reason I had not seen the real Harry Dent previously was "the presence of a veil in our hearts." He described it as "the veil of our fleshly fallen nature living on, unjudged within us, uncrucified. and unrepudiated. It is the close-woven veil of the self-life which we have never truly acknowledged, of which we have been secretly ashamed, and which for these reasons we have never brought to the judgment of the cross." He called it an "opaque" veil. He said, "It is woven of the fine threads of the self-life, the hyphenated sins of the human spirit." These self-sins he listed are: "self-righteousness, self-pity, self-confidence, self-sufficiency, self-admiration, self-love, and a host of others like them." "They are not something we do," he wrote; "they are something we are, and therein lies their subtlety and their power."[2]

In reading through Genesis 3, I had come to realize that the problem Adam and Eve experienced with our creator was a difference of opinion as to authority. God had permitted them to eat of any tree in the Garden of Eden except one. He had set up a test of obedience. Eve, and then Adam, made a conscious decision to heed the advice of another, a crafty, subtle serpent. The serpent suggested to them that the forbidden tree was "good for food," "pleasant to the eyes," and "desirable to make one wise" (Genesis 3:6). So, they did what they selfishly wanted to do as against what God wanted and, indeed, ordered them not to do. It was the authority question and the selfish response which caught my attention. Now Dr. Tozer was more explicitly defining selfishness for me, and God was pointing Dr. Tozer's arrow right at my heart, the center of my strong will.

Dr. Tozer told me that "self is the opaque veil that hides the face of God from us." He said this veil "can be removed only in spiritual experience, never by mere instruction." Then he warned against "tinkering with our inner life, hoping ourselves to rend the veil."

"There must be a work of God in destruction before we are free," he proclaimed. He added: "Our part is to yield and trust. We must confess, forsake, repudiate the self-life, and then reckon it crucified."[3]

I had never quite heard God's message in this way. Dr. Tozer and Genesis 3 had punctured my strong will. Why now? Because God had set up a series of critical events in my forty-eight-year-old life to send me searching for reality. I had been thrust through the very inner recesses of my heart and soul by something "living and powerful, and sharper than any two-edged sword, piercing even to the division of soul and spirit, and of joints and marrow, and is a discerner of the thoughts and intents of the heart" (Hebrews 4:12). What is that sword? It is the Word of God wielded by the Spirit of God.

Dr. Tozer not only was used of God to define the condition of my inner life — the real Harry Dent — but he also spelled out for me the meaning of reality. He wrote: "I mean that which has existence apart from any idea any mind may have of it, and which would exist if there were no mind anywhere to entertain a thought of it. That which is real has being in itself. It does not depend upon the observer for its validity."[4]

When I finished reading Tozer's valuable little book, several others, and God's big Book, I came to comprehend that God is Truth and Reality. I knew I needed His supernatural work to rip that veil from my heart. God used Ananias in Damascus nearly two-thousand years ago to give spiritual sight to Paul. "Immediately there fell from his [Paul's] eyes something like scales, and he received his sight at once; and he arose and was baptized" (Acts 9:18). Spiritual sight is seeing God's perspective and will, not just man's. In my life the scales of pride began to fall away, and I began receiving double vision — God's perspective as well as my view for the decisions of life. God's view started becoming my view.

Previously I would check in with God when I needed Him. I was unfocused and uncommitted. After God had served my purpose, I put Him back on "hold" until I got myself in another bind.

God used another book to reveal more of the truth of Genesis 3 to me, *The God-Players* by Earl Jabay. This little-noted Army officer gave me another insight into the story of Adam and Eve and further revealed to me the real Harry Dent. He explained that what man really wants is to be "in the position of God, the Divine Spirit." Jabay says that in the fall and ever since, man has succumbed to the same siren song the serpent has always used: "You will be like God." Jabay writes, "Ever since the fall, man has schemed, plotted, convinced, and even murdered [the Son of God] in his attempt to be positioned in a place which rightfully belongs to the Ultimate Spirit."[5] Again, I could see Harry here, king of my own hill and heart.

I came to realize that I had been playing God, reigning on the throne of my own life in rebellion against God's inherent authority to be the Lord of my life. That is the same mistake Adam and Eve made. The basic question I found running all through Scripture is this: "Who is Lord, God or man?" This question permeates all of life. It determines the outcome of man's decisions, his choices, even his world view.

Man must have a belief system, values for life and priorities as to who and what gets his attention first and most often. I now see that all of this derives from the first choice man makes: Who is Lord? Who has the authority? Who is accountable? Adam and Eve were the first sinners because they were the first to play God. All sinners are God-players.

In February 1978, I was beginning to see the real Harry Dent as a sinner. Previously I had seen myself as a pretty nice fellow. *Time* magazine (July 11, 1969) portrayed me as a rather good guy. They saw me as one who did not smoke, drink, cuss, chew and who chased but one woman — my wife, Betty. That was my idea of a righteous man, evidently — a self-righteous man. After all, I had been a church member since age thirteen, when I joined First Baptist Church in my home town of St. Matthews, South Carolina, because it was time to join and "the thing to do."

I had been faithful in church and Sunday school attendance. In fact, I had spent four years at a Christian college. There I received the college's highest award, the Founder's Medal, given annually on vote of the faculty and senior class members to "that student most nearly approximating this institution's ideals for young manhood." Also I had been a Boy Scout with the highest award, the rank of Eagle. I had reason to feel good about myself.

In addition to all this, I had established a prayer breakfast group for staff members in the United States Senate. I worked there as chief aide to U.S. Senator Strom Thurmond of South Carolina from 1955 to 1965. The senator and approximately one-third of the Senate membership attended their own weekly prayer breakfast. So I modeled the staff breakfast after theirs.

When I served in the Nixon White House as Special Counsel to the President, I again formed a prayer breakfast group. I served as chairman for the four years I was in the White House, from January 1969 to January 1973.

Also, I had been a Sunday school teacher, Sunday school superintendent, a deacon, church trustee and stewardship chairman. Who could do more than all this? No wonder I was becoming more and more self-righteous. I deserved that accolade from *Time,* I thought. This is how the Pharisees had similarly reasoned about their works of self-righteousness in Jesus' day.

In February, 1978, I settled the question of who would be

the Lord of my life. Jesus Christ took command of my will. Then I began a new quest: how I might grow in this truth in preparation for helping others to see and experience this same truth in their lives.

Behind all of this loomed that major event of 1972.

After covering up the real story of Watergate, our Nixon team had coasted to the biggest presidential election victory in history. The next morning, the President thanked the senior White House staff and the Cabinet members. Then, he directed Bob Haldeman, the chief of staff, to fire everyone. The top people of the Nixon Administration were shocked and chagrined. The President was going to reorganize his Administration for the second four-year term. Some would get their letters of resignation back and be kept for the same or new roles in the next term. Most would suffer the ignominy of having been fired. Nixon had won, but they would lose in the aftermath of this momentous election mandate.

The President moved from the White House to Camp David for a stay of several weeks while putting together his new team. Those Nixonites who would be kept got a helicopter ride on Marine One to Camp David to retrieve their resignation letters and to receive their new assignments. My plans had already been made to return to Columbia. My resignation had been submitted a few months earlier. I knew that if I continued in Washington as a White House workaholic, I might come home one evening to no family. No one had put in more hours at White House work than I — this had been by far the greatest and most exciting experience of my life. I was surprised to get the first call to Camp David. I flew there with Vice President Spiro Agnew, the only person the President could not fire, but at Camp David I found that the President really did not want Agnew to be his successor.

On December 8, 1972, I met alone with President Nixon for almost two hours at Aspen Lodge. The meeting was scheduled to be brief. Nixon expected that I, as an attorney, would be honored to stay as an Assistant Attorney General in the Justice Department. My major assignment would be to implement a plan to derail Agnew from the Republican presidential nomination in 1976 in favor of Treasury Secretary John Connally, then a Democrat.

Even though I had previously suggested the idea of substituting Connally for Agnew to the President, I declined the offer. I did agree to help as volunteer General Counsel for the Republican Party's National Committee. (This I did until Watergate blew apart all future Nixon plans.)

After that ten-minute conversation, I engaged the President in what turned out to be a one and one-half hour talk about Watergate and its potential consequences. I became very candid with the President. I explained how impressed I had been with the first term and with Nixon as my boss and leader. We had made history in national politics by winning all of the South for the first time by a GOP candidate, and we had done it easily with an average vote of 70 percent. I told him that he had performed magnificently in splitting the Communist giants at a time when this was vital to the freedom and future of the world. And he had done it all in "the name of peace, peace with honor, and peace through strength, determination, and resolve." What was worrying me now, I said, was what could happen to this great leader. Watergate could be his downfall. Something had to be done. The infection of Watergate could not come to the President's door.

I explained that fortunately my speaking itinerary as a surrogate candidate in the 1972 campaign had left me uninformed on Watergate except for what I had read or heard in the news. Nevertheless, I did believe it would become uncorked. It was too big, too hot. The cap could not stay on that bottle. I told the President I had no idea what part, if any, he had had in it or if he even knew of Watergate, but I did know that the press and the prosecution believed the infection would lead right back to some of the President's staff. So, in the shuffling of his Administration, it would be most unwise for the President to fire almost everyone except the men under Watergate suspicion. This would be the signal that Nixon was protecting his bad boys. The trail would lead inevitably and inexorably into the Oval Office.

Next I turned the President's attention to his place in history, which I painted in glowing terms provided he could handle Watergate properly. But Watergate could ruin it all — not only the place in history but also all the great good the President had done in foreign policy and was preparing to do in domestic affairs in the next four years.

I shook the President; no question about that. I was pouring out my heart of concern to a man who had done about everything I wanted to see him do for my country. I did not want to see him hurt, much less ruined. Nor did I want to see his programs and policies drowned with Watergate. And I could feel that was coming. He had to act and act now!

As the first step, I suggested he immediately remove anyone under any suspicion. He could do it by throwing them in with the staff shuffle. That meant anyone — all the way to the top. I told him I was against no one on the staff, that I made it my business to get along with them all. But the presidency had to be saved from contamination. I called out the names of what turned out to be most of the roll call of Watergate personnel.

At the close of the meeting the President implored me to stay in the Administration. He insisted that I rethink the matter and get back to him with an answer in two weeks. With that I departed, sad and also glad. I was sad thinking about our conversation on Watergate; I was glad I had had the nerve to pour out my concern. I knew I had upset him, but maybe it would cause him to do what he needed to do. I was glad, too, that he cared enough to want me in the second term. But I was sad that there was no way I would reverse my decision. As much as I wanted to stay, I also needed to leave.

The only advice the President may have accepted from me that day was my suggestion that he not keep Charles Colson in the second term. Several weeks later Colson left his position as Special Counsel to the President.

Before the news broke on Colson's conversion to Christianity, I received a telephone call from my former White House assistant, Peter Millspaugh. He suggested I fly to Washington to attend the White House prayer breakfast the next Wednesday morning. I asked why. He responded, "Harry you won't believe what happened at the prayer breakfast this morning. Charles Colson and Democratic Senator Harold Hughes came into the breakfast professing — with tears — to be born-again brothers in Jesus Christ!"

I blurted out: "I don't believe it!"

Peter then exclaimed: "I told you that you wouldn't believe it! We didn't either until they talked. It was really something, Harry. In fact, it was so good we're having them back next Wednesday morning. So come on up. You won't want to miss this!"

I accepted Peter's advice, and, as he had indicated, it was a memorable meeting. In fact, this is what launched me on my search for truth. I came into the meeting as a skeptic and cynic. I knew how the apostle Thomas, called Didymus, felt when the apostles had their second meeting with the resurrected Jesus in the Upper Room in Jerusalem soon after the crucifixion. I wanted to experience the nails in Colson's hands and the wound in his side, just as doubting Thomas did with the resurrected Jesus. Colson actually wept as he elaborated on his recent new-life experience. I left the meeting convinced that something had happened to him.

On returning to South Carolina after the prayer breakfast, I encountered a problem with Ginny, the third of our four children. She had experienced this born-again phenomenon as a member of Young Life, a Christian organization which works to promote spiritual experiences and values in high school students. Ginny had infected her boy friend, Alton Brant, with this born-again contagion. Earlier I had tried to end their romance because Alton was the son of deaf parents. He was a nice young fellow, but he didn't represent my idea of a "successful" son-in-law. Also, he was now too religious. This born-again thing made him sound crazy to me. He would talk about "the Word." Finally, I asked, "What word are you talking about?" He responded, "God's Word!" Then I said, "But God's got lotsa words, doesn't He?" So much for my biblical knowledge!

Soon Ginny wanted to transfer from what I considered a normal Christian college to an "abnormal" one, Columbia Bible College. Then I learned the reason. Her fanatical boy friend was behind this desire. So I told her to bring him to our home to discuss the question. Alton was working his way through the University of South Carolina by tarring house roofs and by any other odd jobs he could find.

Ginny brought him. I will never forget this conversation, for it was quite an experience for me. For two hours I informed Alton that he could never be a success if he transferred to Columbia Bible College. I picked apart the curriculum as having too much religion and not enough business courses. I suggested that he get his business degree from the University, make a good and successful living and give 10 percent of his income to God's work.

At the end of the one-sided dialogue, I delivered to him this solemn warning: "If you go to Columbia Bible College and Ginny follows you, you will never have the hand of my daughter in holy matrimony!" All I remember Alton being able to say was: "But, Mr. Dent; but, Mr. Dent; but, Mr. Dent." Alton Brant wanted my daughter more than anything the world had to offer. As he later told me, "Mr. Dent, I could never leave Ginny, no matter what. It's not just because I love her. You see, Mr. Dent, she led me to my Lord!"

Ginny was a model and a beauty contestant. Yet Alton walked out of my den that day with an impressive Christian demeanor. He was nice as he departed, and I thought I had prevailed. But Alton went straight to Columbia Bible College and risked what he calls his second love, Ginny. He was listening to a different drummer, his Heavenly Father, his first love. This left me every bit as perplexed as the Colson prayer breakfast meeting had.

Later, however, I gave in to their wedding plans.

After they were married and were students at CBC, Betty and I went to their apartment to get something from them. They were out, so I went looking for the object. Over their bed I spied a written prayer list. I laughed and called Betty to come and see it. I said, "Have you ever seen anything like this?" Then my laughter stopped when Betty read off the name at the top. It was "Daddy." In addition to praying me into God's Kingdom, they were also praying me through Watergate. Since then, in giving my testimony I sometimes have been introduced by young adults who said their prayer group had been praying for me at the request of Ginny and Alton.

Ginny gave me a number of books and tracts. Usually she just left them around, like under my pillow. One day she gave me a plaque. It read: "The Purpose of Life Is to Serve God." Today this constitutes the logo of the ministry Betty and I have, "Laity: Alive & Serving."

I had told Ginny and Alton that they could never be success-ful — never even be accepted in a graduate school. Today, Ginny has two master's degrees. Alton will soon receive his doctorate in education from the University of South Carolina. He has given his life to Christian lay ministry as a father, educator and church member. He has never been called to attend seminary himself, but he has sent several people to seminary. Included on this list is his "successful, know-it-all father-in-law."

The Brants have dedicated their lives to helping the deaf and hard-of-hearing in better communication and in relations with the hearing world. Their specialty is education for deaf children. The Brants lead with their lives. They don't preach; they put forward their best sermon, what Jesus called salt and light (Matthew 5:13,14).

At the same time that I was working on the Brant "problem" I was also undergoing the Watergate involvement in my life. When I left the Nixon White House I assured my wife that there would be no problems for us in the Watergate investigation. However, I came to realize that having been in the Nixon White House constituted an engraved invitation to problems with the Office of the Special Prosecutor for Watergate. I was particularly vulnerable in that all of my duties had revolved around the subject of politics. I had been the political liaison man for the White House with all operations of the Republican Party across the country. This gave me the privilege of participating in just about any meetings involving politics anywhere. And, politics touched everything except national security and foreign affairs, and it even touched there at times. This privilege turned out to be a liability.

In 1974 before the big Watergate trial featuring Haldeman, Ehrlichman, Mitchell, *et. al.,* I was shocked to get a subpeona to appear before the Watergate grand jury. I determined to do two things: to tell the truth but to be careful not to hurt anyone else unless I was absolutely certain in my testimony.

The prosecutors were not pleased with me. They could not understand why I did not know the details of Watergate. I explained that I was insulated by Haldeman from the covert operations because I had resisted him previously on similar types of commands.

Then the prosecutors faced me with a 1970 White House election campaign fund operation in which I was involved. My part in the fund activity was to provide the political intelligence information for Bob Haldeman and the President to decide who should get how much.

One key mistake was made in what came to be called the "Townhouse Operation." Stock collected from one of the contributors was dispensed from a townhouse outside the White House. That action, of which I was unaware, technically gave rise to the question of forming a political fund-reporting committee. So the prosecutors set up one for us on paper, and I was nominated for membership.

Against the advice of my attorneys, I agreed to plead guilty to a misdemeanor charge that said I had no knowledge or intent to violate the reporting law. I admitted the truth that I was a part of a group that technically went askew of the law. In making this agreement with the prosecutors I was not required to do anything but to stand before Judge George Hart on December 11, 1974, and tell my side of the story. When I finished relating my role, Judge Hart turned to the prosecutor, Charles Ruff, and asked if he had any information to rebut my account. Ruff replied in the negative.

Then, Judge Hart banged his gavel, pronouncing to a media-filled courtroom that he was now going to hand down his sentence. My wife, Betty, was seated at the rear of the courtroom prepared for the worst, one year in prison and/or a $1,000 fine. The judge said: "It does sound to me that Mr. Dent was more of an innocent victim than the perpetrator. I sentence you, Mr. Dent, to thirty days of unsupervised probation." This was the minimum sentence allowed in view of my guilty plea.

I jumped up, and joy radiated all over me. I thanked Judge Hart and ran for Betty. She was shocked and was weeping as she had not understood the pronouncement of Judge Hart and assumed I was going to jail. Afterward, the judge asked a lawyer friend of mine, Ken Robinson, why I had entered the guilty plea. A few months later I shared that secret with the Grievance Committee of the District of Columbia Bar Association. I told them I did not believe that as a Southerner I could get a fair trial in Washington in the atmosphere of Watergate and I was concerned about damage to my family. I wanted to do what was right, and I feel that I did.

A month later, January 16, 1975, my old friend and mentor, Senator Strom Thurmond, addressed the United States Senate concerning my prosecution. In so doing, he placed in the *Congressional Record* thirteen newspaper and television editorials which raised questions about the prosecution of this case and sympathized with "the innocent victim." In 1976 President Gerald R. Ford issued to me a presidential commission to serve on the Sabine River Compact Commission. His purpose was to seek to issue something in the form of a presidential pardon. There can be no pardon for a misdemeanor. This came over my protest. I was more concerned about my oldest child's name, Harry S. Dent, Jr. I was sorry I had put my name and burden on him and on my family.

I had told the judge on that day of sentencing, December 11, 1974, that I would go down in history "as a bad footnote because it would be difficult to distinguish what my dilemma was today." There and then I should have turned over my life to the One who pulled me through the Watergate experience. I had prayed and made promises over and over as I sought God's aid in this biggest wrestling match of my life. And God had delivered me. I had no question about that. My hip, like Jacob's at the ford at Jabbock in Israel, had been broken in a wrestling fight for a purpose. The story is told in Genesis. Jacob had faced his Watergate, his upcoming rendezvous with his brother, Esau, whom he had deceitfully robbed of a rightful inheritance. In fear of Esau, Jacob had fled to a far land. Now, the next morning he and the family he had to protect would come face to face with Esau and his army. So Jacob prayed to his Lord God Jehovah: "Deliver me, I pray, from the hand of my brother, from the hand of Esau; for I fear him, lest he come and attack me and the mother with the children" (Genesis 32:11).

An angel of God wrestled with Jacob that evening. He knocked Jacob's hip out of joint. But Jacob would not turn loose of God's angel until He blessed Jacob. The wrestler did bless Jacob and consequently delivered him from his greatest fear, a revengeful and more powerful Esau. The next day the two brothers made peace.

Jacob realized that his prayer had been answered by God. He had been delivered. He said, "For I have seen God face to face, and my life is preserved" (Genesis 32:30). From that day forward, the crafty Jacob became the obedient Israel. His name and life were changed by God that day at the place Jacob named Peniel. No longer would Jacob, now Israel, be first. Now the Lord God Jehovah and His will would be the top priority in this new life. Jacob is just one of many examples God places before us in the Bible to show us the blessings and/or curses surrounding the question of authority and obedience in the wrestling bouts we face in life.

For my own deliverance I thanked God profusely. However, He did not yet become first in my life. Harry was still number one.

The aftermath of Watergate kept popping up. Various side investigations either by reporters or the law made me uneasy every time the phone rang or the mail arrived. I lived with heartburn.

I had another minus (and plus) in my personality. I was always accommodating to people, some of whom took advantage of me. I had been influenced by my grandfather, William P. Prickett, to be a "good Samaritan." I was born and reared in the back of his house in St. Matthews, South Carolina. My father had an alcohol problem so Poppa Prickett became my role model. He would give or do anything for anyone, and I followed my model. Several times this got me in jams.

I had become caught up in the drive for success. I found that the harder I worked and the more risks I took, the more I succeeded. Thus, I became more and more self-confident. I could out-work and out-think so many people. Looking back now, I believe I was seeking to overcome my young days of embarrassment over my father's alcoholism and failure. Also, my mother had taken great delight and comfort in the successes of her five sons. She had lost two in World War II. So I evidently sought more achievements to provide her with the one point of happiness in her life — bragging on her Dent boys — and to make up for the loss of Jack and H.N.

I grew to young manhood wanting to do my best and to be my best. My dream was to help people, my country (for which these two brothers had died and a third convalesced in a hospital for a year), and to be somebody.

When at age twenty-one I married eighteen-year-old Betty Francis, I acquired a more sensitive conscience than my own.

She wanted me first of all to be my best and then to do my best. To her, success was being godly and humble. She is one of those with a real servant's heart.

I was doing very well financially in a variety of law work, including lobbying in Washington and in South Carolina government. As I practiced law, God enabled me to engage in various ventures that gave me a view of the operations of the business world. The more I grew in strength, power and wisdom the more I could help less fortunate people who came across my path. That's the way I wanted to see it.

In my church I was taking on more and more duties. Betty was hauling me off to Bible retreats. She was not only a deacon but she was also chairman of the board of deacons, although not by her design. I was in a prayer breakfast group of movers and shakers. This group would go on annual weekend retreats to Young Life's Windy Gap camp near Asheville, North Carolina.

In all of this God was communicating to me bit by bit. What ultimately pushed me into the Bible, studying and then teaching through it, was a failure and embarrassment on my part. In a Bible study the question was raised about the humanity and deity of Jesus Christ. A statement was made by the teacher to the effect that Jesus did not know He was God, did not believe He was God, and never said He was God. Many in attendance wondered about the statement, and so did I. However no one challenged it, so I did. The teacher asked me to prove my point.

I said: "I've taught enough Sunday school to know that the Gospel of John is all about the deity of Jesus Christ."

She responded: "You can't believe John! Where else in the Bible?"

This caught me off guard. I was considered to be a good Sunday school teacher; I had the "gift of gab." I would study the student lesson and the expanded teacher's guide on Saturday night, absorbing the lesson and spewing it out almost by rote on Sunday morning. Now I began to realize that I could not go left or right of the Sunday school lesson. Nor could I go deeper in Scripture references and teachings than the written materials had supplied. Nor could I connect the teachings with the big picture of the Scriptures or with other related teachings. That evening all this weakness in my ability to handle God's Word was being exposed to the key leaders in my church. And I was the superintendent of the Adult Sunday School department!

All I could do was to stammer. This was very unusual for the only attorney and political speaker in the church. I was humiliated more that evening than ever before in all of my many political debates and law arguments. In 1970 I had debated Governor Jimmy Carter, but he was easy compared to this teacher, probably because I knew politics better than the Bible.

In my Sunday school classes where I had had the advantage of having studied the lesson, I never had anyone stump me like this. Now, here I was up against a seminary graduate who showed me and the crowd that I could not defend the deity of Jesus nor the authority of John and his Gospel. That being the case, I could not vouch very well for the authority of the rest of the Bible either.

That evening I went home with a deflated ego. I began to study the Bible, looking for answers. I had to be able to defend my faith, whatever that might be. If I were to be a winner, this would include being literate not only in business, politics, government and law, but also in God's Word and my belief therein.

In the midst of this beginning odyssey into His Word, God provided another lesson at First Baptist Church in Hilton Head Island, South Carolina. Betty and I arrived in time for Sunday school where I was impressed with the teacher's ability to relate the lesson to various passages and teachings in other parts of the Bible. At the end of the class, he tied the teachings together — from the Gospels, the Epistles and even back into the Old Testament. He wasn't reading all this. He really knew the Bible.

After class I waited to compliment him. Also, I asked how he could relate Scripture to Scripture outside of the lesson. He responded, "I just study the Bible as often as possible and keep focused on God's big picture as it is laid out for us progressively from Genesis to Revelation." I thought, "It never occurred to me to look at it that way." But from then on it did!

As I began looking for the deity of Jesus in the Bible, I became acquainted with the concordance, the cyclopedic index and other tools. I thought that since the Bible is a progressive revelation, why not begin my study the way God laid out the Bible, with the first things first? That way my study should be able to give me the big picture so I could then relate all the teachings to God's master plan.

Thus I stepped into a study of the Bible that has never ended. The Bible, I discovered, is not only full of truth, but it's also practical. The nature of man came into clearer and clearer focus as the Lord opened my heart to receive the real truth about the real Harry Dent.

Despite the fact that I prayed, did all this church work and lived a fairly decent life, I had concluded that I did not have that right, saving relationship with Jesus as my Savior. I kept trying to save myself. As much as I had taught in Sunday school about Paul's doctrine of justification by faith, I was still operating on the basis that being and doing good equals salvation. Then I saw a film on John Wesley. I had read that he had a strange warming of his heart after being a missionary from England to Georgia. The film showed me — as did Paul's teachings in Romans, Galatians and Ephesians — that salvation is a work of God's grace (unmerited favor) toward man as set forth in Ephesians 2:8-10:

> For by grace you have been saved through faith, and that not of yourselves; it is the gift of God, not of works, lest anyone should boast. For we are His workmanship, created in Christ Jesus for good works, which God prepared beforehand that we should walk in them.

I connected Paul's teaching to Jesus' admonition to Nicodemus in John 3. Jesus was saying that membership in the church, even on the board of deacons, stewards or elders, does not necessarily mean one is saved and thus in a right relationship with the Father.

Jesus told Nicodemus, "Most assuredly, I say to you, unless one is born again, he cannot see the kingdom of God....That which is born of the flesh is flesh, and that which is born of the Spirit is spirit" (John 3:3,6).

This teaching hit me squarely. What a revelation! Church membership *per se* is not salvation. And all this church work and those prayer breakfast meetings do not *per se* constitute salvation either. They are just signs that one may have submitted to Jesus Christ as Savior.

Then, in studying through the Bible I found another startling prerequisite to salvation. That is called lordship. Scripture stresses that if Jesus is not Lord, then Jesus is not Savior. The key I kept seeing was a submission of our life, our will, our authority to the life, will and authority of Jesus Christ indwelling our own beings and ruling our lives. This concept is recited in what we call the Lord's or Disciples' Prayer: "Thy kingdom come. Thy will be done in earth, as it is in heaven" (Matthew 6:10, KJV).

More and more the whole question kept going back to Genesis 3 and the question there: Who is lord — God or man? The question of salvation, how to be born again and how to have a right relationship with God, came roaring through God's big picture and key individual teachings to be this: "Harry, get off the throne! Invite Jesus through the Person of the Holy Spirit to come into your center of volition and let His will be your will!"

For a strong and determined personality this is a tall order. This was my problem. I had been flirting with Jesus Christ for almost half a century. However, I had never committed my will to be His will. Was this submission worth the price of my most precious possession, my volitional and free will? That was the question I faced.

On a Monday morning in February, 1978, I made that decision. I was traveling in a hard rain from Columbia to Greenville, South Carolina, to face a tough legal problem.

That morning I abdicated the throne of my life in favor of Jesus Christ. There was rain inside the car as well as outside as with misty eyes I prayed all the one hundred miles to Greenville. I had made promises to Him so many times before. However, I had never really followed through with a heart and life commitment such as Paul calls for in Romans 12:1,2. On this Monday morning I realized this meant surrender of my determined will to live no longer by Harry's law but by God's Law. This was going to require even more in worship, commitment and work from me. I remembered that the Bible teachings promised that the Holy Spirit would help as my "Special Counsel."

I knew this would last forever. I had come to understand the difference between finite and infinite, between today and forever, between man's hidden agendas and God's open agenda. I felt truly free for the first time in my life. Freedom is what I had wanted all my life, but I had wanted to be free to do everything my way. Now I would have a Chairman of my board to help me make the decisions of life. Surrending this self-control for supernatural guidance turned out to be the best deal I have ever struck. And it was really God's grace, not my work. I had finally appropriated that gift by accepting the Giver as my Lord and Savior.

My study of the Bible now intensified more than ever and has continued unabated. Soon I decided that I should share these truths with others. Thus I requested and received approval to teach the Bible through from from Genesis to Revelation in my church. I began a nine-month course during the Sunday school hour. I did this again in my home the following year. Then, in 1981-82 I made the presentation in the largest church in South Carolina, First Baptist Church of Columbia. It was soon after initiating the First Baptist study that Betty and I closed my law practice and I entered Columbia Graduate School of Bible and Missions to study in a one-year, in-depth bible program designed for lay people. Ginny and Alton really enjoyed this decision! The year at the graduate school was precisely what I needed in structured, in-depth teaching and in the modeling of the life and teachings of Jesus Christ by faculty, staff and students.

This also resulted in my appointment to have further opportunity to grow spiritually as director of The Billy Graham Lay Center, a ministry arm of CBC in Asheville, North Carolina. Dr. Robertson McQuilkin, president of CBC, recruited Betty and me to spend three years in this great laboratory experience. Soon I was speaking and teaching God's Word, His big picture, and man's responsibility to find his place of service therein. Ultimately, I had to decide whether to spend most of my time filling beds in a conference center or filling "old Harry Dents" with God's master message in the pews, where the "old Harrys" habitate far more frequently than in retreat centers. If I established my own ministry, I could speak and teach during the week — and Betty could too.

Therefore, Betty and I established a new ministry entitled "Laity: Alive & Serving". Now we are putting our time, talents and treasure into God's calling for our lives. God is so good! He has taught us how to tune in for His calling — for what Dr. E.V. Hill proclaims to be God's unction.

There was a time when I was convinced that the greatest pleasure of my life was the day I raised my right hand to recite and commit to the oath of office as Special Counsel to the President of the United States, "the most important person in the world," as I had been instructed. Now I know better. The most important commitment and oath I ever recited was when the One who created the "most important person in the world" and all the rest of us opened up my heart to follow the Bible's teaching to be an "ambassador for Jesus Christ" (2 Corinthians 5:20).

CHAPTER III

MAN'S PURPOSE IN GOD'S PLAN

Which choice will be made an actuality once and forever, an immortal "footprint in the sands of time"? At any moment, man must decide, for better or for worse, what will be the monument of his existence.

Dr. Viktor E. Franklin[1]

Many questions intrigue or haunt us but perhaps none more than a person's own origin, purpose and ultimate end. It took about half a century for me to discover the answers to these key questions regarding my life.

In the Nixon White House we thought we knew where we were — at the top of the world. Yet before long, some had plummeted to the pits, and our mandate had vanished. Why? Because the answers to these vital questions of life had not been probed and resolved. Even more important, the bigger question of what is truth had not been resolved and applied in our lives. Although I was chairman of the White House prayer breakfast group I had not arrived at the point in life where I could definitively articulate truth and my world view. Watergate in the White House initiated my search for that truth and my base point for viewing all of the actions in the world.

I had earned three university degrees before becoming really engaged in a structured, in-depth study of the Bible with an open heart, and it changed my life — thanks to God! The more I study His Book and other books about His teachings, the more I understand my own life and purpose and that of all mankind.

There are basically two opposing views on the origin of man: the evolution theory and the biblical account called creation. The first is based on theory, the theory of the accidental or chance creation and development of man. This theory never won any credit in my view because it does not consider the supernatural, the miracles we see and experience all around us.

I believe that the account of the creation of the earth and of man introduced in Genesis 1 is the truth. Verse 1 says, "In the beginning God created the heavens and earth,"and verse 27 says, "God created man in His own image; in the image of God He created him; male and female He created them."

I am first convinced of the validity of these "allegations" (as we call such assertions in law practice) because I have always believed in the existence of a God or universal Spirit. But more than that, my experiences in life, my study of the Bible and more than a thousand books about the Bible, my personal communication with God and my experiences with Him have all convinced me beyond any doubt that this God is Jesus Christ. Also, God uses the Bible as His means of revealing Jesus to man. Why do I believe the Bible? Because I know the Author!

How can a man know Almighty God? The hiddenness of a transcendent and sovereign God can be broken only as He chooses to reveal Himself to mankind. God, exalted above and beyond man in His essential being, is not accessible to the sight or full understanding of man. There is the problem of man's limitations. We human beings are unable to attain knowledge of God without His supernatural revelation and help. In addition, we are even more blinded by the ways of the world and by our sin nature.

The Bible tells us of two types of revelations to man: the general (natural) and the special (supernatural) revelations of God. The general revelation is a limited self-disclosure on God's part outside of the Jewish-Christian revelation in the Bible. This comes through the created order, the workings of providence in nature and history and the moral life and capacities of mankind. For instance, how can one deny the existence of a supernatural God when we observe and consider the miracles of the operation of our minds, the birth of a child, the majestic wonders of our mountains, valleys, plains, streams, rivers and oceans?

God's special revelation to us is His written Word, the Bible, and His living Word, Jesus Christ. God's revelation has been given in the form of a person and also in the preparatory experiences of God's people, Israel in the Old Testament, and the subsequent foundation of God's new people, the Church of Jesus Christ as set out in the New Testament.

When we read the Bible we are reading God's holy, authoritative and inspired Word. Two key Bible passages stress the authority of the Bible as being the Word of God:

All Scripture is given by inspiration of God, and is profitable for doctrine, for reproof, for correction, for instruction in righteousness, that the man of God may be complete, thoroughly equipped for every good work (2 Timothy 3:16,17).

For we did not follow cunningly devised fables when we made known to you the power and coming of our Lord Jesus Christ, but were eyewitnesses of His majesty. For He received from God the Father honor and glory when such a voice came to Him from the Excellent Glory: "This is My beloved Son, in whom I am well pleased." And we heard this voice which came from heaven when we were with Him on the holy mountain.

And so we have the prophetic word made confirmed, which you do well to heed as a light that shines in a dark place, until the day dawns and the morning star rises in your hearts; knowing this first, that no prophecy of Scripture is of any private interpretation, for prophecy never came by the will of man, but holy men of God spoke as they were moved by the Holy Spirit (2 Peter 1:16-21).

Paul is saying in his second letter to Timothy that all Scripture is God-breathed. The forty writers of the sixty-six books of the Bible were led and inspired by the Spirit of God to record the messages God wanted to reveal to us. These writings, coming from different men at different times, formed a unified whole.

Peter is assuring us that what he, Paul and the other biblical writers were presenting did not come just from them. He affirms that God's "holy men" wrote "as they were moved by the Holy Spirit." Both Paul and Peter had been eyewitnesses of the living Christ. Paul met Jesus in His resurrected and exalted state in his Damascus Road experience. In a sense of amazement, Paul tells us in Ephesians 3 how God called him and revealed to him God's plan and purpose to proclaim the gospel to the Gentiles.

Peter spent three and one-half years living and ministering with Jesus. He failed Jesus more than once in times of testing. However, he became a new man as he witnessed that greatest miracle of all, the resurrection of Jesus from the grave. This resurrected Lord spoke to Peter and the other apostles just before He ascended back to the Father, and from that time on Peter had no question about authority. The Great Commission Jesus gave to His apostles and to all of us today is recorded in Matthew 28:18-20:

Then Jesus came and spoke to them, saying "All authority has been given to Me in heaven and on earth. Go therefore and make disciples of all the nations baptizing them in the name of the Father and of the Son and of the Holy Spirit, teaching them to observe all things that I have commanded you; and lo, I am with you always, even to the end of the age." Amen.

The writers of the New Testament recorded the specific teachings given them by the authority and inspiration of the Spirit as the early Church members put these teachings into practice. The personalities and the thought processes of the writers were not superseded. Nor did God dictate mechanically to them. The writers described in human language the message given to them by God, consciously applying their minds to the descriptions and exhortations.

The living Word, Jesus Christ, came to earth and modeled for us the revelation of God. Jesus was both God and man. Jesus tells us in John 14:7-15 that He and the Father are one and that "He who has seen Me has seen the Father."

Jesus is my role model and the Bible is my rule book. I know that God — Father, Son and Spirit — created not only Harry Dent, but every person and thing in this world and universe. Thus I acknowledge, "In the beginning God created the heavens and earth" and soon thereafter man and woman "in His own image."

My conviction, like that of Paul and Peter, is substantiated by my experience with the risen Lord through a personal relationship, by the evidence of His handiwork in all of His vast creation, and by the revelation His written Word.

Qualities that are attributable to God are called attributes. They belong to God and to Him alone. It is the possession of these attributes (eternity, infinity and immutability) which distinguishes God from all others. However, there are also communicable attributes which God does — in a measure — bestow upon us. Thus, God has being (Exodus 3:14); wisdom and power (Psalm 147:5); holiness (Revelation 15:4); and justice, goodness and truth (Exodus 34:6,7). But so do men and angels. God has all these qualities in unlimited degree. Men and angels possess these, but only in a limited way.

God is the great original. Everything else is a mere reflection of Him. Only God has independent existence. This is what is meant by the essence of God.

In Genesis 1 and 2 the major creative act of the Godhead is man and woman. Who is this man (in the generic sense) that God has created? Genesis 1:27 states that man is not just a machine but that man is made "in the image of God." This statement stresses the importance God placed on man, the crown of all of His creation.

In Genesis 1:26 we see the working of the Holy Trinity in creating man, "Let Us make man in our image, according to our likeness." Here is another big plus for man: in "our likeness."

And, in Genesis 1:31, "God saw everything that He had made, and indeed it was very good." Here, good is according to God's values. Another plus for man and for human dignity. Look at the charter God gave to man and woman: "Then God blessed them, and God said to them, 'Be fruitful and multiply; fill the earth and subdue it; have dominion over the fish of the sea, over the birds of the air, and over every living thing that moves on the earth' " (Genesis 1:28). Why this tremendous charter for man? God's methodology provides for God to use people to do His work. A study of His calling of so many people in the Bible affirms that God's method is to work through open and willing people.

The Bible illustrates in its overall revelation that God is carrying out two great programs for mankind: to save fallen man and redeem him back into right relationship with God, and to establish His kingdom of righteousness and peace on earth. And we are to be the visible agents of this invisible God. God offers His Spirit to empower us and to work through us to accomplish those goals.

Psalm 24 and other Scripture passages attest to His ownership as creator. Thus, "to be fruitful" and to "have dominion" means we are to do God's work and be His trustees over all of His creation. We are responsible and accountable to Him for our time, talents and treasures.

The making of man "in God's image" is God's way of seeking to express God's life through man. "In God's likeness" means God is seeking to demonstrate His character through man. To "have dominion" is God's way of exhibiting His power in and through man. God is investing in man the power and privilege of being God's steward and trustee here on earth to oversee all the rest of God's creation. What a magnificent purpose!

Next, in Genesis 2:7 God reveals how He created man. God formed man out of the dust of the ground and He Himself breathed the breath of life into man. And man became a living being. God then planted a garden in a land called Eden. He put the man, Adam, there to tend and keep it for Him. And God allowed man to be subjected to the first of many tests of life. Why? God desired volitional love and obedience to His authority, not a puppet response. Therefore man was given the power of reason and choice along with a superior mind and supple hands to use in his role as God's steward over the rest of creation.

God planted two special trees in the Garden of Eden. One, the tree of life, represented eternal life with God. The other was the tree of the knowledge of good and evil.

After this, God came to a conclusion for which I'll always be most grateful to Him: "It is not good that man should be alone; I will make him a helper comparable to him" (Genesis 2:18). In Genesis 2:18-25 and Genesis 3:20 God tells us how and why He created woman.

What is the importance of these revelations in Genesis 1 and 2? What impact do they have on the purpose and meaning of our lives? The Psalms provide many eloquent insights into this creature called man. Psalm 8 says:

> O LORD, our LORD, How excellent is Your name in all the earth, You who set Your glory above the heavens!
>
> Out of the mouth of babes and infants You have ordained strength, because of Your enemies, that You may silence the enemy and the avenger.
>
> When I consider Your heavens, the work of Your fingers, the moon and the stars, which You have ordained, what is man that You are mindful of him, and the son of man that you visit him? For You have made him a little lower than the angels, and You have crowned him with glory and honor.
>
> You have made him to have dominion over the works of Your hands; You have put all things under his feet, all sheep and oxen — even the beasts of the field, the birds of the air, and the fish of the sea that pass through the paths of the seas.
>
> O LORD, Our LORD, how excellent is Your name in all the earth!

In Psalm 139, verses 1-6, we discover how well God knows us. Verses 7-12 show how close God is to us: Nowhere can we hide from His presence, not even in heaven or hell. Verses 13-16 explain how carefully God made us: "For You have formed my inward parts....Your eyes saw my substance, being yet unformed. And in Your book they all were written, the days fashioned for me, when as yet there were none of them." Then, in verses 17-24 we see how much God protects us: "How precious also are Your thoughts to me, O God! How great is the sum of them!....Search me, O God, and know my heart; try me, and know my anxieties; and see if there is any wicked way in me, and lead me in the way everlasting."

These passages from God's Word should fortify us in the deepest travail and trauma. God created us to possess dignity, value, purpose and meaning as human beings. The Bible keeps before us not just our sinful nature but our divine potential. What a difference this message could have made in Watergate. What a blessing this can be in all of our Watergates of life. This is what application is about, putting our Watergates side by side with the Bible and changing to conform to God's will for our lives.

What is the meaning of the phrases "in God's image," and "in our likeness"? While God is unlimited, man is limited yet like God in some important respects. God is all-powerful, He is purposeful, and He loves beyond any limitations. Man is limited in time and space, and he is also limited in his love capacity. Man needs supernatural help.

Yet, man is like God in that he can think, will, feel and speak. Unlike the rest of creation, man can have a conscious relationship with his Creator. Man is triune like God, but in a different way. Man has a body, a soul and a spirit. Soul refers to conscious life. Spirit means "to know." Heart is used synonymously with soul, intellect and mind, sensibility and emotions, and will (the power of choice). The key part of man is spirit. This represents the spiritual life, the "inner man," a God-consciousness one cannot see or touch. Ephesians 3:16,17 uses the terms "inner man" and "hearts."

Proverbs 20:27 says "The spirit of man is the lamp of the Lord, searching all the inner depths of his heart." This means God's abode in man is the spirit of man. "In Christ" and "Christ in me," used so much by Paul, means that the Spirit of the Godhead is ruling in the spirit of a new creature in Christ.

A person's external activity is determined by the inner life, for the doing comes from the being.

Dr. Theodore Epp, in *The God of Creation*, asserts that "the most distinguishing characteristic of man's creation was that God 'breathed into his nostrils the breath of life,' "[2] our essential nature and what distinguishes us from animals. The joining together of spirit and body activates and galvanizes the soul so that it begins to function.

Matthew 10:28 attests to the immortality of man. Christianity promises life after death, with God. Because Jesus Christ lives we also can live eternally, beginning now.

The body of a believer, Paul stresses, is "the temple of the Holy Spirit who is in you [as a Christian]...you are not your own." Paul then drives home the punch line: "For you were bought at a price [Christ's blood]; therefore glorify God in your body and in your spirit, which are God's" (1 Corinthians 6:19,20).

Breathing life into Adam, God then communicated His own personality in a living soul. No other creature possesses this god-like personality.

It is apparent that God created man to be a social and relational creature. God wants man to have a right relationship with Him and with his fellowman. We tend to call this fellowship, which means mutual sharing and mutual love. God also commands man "to be fruitful" and "to have dominion." This dictates stewardship, ministry and service. God desires this not only for Himself but also for all mankind. Scripture underscores that we are to love one another and to serve one another because we love both God and man. God commands man to have a heart and life commitment of love and service to God and our fellow-man. The biblical mandate is unequivocal. Jesus, in giving His followers "a new commandment," explained, "By this all will know that you are My disciples, if you have love for one another" (John 13:35).

The teaching of the creation account and study of the infinite attributes of God versus the finite attributes of man present a picture of a complete God (creator) and an incomplete man (creature). Thus, to be complete, man needs God. Ever since the fall of man, he has been on a search for completeness and fulfillment. He seeks meaning and purpose for life.

Built into man's basic constitution are certain felt needs. Abraham Maslow's chart lists the hierarchy of man's needs in order of importance:

(1) Physiological or bodily needs, such as hunger and thirst.

(2) Safety or concerns for security, physical safety and emotional assurance.

(3) Belongingness and love — the need to receive and give love.

(4) Esteem in the form of self-worth and self-respect.

(5) Self-actualization, that stage in which people give themselves to ultimate individual fulfillment through creative activities.

Few reach this stage five. Dr. Larry Crabb, a Christian psychologist, professor and author, boils down man's two prime concerns to a need for significance and a need for security. The problem in Watergate was that the desire for significance suffocated the concern for security, and Watergaters lost both.

The question is, where will man find fulfillment? In the Watergate dilemma, everyone caught up in having to defend himself experienced deep personal trauma and tragedy. In some cases families suffered as much or more than the Watergater. Yet in most cases, the family had no responsibility for the actions that caused Watergate. Here we see significance and security in grave peril. In times of crisis and intense stress the entire hierarchy of man's needs can be affected: our bodily needs, our security, our belongingness and love, our self-esteem and self-actualization.

John Ehrlichman may have fallen as far as anyone in the Watergate debacle. He was perched at the pinnacle of power.

Soon he was estranged and then divorced from his ideal American family. One of his sons wanted to change his name. Not a man of affluent economic means, Ehrlichman was suddenly several hundreds of thousands of dollars in debt for legal services and expenses in two separate trials.

In his book, *Witness to Power*, Ehrlichman expressed his personal devastation this way:

> When I went to jail — nearly two years after the cover-up trial — I had a big self-esteem problem. I was a felon, shorn and scorned, clumping around in a ragged old Army uniform doing pick-and-shovel work out on the desert. I wondered if anyone thought I was worth anything....
>
> I was wiped out. I had nothing left that had been of value to me — honor, credibility, virtue, recognition, profession — nor did I have the allegiance of my family. I had managed to lose that too. It was all gone, and it seemed hopeless to expect that I could ever get any of it back. But I realized that — unless I was willing to just kill myself — I had to begin to *move:* I had to go slowly in some direction, a step at a time. I wasn't sure that I could take a step and then another, but it was clear to me that I had to try or die....
>
> I was in many respects a person I can neither defend nor condone, nor do I try....Since about 1975, I've begun to learn to see myself, and I care what I perceive about my integrity, my capacity to love — and be loved — and my essential worth.[3]

These are comments by a once very proud and arrogant man with a wonderful wife and five children. John Ehrlichman had probably reached the top tier of personal needs, self-actualization. I can understand his despair. All of this ran through my physical, mental and emotional system as I looked at the same personal end that befell Ehrlichman, a man who said he burned down to "ground zero" in his Watergate experience.

What about Richard Nixon? How far down did he burn? The book, *The Final Days,* by Bob Woodward and Carl Bernstein, gives this moving illustration. The scene: the President's favorite brooding room, the famous Lincoln Sitting Room in the Southeast corner of the Mansion. The time: two nights before he resigned the presidency. Seated with Nixon was his powerful and prestigious Secretary of State, Dr. Henry Kissinger. The President's letter of resignation would have to be addressed to the Secretary of State. But on this dreary evening Nixon just wanted to talk.

> Kissinger really didn't like the President. Nixon had made him the the most admired man in the country, yet the Secretary couldn't bring himself to feel affection for his patron. They sat for a time and reminisced about events, travels, shared decisions. The President

was drinking. He said he was resigning. It would be better for everyone. They talked quietly — history, the resignation decision, foreign affairs.

Then Nixon said that he wasn't sure he would be able to resign. Could he be the first President to quit office?

Kissinger responded by listing the President's contributions especially in diplomacy.

"Will history treat me more kindly than my contemporaries?" Nixon asked, tears flooding to his eyes.

"Certainly, definitely," Kissinger said. When this was all over, the President would be remembered for the peace he had achieved.

The President broke down and sobbed.

Kissinger didn't know what to do. He felt cast in a fatherly role. He talked on, he picked up on the themes he had heard so many times from the President. He remembered lines about enemies, the need to stand up to adversity, to face criticism forthrightly.

Between sobs, Nixon was plaintive. What had he done to the country and its people? He needed some explanation. How had it come to this? How had a simple burglary, a breaking and entering, done all this?

Kissinger kept talking, trying to turn the conversation back to all the good things, all the accomplishments. Nixon wouldn't hear of it. He was hysterical. "Henry," he said, "you are not a very orthodox Jew, and I am not an orthodox Quaker, but we need to pray."

Nixon got down on his knees. Kissinger felt he had no alternative but to kneel down too. The President prayed out loud, asking for help, rest, peace and love. How could a President and a country be torn apart by such small things? Kissinger though he had finished. But the President did not rise. He was weeping. And then, still sobbing, Nixon leaned over and struck his fist on the carpet, crying, "What have I done? What has happened?"

Kissinger touched the President, and then held him, tried to console him, to bring rest and peace to the man who was curled on the carpet like a child. The President of the United States. Kissinger tried again to reassure him, reciting Nixon's accomplishments.

Finally the President struggled to his feet. He sat back down in his chair. The storm had passed. He had another drink.

Kissinger lingered. He talked on, building a case, pouring his academic talents into a lecture on why Richard Nixon would go down in history as one of the great peacemakers of all time. "You made the tough decisions," he said.

The two men had another drink. Their conversation drifted around to personalities and to the role Nixon might be able to play once he was out of office. He might be an adviser, or a special ambassador. Nixon wondered again if he would be exonerated by history. Kissinger was encouraging; he was willing to say anything. But he was certain that Nixon would never escape the verdict of Watergate.

At last Kissinger got up to leave. Nixon had never really asked as much of him as he had that night. Vietnam, Cambodia, Russia, China — they all seemed easier. Weak in the knees, his clothes damp from perspiration, Kissinger escaped. Though he was the

President's only top adviser to survive Watergate, he had never really been consulted about resignation.[4]

Kissinger went back through the Mansion and the West Wing of the White House to his office. Here is his reaction to what he had just experienced with the President: "It was the most wrenching thing I have ever gone through in my life....The President was a broken man. What a traumatic experience."[5]

After a time of conversation with two of his assistants, the phone rang in Kissinger's office. It was the President. As usual another staffer would monitor Kissinger's conversation with his callers. On the phone with Kissinger and the President was Larry Eagleburger, a top foreign affairs expert. Here is the brief but sad conversation:

"It was good of you to come up and talk, Henry," the President said. "I've made the decision, but you must stay on for the good of the country."

Eagleburger could barely make out what the President was saying. He was almost incoherent. It was pathetic. Eagleburger felt ill and hung up.

The President had one last request: "Henry, please don't ever tell anyone that I cried and that I was not strong."[6]

Here was the base of all sin, *pride,* hanging on when all else of value was slipping away. And pride was demanding a cover. But, as promised in the Bible, the pride became uncovered by the one who promised to keep the secret with another silent listener hanging on the phone. Such is the nature of any cover-up and any man.

Jeb Magruder and his wife Gail had many traumatic moments and hours as Watergate began to break over their heads in the spring of 1973 and they sought cover. Here is an excerpt from his book, *An American Life: One Man's Road to Watergate:*

Gail's and my bedroom overlooks our front yard, and the next morning, as I was waking up, I heard strange noises outside. Then, when Gail arose and pulled open the shades, she suddenly screamed and threw herself to the floor. There, on our lawn, were twenty or so reporters and photographers with their cameras focused on the house. My car was in the driveway, so I had no choice, when it was time to leave for work, but to make my way through them and mutter my "no comment" to their questions. But the representatives of the media are not easily discouraged, and they became a fixture on my lawn for the next two months, sometimes just two or three, sometimes twenty or thirty. Eventually I could anticipate, depending on the day's Watergate developments, how many reporters would

be out front the next morning. Sometimes, when it was obvious
that a big morning was ahead, Gail and I would take the children
and spend the night with our closest friends, the Gillespies. It
became quite a cat-and-mouse game. After a while I began parking
on the next street over and going out the back door and over the
back fence to make my morning get away. The reporters caught on
to that and began stationing people in strategic points around the
neighborhood where my comings and goings could be observed.
Some of the reporters were particularly diligent about poking around
our back yard and peering in the windows to see if I might be
hiding inside. One of my few triumphs in the next few months was
that the press never caught me after that first morning.[7]

When man fell from God's grace the godly image was marred
but not destroyed. The lesson of the Bible is that God gives
second chances — even third and fourth chances. "The Hound
of Heaven," as Francis Thompson described God, is always pur-
suing man.

Both the Bible and history testify to the fact that man is
religious by nature. This is to be seen in man's relentless search
for the meaning of life and in his restless quest for truth, reality
and the highest good — man's search for God. What most don't
realize is that God is likewise in pursuit of us.

King Solomon, the most powerful king of Israel, left us with
a tremendous legacy for our study and application. If only we
in the Nixon White House had understood Ecclesiastes, Solomon's
log book of a voyager seeking truth...

These twelve chapters record an intense search for meaning
by the man who prayed for wisdom and was granted a good
measure by God. But, after having everything the world had to
offer, Solomon saw the emptiness and futility of man's power,
popularity, prestige, and pleasure apart from God. Ecclesiastes
holds that man's search must end in God, not man. Life "under
the sun" — purely horizontal, leaving out God — is the "vanity
of vanities." And Solomon pointed to the void that St. Augustine
and Blaise Pascal said exists in every person and can be filled
only by God's Spirit. Man is incomplete and can be made whole,
mature and complete only by our complete creator.

King Solomon had much more wise advice for man in the
book of Proverbs. These wise sayings are designed to instruct
us in the principles of wisdom; they stress our duty to trust in
God and His unlimited wisdom, not man's, in all of our social
relationships.

Proverbs 3 records Solomon's exhortation not to forget God's
law:

My son, do not forget my law, but let your heart keep my commands; for length of days and long life and peace they will add to you.

Let not mercy and truth forsake you; bind them around your neck, write them on the tablet of your heart, and so find favor and high esteem in the sight of God and man.

Trust in the Lord with all your heart, and lean not on your own understanding; in all your ways acknowledge Him, and He shall direct your paths.

Do not be wise in your own eyes; fear the Lord and depart from evil. It will be health to your flesh, and strength to your bones (Proverbs 3:1-8).

The teachings in Proverbs 3 are powerful and practical. In verse 4, we are promised that by keeping God's law we will "find favor and high esteem in the sight of God and man." This is what happened in the life of Charles Colson. Very few question his integrity today, and many, many yearn to sit under his teaching. He doesn't need to apply for a presidential pardon to restore his civil rights. His peace lies in the larger pardon on high. Truly, Chuck now has two prized possessions he never knew in pre-Watergate days. He has "favor and high esteem in the sight of God and man."

Jesus admonished in the Sermon on the Mount that in order to find purpose and meaning we need to get our priorities in proper order: "But seek first the kingdom of God and His righteousness, and all these things shall be added to you" (Matthew 6:33). That's the way to find real purpose and meaning in this life. At the seat of power we in the Nixon White House were looking to our own limited means, unaware that as the marred image of God we were blinded by the logs in our own eyes. Would that we had obeyed Proverbs 3, especially verses 5 and 6 commanding us to trust in God and not in ourselves. One more nugget from Proverbs 3 should have influenced the Watergaters: "My son, do not despise the chastening of the Lord, nor detest His correction; For whom the Lord loves He corrects" (Proverbs 3:11,12).

What a difference there would have been had we in the White House understood and assimilated the teachings of Proverbs 3 in our lives. There would have been no Watergate break-in springing from the fear of insecurity. And there would have been no cover-up or lying out of the fear of chastening. Indeed, our God is the God of truth and justice!

CHAPTER IV

MAN'S PROBLEM: SIN

As it is written: "There is none righteous, no, not one;..." for all have sinned and fall short of the glory of God.

Romans 3:10,23

Ever since I experienced Watergate I have been absorbed with the question of the nature of man. What is it in our nature that causes us to get our lives and the lives of others so twisted and torn, as it did in Watergate? Or, as it does in all the other Watergate crises of life? It is almost as though we pursue self-destruction. We seem to have a bent toward doing the things we know we should not do.

John Ehrlichman tells me that he doesn't like what he has seen of the old John Ehrlichman in the Senate Watergate hearings and in the transcripts of taped White House conversations. He knows there was something wrong in the old John. The apostle Paul grieved over this problem too. In Romans 7 he addressed the subject of his struggle. In verses 14-25, Paul expressed this concern about his human nature and inclination toward sin and evil:

> For we know that the law is spiritual, but I am carnal, sold under sin. For what I am doing, I do not understand. For what I will to do, that I do not practice; but what I hate, that I do. If, then, I do what I will not to do, I agree with the law that it is good. But now, it is no longer I who do it, but sin that dwells in me. For I know that in me (that is, in my flesh) nothing good dwells; for to will is present with me, but how to perform what is good I do not find. For the good that I will to do, I do not do; but the evil I will not to do, that I practice. Now if I do what I will not to do, it is no longer I who do it, but sin that dwells in me.
> I find then a law, that evil is present with me, the one who wills to do good. For I delight in the law of God according to the inward man. But I see another law in my members, warring against the law of my mind, and bringing me into captivity to the law of sin which

is in my members. O wretched man that I am! Who will deliver
me from this body of death? I thank God — through Jesus Christ
our Lord!

So then, with the mind I myself serve the law of God, but with
the flesh the law of sin.

If Paul, the great apostle, had this problem with his human
nature after his Damascus Road experience, then what about me,
you and all the rest of us? Since studying the Bible in detail and
connecting the teachings of Scripture to what I have experienced
in my life and what I have seen in the lives of others, I have
come to some convictions about the nature of man. The enemy,
to echo Pogo, the comic strip character, is me, and you. The
enemy is all of us. Paul refers to our sin nature — it is common
to all. Our nature to do what we know we should not do and
not to do what we know we should do is endemic to the whole
human race.

Genesis 3 records the first instance of man's sin and the
consequences of that sin. It depicts a pattern of sin. Essentially,
all that happened in the Watergate political scandal first occurred
in the Garden of Eden, man's first paradise and the first Watergate.
The White House represents the paradise of power. The Garden
of Eden was the paradise of innocence and of a loving and
personal relationship with the creator.

The events related in Genesis 3 and the consequences of
those actions on all of mankind make Genesis 3 a critical chapter
in the Bible. From verse 24 on, the remainder of the Bible relates
to the events and consequences of Genesis 3. There is no way
we can comprehend the rest of the Bible unless we understand
this important chapter.

Genesis 3 is a revelation of the beginning of sin in human
history. It is the account of the source of the poison that has
contaminated human life, the cancer in our souls.

In the garden God had entered into the Edenic covenant
with man and woman. By this first of many covenants God was
to make with His people, Adam and Eve were to be in perfect
obedience to their creator and they were to have freedom of
choice. God promised eternal life to them and vowed the penalty
of death if they should break this agreement. The life that God
promised the first couple was a happy, holy and immortal existence
of the soul and body.

The Bible teaches only two ways for man to have eternal
life: through perfect obedience (a covenant of works) or by the
faith of man through the working of God's covenant of grace
(unmerited favor) not based on man's having to earn eternal life.

The only life of perfect obedience on record is that of Jesus Christ.

In creating man, God made him a volitional being, meaning one possessing a free will and with it the power of reason and choice. Then he put man in the garden.

> The LORD God planted a garden eastward in Eden, and there He put the man whom He had formed. And out of the ground the LORD God made every tree grow that is pleasant to the sight and good for food. The tree of life was also in the midst of the garden, and the tree of the knowledge of good and evil....
> Then the LORD God took the man and put him in the garden of Eden to tend and keep it. And the LORD God commanded the man, saying, "Of every tree of the garden you may freely eat; but of the tree of the knowledge of good and evil you shall not eat, for in the day that you eat of it you shall surely die" (Genesis 2:8,9,15-17).

Adam was placed in the garden for two purposes. Pastor and author Ray Stedman says that Adam's task was to learn the secrets of the garden so that he might be used of God to turn the rest of the world into a veritable Garden of Innocence and right relationship with God and man. Man was also to stand the test of obedience for his free will. The aim was to ensure a strong sense of responsibility in man.[1]

Thus man came to face his first test of works (or obedience). God commanded Adam not to eat of the tree of the knowledge of good and evil. However, man could eat of any other tree in the garden. God determined that the penalty for disobedience would be not only physical death but also spiritual and eternal death. Upon violation, man was to be separated from the presence, holiness, fellowship and, thus, happiness associated with this right relationship to God. The story of Adam and Eve and their disobedience to God's command is known as the fall of man. Adam informed Eve of the prohibition so that they both knew they should not eat of the fruit of that off-limits tree. However, they surrendered to the lure of the sin that concerns Paul in Romans 7 and that taunts and haunts all of us today.

In Genesis 1 the first four words announce God: "In the beginning God...." Then we meet man in Genesis 1:27 ("So God created man....") The first words in chapter 3 announce the evil spirit of the universe: "Now the serpent...." Now we see the two forces — that of good and that of evil — coming together to battle for the soul of all mankind in the garden. In the middle of the struggle is the prize, man. Evil won this first round to take command of the nature of man's heart, the biblical expression for man's will. The outcome was to reverberate through history.

What we need to glean from Genesis 3 is the satanic method, the human experience, and the divine action in response to man's dilemma in this experience with the lure and power of evil. After the Lord gave me spiritual eyes to see, I began correlating the events and lessons of our Nixon Watergate and the first Watergate of Adam and Eve. I could see that the problem of man from the garden continues to reproduce itself not only in the Nixon Watergate but in the lives of all men and women. Our problem, like Paul's, is that we have a Watergate nature and mentality.

The serpent is the representative of Satan who is also known as the devil or Lucifer, the fallen angel. The Bible mentions three angels: Michael, Gabriel and Lucifer. Lucifer is the angel who revolted because he could not be equal with God, and he was cast out of heaven (Luke 10:18).

Satan, the name of the prince of evil, means adversary. Indeed, Satan is God's adversary. He is also called the devil, Beelzebub, the ruler of this world, the prince of the power of the air and the antichrist. Everywhere he appears in the New Testament, Satan is seen as the head of the forces of evil. He is relentless. Peter reports that he "prowls around like a roaring lion seeking someone to devour" (1 Peter 5:8, NIV). Paul says Satan is so cunning that he "transforms himself into an angel of light" (2 Corinthians 11:14). Paul exhorts all Christians to "put on the whole armor of God, that you may be able to stand against the wiles of the devil" (Ephesians 6:11).

Satan is no figment of the imagination. He persuaded Judas, one of the twelve apostles, to betray Jesus, and he is working on each person today.

Consider what Satan did to the world through Adolph Hitler. Look at what he is doing today to destroy American homes and families. What is the source of all addiction to drugs, alcohol, and tobacco, as well as of hard core pornography and criminal acts? What is the cause for all of the brokenness and shattered relationships in the world today — people against people, nation against nation? This enmity and strife comes at a time when more and more countries are producing nuclear weapons. Never have we had so many potential holocausts threatening the world. All these outward evils are products of evil selfishness breeding and brooding in the hearts of men and women. The source? The same Satan who beguiled Adam and Eve — the Satan who deceives us every day.

In the initial encounter in the garden, Satan took the guise of the serpent, "more cunning than any beast of the field which the LORD God had made" (Genesis 3:1). This tempter approached Eve and asked the first question recorded in Scripture, a question crafted to distort God's prohibition regarding the forbidden tree and to cast doubt on the law God had laid down. The question Satan asked was: "Has God indeed said, 'You shall not eat of every tree of the garden'?"

The serpent was questioning God's Word, His authority and His motive. Also he was encouraging Eve to indulge her desires, which she and Adam did. He told them they could "be like God"; Adam and Eve could be the lord of their own lives.

The serpent urged Eve to go ahead and satisfy her own desires, saying, "You will surely not die. For God knows that in the day you eat of it your eyes will be opened, and you will be like God, knowing good and evil" (Genesis 3:5). Here is the heart of temptation.

The first appeal to secular humanism and the acceptance of secular humanism is portrayed for us here in this verse. Protagoras stated that "man is the measure of all things" — secular humanism means man operating on his own as the measure of all things without God. In other words, man is his own god. His will belongs to himself and Satan, not God. This philosophy has been with us for ages. Now it is virtually a religion.

Genesis 3:6 relates Eve's response: "So when the woman saw that the tree was good for food, that it was pleasant to the eyes, and a tree desirable to make one wise, she took of its fruit and ate. She also gave to her husband with her, and he ate." Now the temptation was completed. The will of Satan and man prevailed over God's will.

What were the consequences of this original sin by the first man and woman? There was an immediate sense of guilt and shame. A void came into their lives. This hollow still exists in people today. Adam and Eve immediately became conscious of their nakedness. Previously their nakedness had no meaning. So they began a cover-up, the original pattern for the cover-up of Watergate. They "sewed fig leaves together and made themselves coverings" (Genesis 3:7). Then they sought to hide in the garden from God. Verses 8 and 9 report, "Then the man and his wife heard the sound of the LORD God as He was walking in the garden in the cool of the day, and they hid from the LORD God among the trees of the garden. But the LORD God called to the man, 'Where are you?' " (NIV).

Haven't we human beings been covering up ever since? How many transparent people do you know? A transparent person is one who is open and honest in his thoughts and actions. We can see right through such a person and ascertain that person's real agenda and purposes. He does not have a double, secret or hidden agenda.

A hidden agenda creates one of the prime difficulties in our relationships. Our real motives are covered up, hidden because of our selfish thoughts, desires and plans. We do not want to be caught or exposed because we are ashamed and feel guilty about the dark thoughts, motives and actions of our marred nature.

Many people never realized that to cover up is a crime until Watergate caught their attention. Even Nixon, Dean, Ehrlichman and Haldeman did not know until they had gone too far that to cover up means to obstruct justice, which is a crime. All but Haldeman were attorneys. I never paid any attention to the seriousness of covering up until Watergate. Yet this has been a natural instinct in me all of my life — as it is for all of us. Since studying Genesis 3, I now understand why the urge to cover up is so strong in us.

To protect himself even more, man not only hides, he hurls. He casts the blame on others. That happened in the garden, it happened in Watergate, and it happens now.

In Genesis 3:11, God fires His second and third questions at Adam. This precipitates the first shifting of blame to others. Adam blamed God and Eve for his sin. He said: "The woman whom You gave to be with me, she gave me of the tree, and I ate." Remember that in Genesis 2:18 God had decided Adam needed a helper. Thus Adam used this as an excuse to blame God.

Then the Lord asked Eve in verse 13: "What is this you have done?"

The woman responded: "The serpent deceived me, and I ate." Or, "The devil made me do it." Now the serpent is "getting it in the neck." This is typical of the way many of the people reacted in Watergate. A team that prided itself on loyalty began falling apart as the game of passing the blame was instigated "to save one's own hide." Before long, fingers were pointing in all directions.

When Jesus was in Jerusalem, He charged the Pharisees with hypocrisy, cover-up and hidden agendas. Hypocrisy comes from a Greek word meaning to play a part. Jesus tells us in the Sermon on the Mount that we are to let His light of salvation shine through our lives as a clear witness of His saving grace to the world (Matthew 5:16). We are to be, Paul says, living epistles so our lives exemplify the truth of Jesus Christ and His gospel (2

Corinthians 3:2,3). Yet a cover-up or hidden agenda can obstruct that light of salvation.

Evidently Adam and Eve perceived the price of their disobedience to their creator. As a result of their conscious decision to rebel against God, they set off a series of actions which resounded like trip hammer blows from century to century. Adam acted as the head of the whole race of man. Everything granted to Adam was given to all mankind, including life or death. God did not give dominion over the whole earth to Adam alone, but as the heritage for the entire human race. Thus, the penalty Adam was to incur would fall on everyone — all of Adam's descendants.

Satan worked an evil seduction. There followed a fall — in fact, the fall of man — with consequent curses which would continue for long centuries.

Satan always intends temptation for evil. However, God uses the trials of life as opportunities for spiritual growth and as visual aids for teaching. Trials can work good for men as well as work for God's own glory. There can be a silver (spiritual) lining in every dark cloud.

Making good out of evil is God's way; making evil out of evil or good is Satan's way. God's way requires our obedience; Satan's way is to entice us into disobedience to God.

Satan proffered the first lie, the "big lie" of the Bible and of all time. The Old Testament prophets recognized lying, whether the lies are big or little, as being a specific evil. Jesus attributed lies to Satan, declaring Satan to be "a liar and the father of it" (John 8:44).

Lying is a way of life today. And the biggest lie of this day is the same big lie of Genesis 3: Don't believe God! Lying and covering up sent more key Nixon people to jail than all the other charges combined. In legal terms, this type of lie is known as perjury, and covering up is called obstruction of justice.

Dr. Richard Halverson, chaplain of the United States Senate, preaches that out of Genesis 3 issue all the decisions and choices of life. "Whom shall I believe, God or Satan? Whom shall I follow, God or Satan? Whom shall I serve, God or Satan?" Dr. Halverson says that "out of Genesis 3 flows our world view, our belief system, our values, our priorities — all the issues of life and the consequences of our choices."[2] We must learn to look instinctively for the mind of Satan when we are being assaulted with trials, temptations and the big lie: "Go ahead, don't listen to God; you can be like God!"

The first choice set before man in Genesis 3 arises out of the power of reason that God gave Adam to use on Earth. Adam and Eve used their reason and exercised their choice to obey the agent of Satan with all of his appeals to selfishness and freedom from God's authority. The power of choice can be used for good or evil, for salvation or death. The choice is man's to make.

Adam and Eve were created in innocence — they did not know evil or death (physical or spiritual). But they permitted their power of reason and choice to become distorted with doubt, unbelief and pride. We inherited the same problem from them. We choose or decide by our will. In criminal law willfulness can make the difference between a transgressor's going to jail or just paying a fine or being placed on probation. If God is to get complete possession of us, He must possess our will, not just our feelings or emotions. Indeed, the will is "the stronghold of our being."[3]

Scripture speaks of the will as being located in the heart, "the hidden man of the heart" reports Hannah Whittal Smith. Heart is used at least 195 times in the Bible to mean volition or purpose, the act or power of willing. Today man thinks of the will as being directed by the power of reason and choice in the brain. As with Adam and Eve, we choose by acceding to the will of Satan and self versus that which God wills for us. The choices we make determine our quality of life here on earth and also into eternity. They determine whether we are in fellowship with God or separated from Him. They invite God's judgment or blessing. The first curse, first judgment, first (and ultimate) punishment were meted out to Adam and Eve because of their choices. Separation from God was the result (Genesis 3:14-24).

Why does sin separate and alienate? Because God is holy — that is, God is perfectly righteous, and He hates sin and unrighteousness. The prophet Isaiah explains God's hatred for unrighteousness as he warns the people of Israel: "But your iniquities have separated you from your God; and your sins have hidden His face from you, so that He will not hear" (Isaiah 59:2). God's holiness is one reason God not only expelled the first man and woman from fellowship with Him in the garden but also barred their access to the tree of life, which symbolized the divine presence and eternal life.

In addition to the judgment of separation, though, God made provisions to restore man from his fallen condition. Only God can put Humpty-Dumpty back together again, spiritually and physically. Man cannot accomplish his own restoration with fig leaves, blue smoke and mirrors or magical elixir from political advance men. Everyone from the White House to the nation's pulpits and TV tastemakers needs to understand this fact.

The first view we see of God's pursuit of man is here in Genesis 3 where He asks His first question of man. God seeks Adam and Eve to call them to the first accountability and to issue the first forgiveness. Why this effort to question, pursue, forgive? Because of God's unconditional love, His bountiful mercies and His overflowing grace. This is what God is about. God is calling man to confession, openness and repentance. The Bible speaks of this from Genesis to Revelation. God punishes, God prunes, and God disciplines because He loves His creatures. For this reason He uses His chastening rod to help us grow and mature in our relationship with Him and our fellowman. God also curses evil and blesses good, and He abounds in hope and promises. We see Him acting in all of these ways in response to the commission of the original sin. God illustrates with His first question that man is lost and stands in need of redemption and salvation. This is the message of Genesis 3.

After the excuse episode, God placed a curse on the serpent. In so doing, He presented the first gospel message and prophecy in a significant verse, Genesis 3:15: "And I will put enmity between you and the woman, and between your seed and her Seed; He shall bruise your head, and you shall bruise His heel."

God intended to grant mercy to Adam and Eve as He dispensed judgment. But for the serpent, who represented evil, there was an eternal curse. This representative of Satan was sentenced to crawl on his belly and eat dust all the days of his life. This curse was concluded with a prophecy. It was the first promise of God's grace.

The Bible is consistent in its teaching that God's absolute justice requires that sin be punished. It is an integral part of God's moral realm. He is now turning His wrath from the serpent to Satan, the power behind the serpent. God decreed in verse 15 that man's enmity must be turned in the direction of his true enemy. Man tends to resent authority and the lawmaker but overlooks the real culprit, the instigator of law-breaking. So, Adam's perception of who is friend and who is foe needed to be changed. In a book entitled *Genesis 3,* Old Testament scholar Edward J. Young makes this point about enmity: "To be at enmity with the wrong object is to lose one's life. To be at enmity with the right object is to be delivered. Not God, but the serpent is the object to be hated."[4]

The woman needed to understand this too, and the enmity God put between her and Satan was extended to their seed. Verse 15 has momentous implications. Notice that God says that the children, the posterity of Satan and of the woman, will be at odds. And it is not the seed of man. This prophecy is of the coming Messiah (Savior) who would be born of the Seed — with a capital S — *of the woman.* Thus, we have the first teaching of the virgin birth of the Savior. He will be God and man, as Jesus is presented to us in the Gospels.

The message in the second part of this verse is one of ultimate victory over Satan by the Seed of the woman. It is the Seed of the woman, the Redeemer (Savior), that will deliver the fatal blow to the head of Satan. Satan bruised Jesus on the cross, but not mortally. However, Satan was dealt a death blow to the head at the cross and the empty tomb, where Jesus won. The ultimate victory will be consummated when Jesus comes again.

The apostle Matthew reports the victory of Jesus over death on that first Resurrection Sunday:

> Now after the Sabbath, as the first day of the week began to dawn, Mary Magdalene and the other Mary came to see the tomb. And behold, there was a great earthquake; for an angel of the Lord descended from heaven, and came and rolled back the stone from the door, and sat on it. His coutenance was like lightening, and his clothing as white as snow. And the guards shook for fear of him, and became like dead men.
>
> But the angel answered and said to the women, "Do not be afraid, for I know that you seek Jesus who was crucified. He is not here; for He is risen, as He said. Come, see the place where the Lord lay. And go quickly and tell His disciples that He is risen from the dead, and indeed He is going before you into Galilee; there you will see Him. Behold, I have told you."
>
> So they went out quickly from the tomb with fear and great joy, and ran to bring His disciples word (Matthew 28:1-8).

Revelation 20:10 records the ultimate end of Satan this way:

> And the devil, who deceived them, was cast into the lake of fire and brimstone where the beast and the false prophet are. And they will be tormented day and night forever and ever.

For man, the marvelous grace of God is shown in that God promised a Redeemer (Savior) before He pronounced judgment on Adam and Eve.

Genesis 3 concludes with the final sentence for Adam:

> Then the LORD God said, "Behold, the man has become like one of Us, to know good and evil. And, now, lest he put out his hand and take also of the tree of life, and eat, and live forever" — therefore the LORD God sent him out of the garden of Eden to till the ground from which he was taken. So He drove out the man; and He placed cherubim at the east of the garden of Eden, and a flaming sword

which turned every way to guard the way, to the tree of life (Genesis 3:22-24).

God cut Adam off from eternal life by barring him from the tree of life. However, through the killing of animals to provide clothing for Adam and Eve (verse 21), God initiated the process by which Adam and Eve and all of mankind may have restoration to eternal life in fellowship with Him. He established the prerequisite of the shedding of blood as the only way to cover man's sins. In Hebrews 9:22 we are told that "without shedding of blood there is no remission [of sin]." Later God impressed upon the Israelites at Mount Sinai the importance of blood. He told them: "For the life of the flesh is in the blood, and I have given it to you upon the altar to make atonement for your souls; for it is the blood that makes atonement for the soul" (Leviticus 17:11).

Since the blood is the essential life of a creature, it belongs to the God who gives life to all. The blood was given back to God for two reasons: to prevent man from usurping the creator's lordship over His creatures, and to show that the lifeblood of one of God's creatures was regarded as possessing atoning (forgiving) value, making forgiveness the costliest of God's gifts. Sacrifice was the appointed means of forgiveness and atonement, and in the New Testament, Jesus became the superior satisfaction for the sins of man by the shedding of His blood.

In Genesis 3:21 God created the first blood sacrifice when animals were slain "to provide tunics of skin" to clothe Adam and Eve. For one to stand in the presence of God, he must be clothed in the robe of righteousness (holiness) because God will not countenance any sin. Adam and Eve had thought that with their fig-leaf coverings they could cover their own shame. Too many people are living, as did I, under the same great deception, that fallen and sinful man can save himself. But Scripture teaches that only God, the righteous one, can provide and restore righteousness to man. Paul explains it in Romans 3:25,26:

> God set forth [Christ Jesus] as a propitiation by His blood, through faith, to demonstrate His righteousness, because in His forbearance God had passed over the sins that were previously committed, to demonstrate at the present time His righteouness, that He might be just and the justifier of the one who has faith in Jesus.

The purpose of redemption and salvation is to restore to fallen man the original image of God. In man's marred image, with its nature to sin, man habitually transgresses God's will for him. Man is easily tempted and led by the prodding of Satan to be selfish and do things his own way. But God wants us, in our own interest, to obey habitually rather than habitually to disobey Him.

The consequence of man's sin is to incur the wrath of a holy God and thus to break fellowship and relationship with Him. But God's whole purpose for man, to have a right relationship between God and man and between man and his fellowman, is based on His unlimited wisdom and is motivated by His unlimited love. Man's welfare, happiness and fulfillment is the eternal purpose of a living and ever-loving God.

CHAPTER V

MAN'S NEMESIS: SATAN

> There are two equal and opposite errors into which our race can fall about the devils. One is to disbelieve in their existence. The other is to believe and feel an excessive and unhealthy interest in them.
>
> C.S. Lewis

The original "dirty trickster" was not any of the individuals of Watergate infamy. The first and most masterful trickster was and continues to be the master of that serpent we meet in Genesis 3. He is the tempter; his best work is his wiley temptation which invariably issues in sin. What happened in Genesis 3 is repeated over and over every day in our own lives. It is what Paul bemoaned in Romans 7:7-25 about his own carnal and sinful nature. Paul knew that sin can cause what should concern all of us the most — separation from God.

The consistent theme of the Bible from Genesis 3 to Revelation 20 is the conflict between good and evil, between God and Satan, in a cosmic struggle over the heart (will) and soul (spirit) of man. Genesis 1 and 2 show us innocence and peace in the Garden of Eden. War then rages from Genesis 3 onward and is concluded in Revelation 20. There Satan is eliminated in the final battle. In Revelation 21 and 22 there is unfolded for us the creation of the new heaven and earth, the new city of Jerusalem and the new garden featuring the tree of life and its life eternal.

What is the nature of this war? It is unlike any military conflict man has ever experienced. The stake in the war of good and evil is eternal life — forever and ever. Yet most people, even many in the church, do not live consciously aware of this invisible reality. Why? Because to most people the devil is a myth, a joke. The popular concepts of Satan are based on the word pictures of Dante in his *Divine Comedy* and Milton in his *Paradise Lost.*

Cartoons and other drawings picture the devil as originally concocted in medieval times, a caricature of a half-man, half-beast
with horns, cloven hoofs and a tail. The pitchfork also is a part
of a masterly gambit that Satan himself no doubt helped devise
to carry out his most clever ruse: to make man believe that the
devil is only a mythical character concocted to amuse and entertain
man. The trick is on man, as Adam and Eve discovered too late
in Genesis 3; it is on all today who choose to ignore the teaching
of Genesis 3 and the rest of Scripture regarding Satan and his
M.O. (method of operation).

Is Satan real? Ask Dr. M. Scott Peck, a brilliant psychiatrist
and Christian and the author of two best-selling books.

> Having come over the years to a belief·in the reality of benign
> spirit, or God, and a belief in the reality of human evil, I was left
> facing an obvious intellectual question: Is there such a thing as evil
> spirit? Namely, the devil?
> I thought not. In common with 99 percent of psychiatrists and
> the majority of clergy, I did not think the devil existed.
>
> (*People of the Lie* p. 182)

Then after examining so-called demon possession cases, Dr. Peck
declares: "I now know Satan is real. I have met it."

> Conversion to a belief in God generally requires some kind of
> actual encounter — a personal experience — with the living God.
> Conversion to a belief in Satan is no different.[2]

For years I could not accept the reality of this invisible
malefactor called the devil. I was too much of a realist and
rationalist. What I could not see through human eyes I could
not accept as fact. If it did not meet the lawyer's rule of reason,
it was irrational. Yet I accepted God the Father as a reality. His
general revelation alone met my test for reality and reason. I
had no problem reasoning that Jesus had lived on this earth as
God's man, but I was not certain that Jesus was God. I did not
comprehend the Holy Spirit or the devil because they were not
visible to me in the real world. Yet I experienced the work of
God in me and all about me. Also, like Paul, I knew something
was making me do what I did not want to do and was keeping
me from doing what I knew I should be doing. This something
was certainly alive and active in others too, especially my political
foes — Democrats or Republicans.

Now I understand why I missed the invisible spirit world:
It was beyond my human sight and earthly vision. I was an

unwitting humanist. Once I really committed my life to Jesus Christ, I began receiving spiritual sight. It was as though I had been half blind all of my life.

As with Paul, an Ananias came alongside my life and helped remove the scales from my eyes. In privately tutoring me, Professor Charles Wenzel of Columbia Bible College pointed me first to a passage of Scripture I had overlooked in all of my "bits and pieces" study of the Bible. This is 1 Corinthians 2:6-16. Here Paul introduces us to the "old Harry Dents," the natural man:

> However, we speak wisdom among those who are mature, yet not the wisdom of this age, nor of the rulers of this age, who are coming to nothing. But we speak the wisdom of God in a mystery, the hidden wisdom which God ordained before the ages for our glory, which none of the rulers of this age knew; for had they known, they would not have crucified the Lord of glory.
>
> But as it is written: "Eye has not seen, nor ear heard, nor have entered into the heart of man the things which God has prepared for those who love Him." But God has revealed them to us through His Spirit. For the Spirit searches all things, yes, the deep things of God. For what man knows the things of a man except the spirit of the man which is in him? Even so no one knows the things of God except the Spirit of God. Now we have received, not the spirit of the world, but the Spirit who is from God, that we might know the things that have been freely given to us by God.
>
> These things we also speak, not in words which man's wisdom teaches but which the Holy Spirit teaches, comparing spiritual things with spiritual. But the natural man does not receive the things of the Spirit of God, for they are foolishness to him; nor can he know them, because they are spiritually discerned. But he who is spiritual judges all things, yet he himself is rightly judged by no one. For "who has known the mind of the Lord that he may instruct Him?" But we have the mind of Christ.

In the next chapter, Paul addresses the Corinthian church members as carnal or fleshly Christians, babes in Christ (1 Corinthians 3:1-4). Then in verses 18-23, Paul revealed to the wayward Corinthian church members and to me the difference between man's reason and wisdom and God's:

> Let no one deceive himself. If anyone among you seems to be wise in this age, let him become a fool that he may become wise. For the wisdom of this world is foolishness with God. For it is written, "He catches the wise in their own craftiness"; and again, "the LORD knows the thoughts of the wise, that they are futile." Therefore let no one boast in men. For all things are yours: whether Paul or Apollos or Cephas, or the world or life or death, or things present or things to come — all are yours. And you are Christ's, and Christ is God's.

Paul completes his teaching on the man with little or no spiritual sight in Galatians 6:6-10:

> Let him who is taught the word share in all good things with him who teaches.
> Do not be deceived, God is not mocked; for whatever a man sows, that he will also reap. For he who sows to his flesh will of the flesh reap corruption, but he who sows to the Spirit will of the Spirit reap everlasting life. And let us not grow weary while doing good, for in due season we shall reap if we do not lose heart. Therefore, as we have opportunity, let us do good to all, especially to those who are of the household of faith.

According to the Bible, the term that describes most individuals is natural man — that is, the Spirit of God is not in that man and thus he cannot see God or the spirit world. Paul introduces us to three kinds of spiritual persons in the above verses. They are (1) the babe in Christ or carnal Christian, as were many of those in the church at Corinth; (2) the progressive Christian who is growing in Christ; and (3) the mature in Christ, those who are grown up in Christ through the indwelling and work of the Holy Spirit.

There are three kinds of Christians and thus, with the natural man, four kinds of persons. Three are spiritual to some degree, and one is unspiritual. Where was I at the time of Watergate and in my days as chairman of the White House prayer breakfast group? A pastor friend referred me to 1 Timothy 1:6 for his view that I had "strayed" along the Christian path, "turning aside to idle talk." Maybe so. I believe, though, that I had never really made a commitment to Jesus Christ. I had made a decision about Jesus, but not a commitment to Him.

Now when I study the whole big picture of Scripture I see the command of commitment to the lordship and not just the saviorhood of Jesus Christ. For every time I see Jesus referred to as Savior, I find ten or more times that He is called Lord. Almost everyone wants a Savior, but too few crave a Lord of their lives, other than the self-lord Satan proposed to Adam and Eve. The end result is rebellion against God and His love and best intentions for us. I contend that man must be either blind or irrational not to accept God's free grace.

In a conversation with Bob Haldeman in August, 1985, about the good and bad that emanated from Watergate, Bob remarked, "There's a mixture of Cain and Abel in each of us." Cain and Abel illustrate the continuation of the sin disease in Genesis 4.

Genesis 3 dealt with individual sin and the root of sin. Genesis 4 displays family and societal sin and thus the fruit of sin not only against God but also against man. These two sons of Adam and Eve were prototypes of two forms of behavior — the way of the ungodly, governed by Satan, and the way of the godly, governed by righteousness. Cain represents disobedience to God's will. Abel represents obedience to God's will.

Cain, the elder brother, brought to the Lord his own type of offering. Abel pleased God by acceding to Him with an offering in accord with His will. In Genesis 4:5 Cain became "very angry, and his countenance fell." God warned Cain that "sin lies at the door" (verse 7). Then, "Cain rose against Abel his brother and killed him" (verse 8). This was the first murder recorded in the Bible.

Subsequently, God gave Adam and Eve another son, Seth. Beginning in Genesis 5 the Bible traces the development of the ungodly line of Cain and the godly line of Seth, the substitute for the righteous Abel. The lessons of obedience versus disobedience continue through Genesis 8. After the time of Noah, who stood alone for God in faith (Genesis 6-9), another major act of disobedience, this time by the descendants of the flood survivors, is recorded for us in Genesis 11. In verse 4, the Bible relates the rebellion of these people against God's will:

> And they said, "Come, let us build ourselves a city, and a tower whose top is in the heavens; let us make a name for ourselves, lest we be scattered abroad over the face of the whole earth."

This is another act of secular humanism. God's will was that mankind scatter over the world to take dominion and multiply. Yet they were going to build their own stairway to heaven and make a name for themselves and avoid obedience to God. Here it is again — my will versus God's will.

What is behind this contempt for God's way and will? It's the same problem: the temptation to sin by the secret machinations and manipulations of the tempter. It's this war between God and Satan, good and evil. As in Genesis 3, as in Watergate, and as in our everyday trials, Satan was seeking to frustrate God's plan and purpose for every person in this world: to love and serve God and man. Satan's strategy is known as spiritual warfare. It's God's will versus Satan's will. The question for man is this: Whom shall I believe, trust, follow? Who has the authority? Satan would lead us to believe that we have authority: "Go ahead; you can be like God." Satan tells us what we selfishly want to hear, that we can be the lords of our own lives, have our own way. This was my problem; it continues to be so, although to a much lesser extent now.

Richard Lovelace informs us in his book, *Dynamics of Spiritual Life,* how blind we are to spiritual warfare:

> Much of the church's warfare today is fought by blindfolded soldiers who cannot see the forces ranged against them, who are buffeted by invisible opponents and respond by striking one another.[3]

We are under spiritual attack: all of mankind — those in the church and those outside of the church. Satan is constantly seeking to weave his web of deceit and distortion over our eyes so we can see only man's ways and not God's. The Bible is replete with teachings about spiritual warfare. Yet this is a subject rarely preached and taught, much to the delight of Satan.

Jesus had to deal with spiritual attacks by Satan. He was tempted by the devil as soon as He was baptized. Satan urged Jesus — when He had been without food for 40 days — to "command these stones to become bread," appealing to the bodily senses (to have). Then, Satan challenged the courage of Jesus with the appeal to "throw yourself down" from the top of the Temple (to make a show). And, finally, Satan promised Jesus all the kingdoms of the world and their glory in exchange for Jesus' worship of Satan (to be glorified). Here in Matthew 4:1-11 was a direct appeal to the spirit and our creator's number one concern: that we worship Him "in spirit and in truth" (John 4:24, KJV).

These are the same subtle seductions we face today. They are (1) the issue of submitting to the will of God or Satan; (2) the issue of trusting in the truth of God's Word or the falsity of Satan's big lie; and (3) the issue of worshiping only God or giving in to the temptations of this world thrust at us by the original dirty trickster. These temptations add up to the appeal for possessions, power and pride.

Jesus met His test with victory. This is what we need to be able to do: to win over snaky, slimy desires and not become a dupe of the original dirty trickster. We must do God's will, accept His Word as truth, walk in His way and worship only Him. This is not only for God's glory but to follow God's concern for man's well-being and eternal life.

Again Jesus was tested, almost successfully, on the night before His crucifixion. The site was another garden (as with Adam) the Garden of Gethsemane across the Kidron Valley from the Upper Room of Last Supper fame. Jesus prayed: "O My

Father, if it is possible, let this cup pass from Me; nevertheless, not as I will, but as You will" (Matthew 26:39).

Jesus' human side shows here as He was depressed and in a poor state of heart and mind. He did not want to die on the cross — His prime mission on earth. Satan was working on Him at His lowest moment. This is when Satan tempts his best, when we are at our weakest and worst.

This was the time Satan pushed the Watergate cover-up in so many brilliant White House minds. Their backs were up against the wall of Watergate. Fear paralyzed their hearts. As Jeb Magruder said, "The cover-up was immediate and automatic."[4]

With Jesus, however, there was a pause — "nevertheless"; then He recovered His presence of mission — "not as I will, but as You will." Many times we win or lose in split-second decisions as to whether we will operate with or without God. Without God we fail and lose. With God we win! This is why we must be prepared to meet our own Watergates of life. Jesus knew that His mission in life on earth was "to do the will of Him who sent Me, and to finish His work" (John 4:34). In Luke 2:49, Jesus, at age 12, told Joseph and Mary, "Did you not know that I must be about My Father's business?" He knew whom to believe, trust and follow. In addition, He understood His mission and purpose, as did that Old Testament leader Nehemiah as he faced his enemies and their temptations in rebuilding the walls of Jerusalem (Nehemiah 2-6). Jesus and Nehemiah rejected the big lie of Satan. In Watergate, Satan convinced the White House and CREEP leaders that the power of government in being like God was the answer and that the end justified the means.

The biggest deceit in Satan's bag of dirty tricks is the ruse that he does not exist. However, Satan is real, just as hell is real. Both are revealed to us by Jesus and others in the Bible, the only authentic source of knowledge we have about Satan and hell. Yet, many in the church dismiss Satan and hell because they do not fit their predilections and because of biblical ignorance.

After coming across Satan's agent, the serpent, in Genesis 3, we next meet Satan himself in Job 1:8. There God removed the protective hedge from around a good man, Job, to permit Satan to tempt and test him. Job probably lived in the time of Abraham, but we see no mention of Job in Genesis. The book of Job proves the sovereignty of God and the limitation of Satan. We must always remember: Satan is no match for God. Just as man is limited, so is Satan. Satan wins his battles by our default or acquiescence. God's restraining hand is upon Satan, even though he is "the god of this world" (2 Corinthians 4:4, KJV). His power is inherent but delegated. His fate, as we read in Revelation, is one of doom. John, Paul and Luke tell us that a part of Jesus' mission was to destroy the works of Satan (1 John 3:8, Colossians 2:15 and Luke 10:18,19). The *coup de grace* was administered by Jesus at the cross and especially when He arose triumphant over death on that Easter Sunday morning.

Just because Satan is on God's leash, however, is no reason to ignore him. He is so clever, so cute, so invisible, so charming, so tempting. He is the pre-eminent con man and cover-up artist. He even tries to imitate God. But his ways are the opposite of God's ways. His world system, over which he presides — and which he offered to Jesus — is not built on love and self-sacrifice. Rather, its foundation stones are selfishness, greed, inordinate ambition, hedonism (pleasure-seeking), humanism, hate, force and an assortment of anti-God, anti-Bible and anti-church strategems.

Chief among Satan's weapons is the big lie that he used so effectively against Adam and Eve, and that he uses every day against us. There are all kinds and forms of lying. In the book, *Lying,* Sissela Bok arrives at this summary on the subject:

> Nearly every kind of statement or action can be meant to deceive. Clearly intended lies — the most sharply etched forms of duplicity — have been in the foreground throughout this book. More marginal forms, such as evasion, euphemism, and exaggeration, have been close at hand, ready to prop up these lies or take their place. And all around have clustered the many kinds of deception intended to mislead without even marginally false statements: the changes of subject, the disguises, the gestures of leading astray, all blending into the background of silence and inaction only sometimes intended to mislead.
>
> We lead our lives amidst all these forms of duplicity. From childhood on, we develop ways of coping with them — of believing some, seeing through others, and consciously ignoring still others.[5]

Satan has expanded the first lie in Genesis 3 to all these forms of lying and more. We Americans, with all our stress on individualism and competition, are perhaps tempted to cut corners more than other peoples. In our country the emphasis is on success and winning in business, politics, athletics and even in religion.

Jesus was well aware of Satan and his allies, evils and techniques. So were Peter, Paul, John, James and the other New Testament writers. Jesus called Satan the "evil one" in the Disciples' Prayer, which we call the Lord's Prayer (Matthew 6:13). Jesus also referred to Satan as the father of lies, stating that "there is no truth in him" (John 8:44).

Paul warned that Satan disguises himself as "an angel of light." (2 Corinthians 11:14) Indeed, when the serpent appeared to Eve the word used for his name in Hebrew meant the shining one. This may have been a part of the reason for his attraction and appeal to Eve. In today's advertising we seem to be most attracted by shining displays of grandeur.

Repeatedly we are warned about the devil and his snares in the Bible. Paul exhorts us in Ephesians 6:11 to "Put on the whole armor of God" against the schemes of Satan. Peter cautions in 1 Peter 5:8 that we must "be sober, be vigilant; because your adversary the devil walks about like a roaring lion, seeking whom he may devour."

James tells us God is not the tempter, and then depicts how temptation works: "But each one is tempted when he is drawn away by his own desires and enticed. Then, when desire has conceived, it gives birth to sin; and sin, when it is full-grown, brings forth death. Do not be deceived, my beloved brethren" (James 1:14-16). James, the brother of Jesus, fingers the real tempter and the answer to his temptation: "Therefore submit to God. Resist the devil and he will flee from you" (James 4:7). James has displayed for us the nature of the temptation and the tempter. We are the temptees, legally speaking. The description of temptation in James 1:14-16 is the exact approach the serpent used on the first temptees, Adam and Eve.

The stages of temptation James described for us are threefold: from desire to intent to action (sin), which issues in death. Ray Stedman places between the stages of desire and death the stage of intent and action, which he calls the stage of gestation.[6] In the process of gestation the temptation grows and matures into the act of sin which then issues in death (the ultimate end Satan seeks for us).

This process of sin accomplishes the works of the devil. Paul sets forth Satan's bag of dirty tricks in Galatians 5:19-21 as his Exhibit A:

> Now the works of the flesh are evident, which are: adultery, fornication, uncleanness, lewdness, idolatry, sorcery, hatred, contentions, jealousies, outbursts of wrath, selfish ambitions, dissensions, heresies, envy, murders, drunkenness, revelries, and the like; of which I tell you beforehand, just as I also told you in time past, that those who practice such things will not inherit the kingdom of God.

Interestingly, Paul follows the works of the devil with his Exhibit B, the fruit of the Holy Spirit:

> But the fruit of the Spirit is love, joy, peace, longsuffering, kindness, goodness, faithfulness, gentleness, self-control. Against such there is no law (Galatians 5:22,23).

Needless to say, Exhibit A is Satan's will or agenda for our lives; Exhibit B is God's. How do you vote?

The serpent urged Eve to go ahead and satisfy her own desires, to break the limitation God had put on her. In Genesis 3:4,5, the serpent enticed Eve with, "You will not surely die. For God knows that in the day you eat of it your eyes will be opened, and you will be like God, knowing good and evil."

Genesis 3:6 relates Eve's response, "So when the woman saw that the tree was good for food, that it was pleasant to the eyes and a tree desirable to make one wise, she took of its fruit and ate. She also gave to her husband with her, and he ate." This is the way Satan works, his M.O. He comes at us from the outside. He sets up the outer appeals: food to satisfy the bodily senses; the enjoyment of beauty to appeal to our emotions; and, to pamper our ego and intelligence, pride — the desire to be above others. God begins His work inside — at the heart — and once our will is attuned to His, then the change of heart and will is manifested in outer actions and in our walk (conduct) with God. Satan's aim is to work God out of us and himself into us.

The serpent questioned God's Word, His authority and His motive. He also urged Eve to indulge her desires, and she did. He told her and Adam they could be the lord of their own lives; they could "be like God." Isn't this the same problem we have today when the tests and temptations of life appear before us? Also, aren't the desires that were experienced by Adam and Eve the basis for all our temptations and sins? Apostles John and Paul say so in 1 John 2:16 and Galatians 5:19-21, respectively. John warns us about "the lust of the flesh [sensualism], the lust of the eyes [materialism], and the pride of life [egotism]." Paul lists the "works of the flesh" which issue in sin. In these two passages the apostles point to these desires as the root sins from which the sin tree sprouts and grows to envelope the life (soul) of man.

Temptation is not a sin. It is the action we take as a consequence of temptation that can result in sin. Jesus was tempted, but He did not yield to its appeals.

Sin comes in four basic packages. First, there is the original sin or the bent of our nature to sin habitually. Second, sin can be not only external but also internal, in our inner person and thoughts. Third, there are the sins of omission, failure or refusal to do what we should do. Fourth, there is the gravest sin of all, our rebellion against God. These four types of sin are: our sinful nature, our sinful thoughts, our sins of falling short and our sin against God.

Deception comes in very convincing packages. There is the garb of authenticity and the credentials of intelligence, power, prestige and popularity. Even Christian fakes can fleece us. By the millions, gullible gluttons, still falling for something for nothing, are tricked into swallowing lies that appear to be truth. P.T. Barnum, the great circus promoter, best said it years ago: "There's a sucker born every minute." Paul puts it for us in Scripture this way:

> For such are false apostles, deceitful workers, transforming themselves into apostles of Christ. And no wonder! For Satan himself transforms himself into an angel of light. Therefore it is no great thing if his ministers also transform themselves into ministers of righteousness, whose end will be according to their works. (2 Corinthians 11:13-15).

Our great defense against sin lies in our being shocked at it. There are three well-known steps by which we fall into sin: distortion of God's will or law, insinuation of doubt, and then a flat denial. Finally there follows the last stage of sin, the agony and remorse of sin. This was Satan's game plan in the Garden of Eden. It has worked so well throughout history that he is using it on you and me today in our lives.

The first line of defense in discerning evil is to know Scripture and its truth and the Author of all Scripture, who is Truth embodied. We are tricked because we still seek man's kingdom over God's kingdom, and man's kingdom reeks with deceit, duplicity and downright lying. Jesus commands us to "seek first the kingdom of God and His righteousness, and all these things shall be added to you" (Matthew 6:33). We are also easily deluded because we believe in myths, charms, superstition, chance, luck, hunches, astrology and our own whims. We are patsies of self-deception because we seem to want to believe the worst about everyone but ourselves. We need supernatural help. We need spiritual vision to recognize better the temptation and the tempter.

a child in the way he should go, and when he is old he will not depart from it."

Paul followed this admonition with another in Ephesians 6:4m "And you, fathers, do not provoke your children to wrath, but bring them up in the training and admonition of the Lord."

In Deuteronomy 6:4-9, Moses instructed the new generation of Israelites who were preparing to enter the Promised Land about the family and the home:

> Hear, O Israel: The LORD our God, the LORD is one! You shall love the LORD your God with all your heart, with all your soul, and with all your strength.
> And these words which I command you today shall be in your heart. You shall teach them diligently to your children, and shall talk of them when you sit in your house, when you walk by the way, when you lie down, and when you rise up. You shall bind them as a sign on your hand, and they shall be as frontlets between your eyes. You shall write them on the doorposts of your house and on your gates.

In essence, Moses charged the fathers in the homes to establish a divine school in which the father is to be the teacher and the role model. He is to ensure that the family members know God, that God's love and truth prevail in the home, and that the father's life and that of the family be a witness for God outside the home.

The father is clearly the parent responsible for setting the pattern for the obedience of the children. Both parents are to ensure that the children experience unconditional love for the Lord and within the family. The key role model is the father. This goes with being the spiritual leader in the family. Also, children innately tend to focus on the example of the father.

In the Watergate saga, we see Gordon Liddy as being anything but a spiritual role model. Thus, Frances Liddy seemed undisturbed when she got the news of the Watergate break-in. In his book, *Will,* Gordon Liddy gives this account:

> It was about 3 A.M. when I eased my way into the bedroom, trying not to waken Fran. Light streamed into the room from the streetlight outside, and I could see her still form as I started quietly to undress. After a moment she stirred. I stopped moving, hoping she'd stay asleep. Fran stirred again. "Is that you?"
> "Yes."
> I continued undressing. Fran has a sixth sense. Maybe all women married to the same man for fifteen years do.
> "Anything wrong?"
> "There was trouble. Some people got caught. I'll probably be going to jail."

> Perhaps the experience of the FBI years told Fran it would be pointless to inquire further. She closed her eyes and said nothing more. Neither did I. What more was there to say?
> I climbed in bed and went to sleep.[3]

Frances stood by her husband and his convictions despite his long incarceration and the resulting expenses and other problems. She had to work and handle a family of five growing youngsters. She respected Gordon Liddy's convictions. His silence cost her and their two girls and three boys dearly. Frances maintained that the family would have considered Gordon to be a coward had he done otherwise. Gordon offered her a divorce to end her misery. But Frances loved him too much. In fact, she and the children considered him a prisoner of war.

What is Liddy's view now? In November, 1985, he told an audience at Brown University (Colson's alma mater) that he'd do it (Watergate) all over again. He said the only thing wrong with the break-in is that the burglars got caught. "Anyone who doesn't believe that both sides, Democrats and Republicans, don't do everything they can to get an advantage also believes in the tooth fairy," Liddy said.[4]

Dorothy Hunt supported her husband, Howard, even more. She became involved in the cover-up and was killed in an airliner crash while ferrying $10,000 in cash. Like Frances Liddy, she knew and accepted her husband's cloak-and-dagger existence. Howard Hunt earned his family's livelihood in undercover operations of the Central Intelligence Agency and in writing more than forty-five CIA-type novels.

Dorothy told reporters from *The Washington Post* that "they ordered him [Hunt] to do this and it is wrong for them to prosecute him." Hunt's demands for family living expenses and attorney's fees are what caused the Nixon leaders to obstruct justice and to dig themselves deeper into perjury and conspiracy.

The Hunt children suffered the most of all the Watergate children. Dorothy had kept their father's secret life from them. In the book, *The Women of Watergate,* the views of the Hunt children are related:

> And yet, now that their mother is dead and their family scattered, they are bitter. If only their mother had refused to cooperate. If only their father had not talked her into it. If it had not been that plane. They do not know where to place the blame. They see their mother's death as a terrible penalty for what was, in their view, a mistake, a miscalculation. "It seemed like she paid for every mistake he ever made," says her son. "Her first mistake was getting married. She paid for that one her whole life."[5]

Where is Howard Hunt today? He is back in Miami continuing to grind out more of his spy novels and is now working on a screen play as well. If he moves again, it will be to Mexico, perhaps to find novel approaches to intrigue and covert operations for his pulp fiction. A book on Watergate's intrigues and secrets? No way!

In contrast, the late Martha Mitchell (Mrs. John Mitchell) would not be silenced about Watergate. She defended her husband, but she publicly decried the break-in and cover-up. In fact, she was the first person to sound the alarm five days after the break-in on June 17, 1972. She was present when her husband, the campaign chairman, received the news of the foiled burglary. She telephoned her favorite news reporter, Helen Thomas, longtime White House correspondent for United Press International. Martha continued calling, but her calls were abruptly concluded by her being pulled away from the phone. Martha became famous for her nocturnal calls to reporters.

Martha Beall Mitchell was a charming and loquacious blonde southern belle from Pine Bluff, Arkansas. In addition to her notoriety for Watergate phone calls, Martha had become noted for adding splashes of color and life to an otherwise uncolorful and drab Nixon Administration. We began using her as one of the best political and fund-raising drawing cards in the Administration.

I took Mrs. Mitchell on several political excursions including one to my home city of Columbia, South Carolina. She and Vice President Spiro Agnew could be counted on for conservative and bombastic comments — just what GOP regulars wanted to hear. Martha did not give speeches as such. She would wow the contributors with her southern belle appearance, dresses, accent and charm in the receiving line. And she would throw out enough spicy anti-liberal, anti-Communist and iconoclastic barbs to bring down the house.

On September 11, 1973, John Mitchell walked out on Martha, and the two never talked again. He went on later to be incarcerated in Montgomery, Alabama.

Martha had a problem with tranquilizers and alcohol. This is discussed in various Watergate books, especially the one by Jeb Magruder. When John left her, he commented only that Martha was "a very sick woman." He continues in that view today.

The Mitchells had a daughter named for Martha but called Marty. She was born when Martha was 43 years old. Martha claimed that John turned Marty against her. She reported that

Marty told her, "It's all your fault that Daddy is in trouble. You're the one who talked." Marty was then twelve years old. Today her father is very proud of her morals and good adjustment to life after all she endured in the Watergate days and with her mother's problems.

Richard Nixon went further than Marty. He claimed that had Martha not distracted his close friend John, there would have been no Watergate. Indeed, John Mitchell was the most mature and wisest man in the Administration insofar as judgment was concerned. He was bedeviled by his problems with the International Telephone and Telegraph investigation on Capitol Hill and by his wife's candid, erratic and uninhibited behavior. While Martha liked to travel with the President, she began throwing the blame for Watergate away from her husband and on his friend, "Mr. President," as she began referring to Nixon.

Martha Mitchell had her highs and lows. She was the only Cabinet wife ever voted one of the ten most-admired women in the world. In the 1972 re-election campaign she was second only to the President in speaking invitations and sported an amazing 76 percent national recognition factor.

Her final low came in the summer of 1977 as she grew more lonely for John's return and entered the final stages of terminal multiple myeloma. John and Marty finally came to Pine Bluff, Arkansas for a quick visit. The occasion was Martha's funeral on a beautiful, sunny day, June 3, 1977. The one consolation for Martha was that she died as John's wife. The proposed divorce was never finalized. The former Attorney General buried Martha near her forebears in Pine Bluff.

Never one to be short on words, Martha got the final word at the cemetery. An anonymous supporter — and in Pine Bluff she was and continues to be a heroine — provied a floral wreath proclaiming: "MARTHA WAS RIGHT."

Martha told much of what she knew to the public, but she did keep some secrets for the book she and Winzola McClendon were collaborating on. Winzola published this book, *Martha: The Life of Martha Mitchell,* in 1979. Here are a few of the book's revelations.

1. James McCord confided to Martha in a 1974 meeting that the Watergate entry was "because they [CREEP] had a feeling that the Communists were financing the Democratic Committee."[6]

2. Martha often carried her worn kindergarten Bible when under stress.[7]

3. Martha's childhood disease of dyslexia affected her use of numbers, her spelling, and her reading. Also, she was hyperac-

tive and always talked too much. These problems, plus her cover-up about her father's abandonment of her and suicide in Texas in 1943, all contributed to her severe emotional problems. For relief, she mixed prescription drugs and alcohol.[8]

Was Martha right, or was Martha crazy, as alleged by CREEP aides? Dr. Klaus Mayer, the doctor who treated Martha in her final illness, declared her to be "normal" with this comment: "Oh, God, yes! She was a character, but she was normal."[9]

The record shows that Martha was far more right than wrong!

There was another lady — a young, pretty, and then pregnant one — who also sounded an early alarm to her husband, Hugh (Duke) Sloan. This was Debbie Sloan. I knew both of them very well. In fact, I kidded them more than once in the White House staff mess that Watergate would get them. What I did not realize at the time was that Hugh was already sweating over the Watergate break-in. He had supplied the $190,000 in cash to Gordon Liddy for his covert operations. Some of the currency bills had been captured and were traced to the Committee to Re-elect the President. Hugh was the campaign treasurer and thus the disburser of spending money.

Hugh Sloan was one of several people Jeb Magruder tried to bring into the cover-up and perjury conspiracy. Even John Ehrlichman had assured Hugh that executive privilege would cover financial details.

After a vacation in Bermuda, the Sloans returned to Washington, and he resigned on July 14, three weeks after the Watergate break-in. Debbie refuses to take credit for the decision, but Washington believed her influence was responsible. She once told an inquiring reporter, "This is an honest house!"

Debbie had been an assistant in the office of the First Lady, Pat Nixon. She and Hugh were strong Nixon loyalists, but they believed the truth would help the President the most. They drew a moral line over which they refused to transgress.

Today the Sloans are living in Waterloo, Ontario, Canada, where Hugh is running an automotive parts supply business. They now have four children, ages thirteen to five. The Sloan family is much involved in the Anglican church, and Debbie and Hugh are much wiser because of their Watergate experience. They were among the few who refused to cover up from the beginning.

"I thought my productive life was over," Hugh says, "because I thought they would be able to cover up Watergate and get away with it. I just knew they would then go after me. But, we didn't feel comfortable doing anything but what we knew was right.

"Debbie and I learned so much from that experience. We grew together as a couple. We grew spiritually and in maturity, and our value system firmed up. Now I tell young people: 'In a crisis, do what you know is right even if you stand to lose by doing so. That way you can always live with yourself.' "

Debbie reminds me very much of my wife, Betty. Betty and I were in Columbia buying a lot when the break-in at Watergate became news on that weekend of June 17-18, 1972. She had tried to dissuade me from accepting the prized job in the White House in 1968. She cried when I said yes over her objections. I commuted each year until 1972, and she continued to beg me to resign. She was always fearful of something like a Watergate in the White House. After the break-in, her protective radar sensed the ultimate tragedy of the cover-up. It was because of my respect for her judgment and concerns that I decided against staying for the second Nixon term and what could have brought involvment in the escalating cover-up.

Before Watergate I did not heed her advice on many matters, especially my career in politics. After Watergate I over- listened. In doing so, I discovered what profitable wisdom and advice women have to provide. When the "E.F. Hutton" named Betty Dent speaks, Harry Dent listens as never before!

Another woman and her children stood staunchly behind her husband both privately and publicly in Watergate. However, Joanne Haldeman had nothing to do with fostering the cover-up. Harry Robbins (Bob) Haldeman praises his family's encouragement and says that this family backing plus his Christian Science faith have accounted for his ability to survive Watergate and imprison-ment without breaking, as did some. Today he is president and chief executive officer of a growing and successful hotel and real estate development corporation in Los Angeles. "My wife, Jo," he says, "has always been very strong. We've had to help some of our children recently work through some problems, but none are related to Watergate."

Jo's best friend at UCLA, the former Jeanne Ehrlichman of Seattle, Washington, has not fared as well. Jeanne and John Ehrlichman were among the many couples whose marriages were destroyed by Watergate. She is now happily remarried in Seattle to a state senator — back in politics again. John and his second wife, Christy, live together in Sante Fe with their five-year-old son, Michael. Recently Christy arranged a surprise sixtieth birthday party for John in California with all of his children present, including their mates and John's grandchildren. John feels that he has a good relationship with all family members.

The Haldemans and Ehrlichmans were Christian Scientists when they came into the White House. This received much attention, especially when a Christian Science church building was erected within two blocks of the White House soon after their arrival.

John Ehrlichman brought with him a handsome and capable young attorney from his Seattle law firm, Egil (Bud) Krogh, husband of Suzanne Krogh. The Kroghs were also Christian Scientists. Suzanne survived tough marital problems with Bud for a while. In fact, they were separated at a critical time, from 1970 to the summer of 1972. During this time Bud made decisions that sent him to jail, shortcutting the potential of a brilliant career. From the White House he had moved in 1973 at age thirty-three to the number-two position in the Transportation Department. All of this was undone, however, by decisions he made and executed in using Liddy, Hunt and most of the Watergate break-in team to do the black-bag job in Los Angeles several months before Watergate. The break-in at the office of Daniel Ellsberg's psychiatrist was one of the actions that sent Bud to prison for six months and caused his disbarment from the practice of law for several years. When Bud made these mistakes he was separated from his wife and his religion.

Suzanne and Bud became reconciled in the summer of 1972. He returned to his wife and his religion. As the Watergate cover-up began cracking, Bud and Suzanne decided that Bud also had to come back to the truth. So in the summer of 1973 they together prepared an affidavit of truth for the prosecutors. Bud took full responsibility for the Ellsberg break-in and his previous lying. Unlike Dean and Magruder, Bud did not seek immunity from prosecution by implicating others. He kept in mind the Christian Science teaching, "injure no man." Bud was sentenced to prison and moved to serve his several months immediately.

In a conversation with me on October 4, 1985, Bud related his reliance on the Bible this way:

> In prison I determined to look to the positive (a Christian Science precept), to be active, to be influential for good, and not to pine or give up. So I started a study of the Bible to discover what all those characters who had done time in jail had done. Daniel, Paul, Peter — they all impressed me to no end.
>
> The Bible and my bad experience showed me I had to turn to a higher power. It was more like a quickening type of experience that happened in my life. I'm not the type to easily give a verbal witness. I try to do it with my life — how I live my life.

Bud Krogh won plaudits from Senator Sam Ervin, Special Prosecutor Leon Jaworski and many others, including the news media, for facing his Watergate forthrightly though belatedly. As a consequence, several years later in 1980, the state of Washington's Supreme Court restored him to the practice of law. Who was one of those backing him? Leon Jaworski. Today Bud is a partner in a prestigious Seattle law firm.

Although Suzanne influenced Bud to do right, they could not make their marriage work. She is now a professor on the faculty of the University of Florida. One son is in college, and they share custody of the younger son. Bud has been remarried for seven years to an interior decorator, Laura Lee Krogh.

Maureen (Mo) Dean drew the most raves and public notice of any Watergate wife except for Martha Mitchell. Her husband, John, was the star witness in the U.S. Senate's Watergate hearings on television. However, the young, well-dressed ex- White House counsel was hardly any more familiar to television watchers than his attractive wife, Mo. Her dress, style, chic coiffure and spunky comments in support of her husband spiced the television hearings with special color and interest. Her background alone was worth many human interest articles and short TV features. Mo was the daughter of a former Ziegfeld Follies beauty. Also, her background was rather mysterious. She had been involved in two previous marriages and had just married into Watergate. Mo and John were wed four months after the break-in as John was coordinating the cover-up from his office in the old Executive Office Building next door to the West Wing of the White House.

John had been quietly divorced in 1969 from the daughter of a U.S. senator. He wore expensive suits and Gucci loafers, and he was especially noted for his sleek maroon Porsche. The young couple drew special attention when he was forced to admit in the television hearings that he had used $4,850 of cash campaign funds for his honeymoon.

The love between the two showed. John credited "the love of this woman" as being one of the greatest sources of strength in his Watergate ordeal. His love for Mo, he felt, was inextricably linked with his faith in a higher being. He told *Time* correspondent and good friend, Hays Gorey, that he and Mo remind each other to pray every night before going to bed. John also told Gorey he once "almost went into the Episcopal ministry."

Mo Dean had tried to influence John not to write that Watergate report at Camp David and to uncover himself before the prosecutors.

> She was right, but her innocence annoyed me. She seemed so far removed from all the shadings of lies that make up political life....Still, even though she knew nothing of the details of Watergate, or the rationale behind the report, or all that had gone on before, she had hit the mark intuitively.[10]

Where is John Dean today, and what is he doing for a living as a disbarred attorney? John has turned from writing to investment banking in Los Angeles. He owns his own company, Western Mercantile Services Group.

John has found "the world to be very forgiving." What does he think of his old White House boss? "Today, with maturity," he exclaims, "I'd tell him to go to hell with his cover-up."

What does John believe was the critical mistake in Watergate? "Jeb [Magruder] got Gordon [Liddy] excited and pushed him."

What does he think Nixon is about these days? "He's running for ex-President."

How about Mo? "She's as pretty and wise as ever."

While in prison together at Fort Holabird, Maryland, old enemies Colson and Dean became good friends. At the same time, so did Patty Colson and Mo Dean. When Dean was released he wrote Chuck a note promising that his and Mo's prayers would be with them.

However, in 1977 a *Parade* magazine article emanating from a social reunion of the Deans and Colsons caused Chuck grave embarrassment. The article by Lloyd Shearer purported to quote the editor of John's book, Taylor Branch, as saying that "Colson got very drunk" at the private dinner. Twenty-seven million copies of the *Parade* article thus conveyed the impression that Chuck was a phony Christian.

The problem was that Chuck had taken one drink of Scotch whiskey. In his second book, *Life Sentence,* he cited this incident as an example of how new Christians can stumble along the path of spiritual growth. The lesson he learned was that he must "face the issue of social drinking as it related to my Christian witness....In no way do I want to be a stumbling block to others; alcoholism is an epidemic illness in American life and more than 50 percent of all crimes are committed by people under its influence."[11]

Patricia Colson had had no idea how much her life would be changed by her marriage to Charles Wendell Colson. She knew he was a young man in a hurry because she had worked under his leadership in the office of U.S. Senator Leverett Saltonstall of Massachusetts. Patty was a Catholic, an orphan, and had dated a New England political star named John Fitzgerald Kennedy.

Perhaps the biggest shock for Patty came when Chuck "got religion." It was some time before she began to understand the changes she could see developing in his life. Chuck was becoming a staunch evangelical. This was a far cry from her orthodox Catholic faith.

Patty is very proud of Chuck and his ability to deliver God's message so eloquently and effectively in prisons, pulpits, corporate boards and in his best-selling books. She now accompanies him in most of his travels and worships with him in the Presbyterian church they attend in Naples, Florida, and in Columbia Baptist Church in the Washington area.

The stress and strain of all the Watergate trauma have adversely affected some marriages of those touched by the scandal. In addition to those broken marriages already mentioned, Alex and Charlotte Butterfield and Jeb and Gail Magruder also divorced.

Alex was not a defendant. He was the one who answered the questions about the secret White House taping system. As a consequence, he has had some difficulties. Now he is involved as an executive in the retail store coupon redemption business in Los Angeles.

Perhaps the cause of Butterfield's woes has been the persistent reports, even in the 1984 book, *Secret Agenda,* by Jim Hougan, suggesting that he may have been a CIA plant in Nixon's inner sanctum. Butterfield denies this. The late Fred Buzhardt agreed with Butterfield. John Ehrlichman and Steve Bull, Butterfield's former assistant, also stand with Butterfield. However, Bob Haldeman and Nixon's former and longtime personal secretary, Rose Woods, are very suspicious of Butterfield. Charles Colson and others are convinced that the CIA had "unrivaled access to the President's private conversations and thoughts."[12]

The divorce of Gail and Jeb Magruder has received news attention because of Jeb's current employment in Christian ministry work. Gail says Watergate ruined their marriage, and she is convinced that both her parents and Jeb's died as a consequence of the pressures of Watergate. Gail lives in Bethesda, Maryland. Jeb is executive minister of First Community Church in Columbus, Ohio.

Jeb is certain most of his struggle is in the past, but the unwanted divorce hurts. "I look forward to serving the Lord and my fellowman more faithfully as the next chapters of my life unfold," he told me in late 1985. "My job here at First Community Church is an exciting and challenging one."

Both Gail and Jeb were led into a right relationship with Jesus Christ by the Rev. and Mrs. Louis Evans of National Presbyterian Church in Washington, D.C. Colleen Evans was used by the Lord to reach Gail. Louie Evans came alongside Jeb in prison and after he returned to his Bethesda home.

At least one immediate member of the Richard Nixon family turned to the Lord and held on during the Watergate trauma and thereafter. Julie Nixon Eisenhower studied the Bible with a small group of other Washingtonians under the tutelage of Eleanor Page. Mrs. Page was at that time (1973-1974) a Campus Crusade for Christ speaker and teacher. Later Julie joined the Eleanor Page "speak team" for sharing Christian testimonies. In Palm Beach, Florida, Julie told the news media and her audience that God had cleaned out of her life all the bitterness and malice generated by Watergate.

In her 1977 book, *Special People,* Julie chose Ruth Bell Graham (Mrs. Billy) as one of six special people "who have shaped our lives, even shaped our world....Ruth Graham has also lived for a cause. Her commitment has been to helping others develop their own faith in God."[13]

In writing the book, Julie visited with Ruth Graham three times — at the White House, during the 1976 Graham Crusade in San Diego, and later in 1976 at the Graham residence in Montreat, North Carolina. Julie compared Ruth with Julie's grandmother, Hannah Milhous Nixon.

> It seems incongruous to compare Nana with a woman so strongly associated with public displays of belief. My grandmother was so private in her faith....But the reason I link Ruth Graham and my grandmother in my mind is that their faith in God — more important to them than anything else in their lives — had made me want to believe also. And like Nana's, Ruth's faith comes from her Bible.[14]

David and Julie Eisenhower had their political goals altered by Watergate. I worked with the President in devising a strategy to have David elected to Congress from Gettysburg, Pennsylvania, then to the governorship or United States Senate and ultimately to the White House. The first step was cleared in persuading the elderly Gettysburg Congressman to retire from office. But Watergate intervened.

David and Julie now have been writing books in a community outside of Philadelphia. They are involved in an Episcopal church, and their three children are enrolled in a Christian school.

Julie has discussed her spiritual experience with her mother, father and sister. The president feels he had his experience as a youth. Pat Nixon's view is that every person is entitled to his own personal faith. Julie's sister Patricia does not seem interested, the result of a bad experience with a clergyman.

Julie has always been the most gregarious and outspoken member of the Nixon family. Her attention at present is focused on her own family. She very much believes in "the theme that runs through Anne Morrow Lindbergh's writings...'Life is a gift, given in trust — like a child.' "[15] Mrs. Charles Lindbergh was another one of Julie's special people, those who affected her life. Julie believes in the importance of getting the good news of Jesus Christ out to the world, beginning with the family. For Julie understands, as Ruth Graham explained to her, that husband and wife are to become, as the Bible says, "one flesh," and as Ruth proclaims, "a union of two forgivers."[16] I believe the world has not heard the last of Julie's witness.

As I look at the role of the women affected by Watergate and at their husbands enduring the agonies of Watergate, I see two strong teachings. First, every man needs to be open and honest with his mate and vice versa. The women will, in most cases, lead egotistical and erring men toward the truth. Their intuition is invaluable. Second, I see the husbands of these women reaching out for God and the Bible — in most cases. I see them finding consolation and truth there — in prayer with God and in study of His Book — when they can find balm and strength nowhere else.

The teaching is: Stay close to the mate and family, and stay close to God, His Word and His people. Above all, do not play God yourself.

CHAPTER VII

MAN'S BIGGEST TEMPTATION

Unlike the men who were responsible for Teapot Dome, the presidential aides who perpetrated Watergate were not seduced by the love of money, which is sometimes thought to be the root of all evil. On the contrary, they were instigated by a lust for political power itself.

U.S Senator Sam Ervin[1]

If there was one enticement that caused Adam and Eve to commit the original sin, it was the desire for power — to play God. Man wants to have the authority, and Satan understands all too well that this is man's Achilles' heel. So, the will to have power and to resist authority were the principal motives behind the fall in the garden as well as Watergate. They are also the prime motives that unleash other Watergates in our lives. Behind these two motives lurks the root cause of sin: pride. Man wants to be free to have his own way more than he wants to be responsible and obedient in a servant role to authority.

In Genesis 3, we see Adam seeking power and reaping trouble. The same can be said for the conduct of our campaign to re-elect the President in 1972. Jeb Magruder, the day-to-day director of the Nixon campaign, gave three causes for Watergate: (1) too much power in the White House, thus cutting it off from reality; (2) Nixon's obsession with his "enemies" and their criticism of him; and (3) "we convinced ourselves that wrong was right, and plunged ahead."[2]

In all of my occupations in life, I have been subject to the will-to-have-power delusion and have experienced the human drive to manipulate and control others — to be above others — in business, law practice, the news media, government, lobbying and politics. What convinces me that the will to have power is of epidemic proportions in every area of life is that I have also experienced what Dr. Tony Campolo calls the "power delusion" in God's work, the one area where coercion and manipulation are clearly to be off-limits. The life and teachings of Jesus Christ are wrapped around the opposite of power. A long-time Christian teacher and leader — one who is surrendered to Jesus' teachings on servanthood — informed me that approximately nine of ten people who come out of the business world into God's work fail to adjust to Jesus' way of doing business. The most fruitful servants for Jesus that I have come to know have been not the manipulators but those who have relinquished power and thus have won authority by respect and love. In so doing, they have gained authority to lead people for Jesus Christ.

In his book, *The Power of Delusion,* the unconventional Anthony Campolo, Jr., gives incisive definitions of the two words, power and authority.

> I am defining power as "the prerogative to determine what happens and the coercive force to make others yield to your wishes — *even against their own will."* This last phrase is crucial, for the coercive nature of power gives expression to its potential for evil. Coercion is the crux of why power is irreconcilable with Christianity.   When a leader is able to persuade others to do his will without coercion, when he presents himself in such a way that people *want* to obey him, when they recognize him as a legitimate leader with the right to expect compliance with his wishes, I say that he has *authority.*[3]

Jesus had a problem with His disciples on this very subject. They too wanted to be above others and even above one another. Salome, the mother of apostles John and James, asked Jesus to place her boys on His left and right when He returned to heaven (Matthew 20:20,21). In His response to her and to all the apostles, Jesus gave an astonishing teaching:

> But Jesus called them to Himself and said, "You know that the rulers of the Gentiles lord it over them, and those who are great exercise authority over them. Yet it shall not be so among you; but whoever desires to become great among you, let him be your servant. And whoever desires to be first among you, let him be your slave — just as the Son of Man did not come to be served, but to serve, and to give His life a ransom for many" (Matthew 20:25-28).

Jesus ruled out power plays in His kingdom. In fact, humility and servanthood based on love are the keys to the kingdom life. At the Last Supper, Jesus not only preached servanthood but illustrated this value of the kingdom by washing the feet of the apostles. He was showing them that the master must be the servant. He expressed it this way:

> So when He had washed their feet, taken His garments, and sat down again, He said to them, "Do you know what I have done to you? You call me Teacher and Lord, and you say well, for so I am. If I then, your Lord and Teacher, have washed your feet, you also ought to wash one another's feet. For I have given you an example, that you should do as I have done to you. Most assuredly, I say to you, a servant is not greater than his master; nor is he who is sent greater than he who sent him" (John 13:12-16).

Then, Jesus gave the apostles and us these instructions. "A new commandment I give to you, that you love one another; as I have loved you, that you also love one another. By this all will know that you are My disciples if you have love for one another" (John 13:34,35).

People in church pulpits and pews need to re-read John 13. The world must understand this key leadership principle because it is not just idealistic; it actually works. In the best- selling book, *In Search of Excellence,*[4] this principle of service and caring about people is cited as one of the most rewarding policies in the business world. The authors studied sixty-two American companies noted for the excellence of their operations.

Out of this study came eight basic principles that promote excellence and success in business and industry. All eight have to do with how people are handled. Point number two is this: "staying close to the customer — learning his preferences and catering to him." This spells service after the sale as well as before the sale. The chapter on this subject stresses service, quality, reliability and genuine caring. These attributes keep the cash registers ringing in the excellent companies. "All business success rests on something labeled a sale," the authors underscore.

These attributes also work in politics. U.S. Senator Strom Thurmond has been winning elections by big margins because so many people believe he cares about them and gives service to them after as well as before the elections. He taught me to stay close to the voters.

This is what the Bible teaches: Love and care for one another, serve one another and forbear and forgive one another. But man's problem is that, by and large, he prefers to rule rather than to serve. This is a problem even in Christian work.

Professor and author Richard J. Foster delineates between two types of power in his book, *Money, Sex and Power.*

> There is a power that destroys. There is also a power that creates. The power that creates gives life and joy and peace. It is freedom and not bondage, life and not death, transformation and not coercion. The power that creates restores relationship and gives the gift of wholeness to all. The power that creates is spiritual power, the power that proceeds from God....Love is the first mark of spiritual power. Love demands that power be used for the good of others.[5]

In the Garden of Eden, Adam and Eve saw their surrender to the serpent's lure to be like God backfire on them. Like God they came to know good and evil, but they also became marred and perverted in evil and sin. And God hates sin. So they had to be expelled from the garden, and they became subject to spiritual and physical death.

Watergate might aptly be called *The Failure of Success.* That is the name of a book that focused and helped change my thinking on my primary aim of the past: success. The author, Dr. Esther Milner, maintains that our drive for success and "the good life" in America is destroying the very fabric of our society, our homes and our individual lives. She zeroes in on two principal misbeliefs of our day.

> The touchstone fallacy that high occupational and consumer status will somehow transform us into happy, "whole" beings — is the first of these beliefs. The other is the success myth that a sociologist labeled the "American Dream" some time ago: anyone can succeed if only he tries hard enough. We are so sure of the Dream's promise we are convinced that if a man doesn't succeed after trying and trying, there must be something very wrong with him. Both those who succeed and those who fail tend to react to failure as a personal sin, and therefore as a strictly individual matter. In so believing and so reacting, we are rendered incapable of objective appraisal of the external factors which have entered into our failure (as well as into our success), and as a result, we fail to recognize not only that we are one of many with the same problem, but that there are common reasons for our common problem. Our assumption of personal guilt serves to render us incapable of taking intelligent group action in our own behalf.
>
> Most of us subscribe so strongly to the Fallacy and the Dream that these two beliefs can be considered the American middle class's "axioms of life." Yet these two beliefs, developed during and relatively appropriate to an earlier period of our history, no longer have a realistic base because of irrevocably changed social and economic conditions. Persistence of values and practices rendered inappropriate and even socially dangerous by changed economic, social, physical conditions, have in the past led to the decline and fall of once powerful societies — and may be leading to that of ours. Here is reason enough for examination of the touchstone fallacy and its effects.[6]

Tony Campolo defines success as meaning that "an individual has gained for himself one, if not all, of the following: wealth, power, and prestige."[7] In his book, *The Success Fantasy,* Campolo points out that Jesus turned His back on such success in the world. He adds:

> A world that worships power, and sees it as an ultimate mark of success, has a hard time comprehending a kind of success that is based on the mutual submission of love. Frederick Nietzsche, the atheistic, existentialist philosopher, claimed that the "will to power" was the most basic drive of the human personality, motivating all of human behavior. I believe there is more to Nietzsche's claim than we want to admit. Power *is* a mark of success within our society, and the human appetite for it seems insatiable.[8]

Campolo aptly addresses the dangers inherent in wealth, power and prestige:

> Wealth, power, and prestige can corrupt those who possess them. *Wealth* can delude us into a kind of self-sufficiency and denial of our need of God.... *Power* can turn us into megalomaniacs. Desire to dominate can lead us to diminish their humanity, as well as our own....Cravings for *prestige* can lead us into destructive pride and egotism that know no bounds.... Yet we must remember that wealth, power and prestige have great potential for good.[9]

The thrust of Bible teaching is to use the gifts God has given us for His glory and the good of our fellowman. After all, everything was created by God; we are created by God and we are His stewards and trustees. However, the record of history is replete with accounts of man's selfishness and drive for his own success. The stories of those who have followed Jesus' teachings to be fruitful and faithful are less noted.

The madness of man's determination to be like God is nowhere better set out for us than in Albert Speer's classic book, *Inside the Third Reich.*[10] Here the former high-ranking Nazi provides a candid account of the megalomania of the century's most notable despot, Adolf Hitler. As a young man, Speer began working for Hitler as his architect. He knew the difference between good and evil. However, the attraction of being associated with wealth, power and prestige was too much for an outstanding young man reaching out for success and all of its trappings.

As I read Speer's book for a second time and watched the ABC-TV mini-series based on his book, the story became an all too vivid reminder of our Watergate. Speer highlighted the Hitler inner circle's lack of reality, the amateurishness, the stubbornness, the isolation, the enemies lists, the insecurity, the blunders, the bunker mentality, the temptation to sychophancy (currying favor with the leader) and the absorption with monuments and history. In writing this, I do not mean to imply that Richard Nixon and his Administration were taking America in the same direction that Adolph Hitler and his minions led Germany. However, there are similarities and parallels in operations that concern me today more than they did at that time.

On sychophancy, Speer makes the pertinent comment:

> There is a special trap for every holder of power, whether the director of a company, the head of a state, or the ruler of a dictatorship. His favor is so desirable to his subordinates that they will sue for it by every means possible. Servility becomes endemic among his entourage, who compete among themselves in their show of devotion. This in turn exercises a sway upon the ruler, who becomes corrupted in his turn.

In his chapter on "Architectural Megalomania," Speer shows a ruler absorbed, even while bombs fell on Berlin, with his fantasy for monuments to perpetuate his fame and success for posterity as being like God. Malignant narcissism was rampant in Hitler. As to Hitler's addiction to monuments, Speer linked this to the will to have power and to be like God:

> What had remained of the emperors of Rome? What would still bear witness to them today, if their buildings had not survived? Periods of weakness are bound to occur in the history of nations, he (Hitler) argued; but at their lowest ebb, their architecture will speak to them of former power.[12]

Albert Speer met his Watergate with the fall of the Third Reich. He stood trial at Nuremberg, the site of his architectural wonder, for his complicity in the war crimes of the Third Reich. In his trial and tribulations Speer came to know the wrongs of his own heart. He became transparent and truthful, risking the death penalty to testify with candor and in contrition. He received twenty years in Spandau prison rather than death because of that contrition. As a consequence of his repentance he salvaged a sense of honor and respect. He did not permit his Watergate to destroy him.

In his trial Speer turned to God.

> The Sunday divine services became a great support for me. Even as recently as my stay in Kransberg I had refused to attend them. I did not want to seem soft. But in Nuremberg I threw aside such prideful feelings. The pressure of circumstances brought me — as,

incidentally, it did almost all the defendants with the exception of Hess, Rosenberg, and Streicher — into our small chapel.[13]

I find that many Watergate defendants did likewise. Some merely reached out; others took hold for eternity.

Adolph Hitler salvaged nothing as he never faced up to his Watergate. Like Judas, he committed suicide. Speer reports that Hitler believed in himself and "his lucky star." Hitler had a religious root, but evidently one grounded in self. We all have a spiritual root of some nature and to some degree. Some insist on worship of self. Only God knows whether the particular root is one constituting spiritual salvation. Man will worship someone or something. It is his nature to do so.

Aside from self and wealth, power and prestige can become our idols. This was a subject of much concern to the Lord God in both the Old and the New Testaments. Anyone with a hierarchy of values always has something at the top that he worships and serves. Realizing the importance of idols and gods in the lives of all people, God addressed this subject up front in the Ten Commandments:

> You shall have no other gods before Me.
> You shall not make for yourself any carved image, or any likeness of anything that is in heaven above, or that is in the earth beneath, or that is in the water under the earth; you shall not bow down to them nor serve them. For I, the LORD your God, am a jealous god, visiting the iniquity of the fathers on the children to the third and fourth generations of those who hate Me, but showing mercy to thousands, to those who love Me and keep My commandments.
> You shall not take the name of the LORD your God in vain, for the LORD will not hold him guiltless who takes His name in vain (Exodus 20:3-7).

Idolatry was the first of many reasons God took the people of Israel and Judah from the Promised Land and into exile. As the prophet Hosea said, "From their silver and gold they made idols for themselves — that they might be cut off" (Hosea 8:4).

Secularism is the first name for a new religion which has slowly and surrepticiously been emerging from its cocoon. The other name is humanism. This is the conviction that man, not God, is the measure of all things, including authority. This spawns relativism and situation ethics. So secular humanism spells reliance on and worship of man, not God. It declares that man can call his own shots and develop his own value system. This is what tripped up Adam and Eve in the Garden of Eden: "You can be like God." Adam and Eve were indeed the first humanists in the

Bible. They probably did not realize that they had been transformed into secular humanists by the serpent's temptation to
play God.

I can understand their plight because I too have been a
secular humanist without understanding my real nature. The same
is true of many people I know, both in the church and out of
the church. Secular humanism is sweeping lives, homes, society
and institutions today. "Old Harry Dents" are being zapped with
secular humanism and do not realize its nature or recognize its
author, Satan himself. For a prize example, begin viewing TV
with spiritual vision.

The need to play God seems to be a major part of many
White House operations — and for United States senators and
congressmen, too. It goes with life and especially with position.
It also has to do with re-election, with a "correct" record for the
history books, and with wealth, power, prestige and being above
others.

In politics the chief objective is public image. Bob Haldeman
kept adding more and more staff to change Nixon's image and
thus to manage the news as much as possible. The rationale was
that the news media was basically anti-Nixon. And that was
basically true.

Richard Nixon understood the importance of the image of
a President for election, ego and history. Ehrlichman chronicles
this Nixon homily on imagery:

> "He [any President; himself; Richard Nixon] came in with the
> press against him. They said he couldn't handle TV. Now there's
> been a complete shift in 'the man's' image.
>
> "You know, it's been harder because I won't let Ziegler be a pimp
> for me like Jack Valenti was for Johnson. Instead we've built a
> mythology about the President.
>
> "Teddy Roosevelt is a good example. Taft was a much more effective
> President than T.R. But Roosevelt is recorded by history as the
> 'greater' President. It's fine to be the good managers. But we've got
> to get the story out!"[14]

The aim of man, down in his heart, is to play God here and
now. For those who are destined for the history books the aim
may well be to portray the image of God there too.

One of the great purposes of the Bible is to hold a mirror
up before our hearts so we cannot escape seeing our real selves
down in the hidden recesses of our inner beings. John Ehrlichman
has dared to view the real John and thus the real problem of
playing God.

On the other hand, the trials, conviction and imprisonment forced me to confront some very stark and surprising realities about myself. Much good has come from that process. A pardon would have permitted me to escape that confrontation.[15]

What each of us needs is to see ourselves in Genesis 3 playing God, like Adam and Eve, and like John Ehrlichman and the old Harry Dent. Then we can decide whether our salvation in this world lies in man's will to have power or Jesus' will to love and serve.

CHAPTER VIII

MAN'S FIG LEAF SYNDROME

But basically we are sinners. Sinners tend to hide....Sin separates.
Sin alienates. Sin causes people to hide from one another.

Dr. J. Grant Howard[1]

I have long maintained that one of the lessons of Watergate is that no person should be trusted with any secret. If you are planning to do wrong, you should not do so. If you insist on doing wrong anyway, then go into a locked room, pull down the shades, turn off the lights and don't ever tell anyone what you did. Today I realize even this is not foolproof for two reasons: God knows, and you and your conscience know.

One of the reasons the Bible is such a credible book is that it has the answer for every aspect of life. If the architects of the Watergate cover-up had consulted the Bible, they would have discovered that the cover-up would not work. Yet, as bad as that cover-up was, the most serious and on-going cover-up is in you and me, in our private worlds.

There are no secrets from God and precious few even from our fellowman. One day even our fellowman will know. Indeed, Jesus told His apostles that everything done or said in secret will be revealed. "For there is nothing covered that will not be revealed, and hidden that will not be known" (Matthew 10:26). And the Lord God Jehovah warned the chosen people before they entered the Promised Land, "Be sure your sin will find you out" (Numbers 32:23).

In teaching about man's relationship to government, Peter, apropos to Watergate, warns: "Live as free men, but do not use your freedom as a cover-up for evil; live as servants for God" (1 Peter 2:16, NIV.)

In concluding his powerful testimony as to the emptiness of life down here on earth without God, King Solomon also admonished us about the futility of secrecy and hidden agendas.

> Let us hear the conclusion of the whole matter: Fear God and keep His commandments, for this is man's all. For God will bring every work into judgment, Including every secret thing, whether good or evil (Ecclesiastes 12:13,14).

The Bible covers well the subject of covering up and hiding or playing games with God and/or man. As soon as they broke God's law, Adam and Eve moved into an immediate cover-up and began hiding from God. A sense of guilt and fear overcame them. They covered themselves with fig leaves that they fashioned to hide their nakedness. They hid from the presence or sight of God among the trees and shrubs of the garden (Genesis 3:7,8).

However, verse 9 shows that even the first cover-up was a failure. They could not hide from God. In fact, all cover-ups since then have failed to fool God. Paul tells us in Galatians 6:7 that man cannot deceive God, "Do not be deceived, God is not mocked; for whatever a man sows, that he will also reap."

God is all-knowing, everywhere present and all-powerful. He is also eternal, unchanging, and is the truth and the reality. Man is limited to time and space. And every other aspect of man is limited, including his knowledge and wisdom. Yet, man is talkative, and finds a secret difficult to keep, especially if it contains gossip or bad news about another. Man will also talk if he can get immunity from prosecution or a lesser sentence. This is a part of natural man's selfish and sinful nature. We all have that problem. Watergate underscored this nature of mankind.

Stop and ponder the question of whether you have only one agenda and whether it's open and known to God and man. Is everything in your inner life open and available for inspection? In his book, *Ordering Your Private World,* Gordon MacDonald defines that private world:

> It's this private part of life where we know ourselves best of all: this is where self-esteem is forged, where basic decisions about motives, values, and commitments are made, where we commune with our God. I call it *the private world,* and I like to refer to its ideal state as one of *order.*
>
> Let me be perfectly clear that I base this entire treatment of order in one's private world on the principle of the indwelling Christ....To bring order to one's personal life is to invite His control over every segment of one's life.[2]

God created us to be relational and social human beings. That's why He gave Adam a comparable helper. God gifted us with the ability to speak so we could communicate openly and honestly with one another. God created Adam and Eve in innocence — with no guile in them. They were whole persons before their fall from grace. They related to each other mentally, emotionally, volitionally, socially and sexually. There were no secret or hidden agendas in the garden before the original sin. Then came sin, and man and woman initiated the cover-up. This has continued in us ever since. Our tendency is to hide, to speak with what the American Indians called the forked tongue, to deceive, to blame others, to play games with one another and with God.

Why? Because of our sin nature. Adam and Eve have transmitted their fallen nature down the family tree to each of us. What people see in us is not necessarily what they get. All of this cover-up, deceit and misleading started in Genesis 3. It has been the order of the day ever since. The problem is sin, which is rebellion against God and His authority.

As we have already seen, sin stems from our self-centeredness. God is trying to help us to become unselfish and thus less susceptible to sin and broken relationships and communications. Jesus in His sacrifice in unlimited love is the best example of selflessness. The remedy for sin lies in Him, His way and His love and will for our lives.

It is bad enough that we deceive others. Worse than this is the fact that we deceive even ourselves. Self-deception leads to tunnel vision or astigmatism, a principal cause of Watergate.

The prophet Jeremiah told us why we engage in such foul deeds — even to ourselves: "The heart is deceitful above all things, and desperately wicked; who can know it?" (Jeremiah 17:9) In chapter 7, Jeremiah accused the people of God of covering up their wicked hearts with external religion and ritualism.

Jesus spoke of the heart of man in much the same way in Mark 7:18-23.

> So He said to them, "Are you thus without understanding also? Do you not perceive that whatever enters a man from outside cannot defile him, because it does not enter his heart but his stomach, and is eliminated, thus purifying all foods?" And He said, "What comes out of a man, that defiles a man. For from within, out of the heart of men, proceed evil thoughts, adulteries, fornications, murders, thefts, covetousness, wickedness, deceit, lewdness, an evil eye, blasphemy, pride, foolishness.
> "All these evil things come from within and defile a man."

We tend to hide, cover up or wear masks out of fear, anger or shame. The basic emotion behind anger is fear. In the case of Adam and Eve it was both fear and shame. In Watergate it was much the same.

Dr. Charles Swindoll has addressed the subject of masks most eloquently in his book, *Dropping Your Guard.* He lists the masks we wear because we "have learned that survival comes a lot easier behind a mask."

> There's a mask for whatever the occasion — have you noticed? No matter how you really feel, regardless of the truth, if you become skilled at hiding behind your guard, you don't have to hassle all the things that come with full disclosure. You feel safe. What you lack in honesty, you make up for in pseudo-security.
>
> If you wear an "I'm tough" mask, you don't have to worry about admitting how weak and frightened you actually are. If you keep your "I'm holy" mask in place, you never need to bother with people wondering if you struggle with spirituality. Furthermore, the "I'm-cool-because-I've-got-it-all-together" mask comes in handy if you resist stuff like hard questions, vulnerable admissions, straight talk. Another familiar front is the "I'm-able-to-handle-all-this-pain-and-pressure" mask. No tears, not even a frown or hint of bewilderment is revealed. That one helps when you're surrounded by super-pious folks who are impressed with answers like, "Oh, I'm fine" and "I'm just claiming the victory," accompanied by eyelids at half mast and a nice, appropriate smile. There are even "intellectual-and-scholarly" tasks that protect you from having to face the practical nitty-gritty.
>
> There is just one major difficulty in this mask-wearing game — *it isn't real.* It therefore forces us to skate rather than relate. It promotes a phony-baloney, make-a-good-impression attitude instead of an honest realism that relieves and frees. What's worse, as we hide the truth behind a veneer polished to a high gloss, we become lonely instead of understood and loved for who we are. And the most tragic part of all is that the longer we do it, the better we get at it...and the more alone we remain in our hidden world of fear, pain, anger, insecurity, and grief — all those normal and natural emotions we hesitate to admit but that prove we are only human.
>
> The result? Distance. Distance that makes you out of focus with me — removed from me by closed-off compartments that stay locked, keeping us from being able to know each other and, when and where necessary, to help each other.[3]

We seek to hide our failures, imperfections and sins. The characters of the Bible were not perfect, except for Jesus. Yet, God does not hide these imperfect acts of imperfect people — even in His best workers, such as Moses and Peter. The Bible reveals man as he really is — the good and the bad. In fact, the writer of Hebrews tells us about the penetration of God's Word and God's eye.

> For the word of God is living and powerful, and sharper than any
> two-edged sword, piercing even to the division of soul and spirit,
> and of joints and marrow, and is a discerner of the thoughts and
> intents of the heart. And there is no creature hidden from His sight,
> but all things are naked and open to the eyes of Him to whom we
> must give account (Hebrews 4:12,13).

The Bible removes all facades and masks and uncovers all cover-ups. We are forced to face our imperfections, get them out on the table in full confession and view and then find and apply God's solution. We are to open up our lives, become transparent and let the love and life of Jesus Christ shine through us. In the Sermon on the Mount, Jesus commands all of His followers to "let your light so shine before men, that they may see your good works and glorify your Father in heaven" (Matthew 5:13-16). How can God's light shine through a darkened and covered-up life? The best witness is the open Christian who displays a contrite and humble heart.

To be transparent is to be lovingly candid; open; honest; easily understood, recognized and detected. Jesus identified a good example of transparency when he first encountered Nathanael. John 1:47 says, "Jesus saw Nathanael coming toward Him, and said of him, 'Behold, an Israelite indeed, in whom is no guile.' "

"No guile" equals no deceit, no hidden agenda. Would Jesus see "no guile" in you or me? Unfortunately, the world is built on guile, the original sin of self-interest, a cancer implanted deeply into man by Satan.

The Bible has many cover-ups and guile-motivated actions to report. The "man after God's own heart," King David, is a prime exhibit. Evidently, David had a heart for God like no other man of his day. His will was tied into God's heart and will for David's life. Yet David, like us, was not perfect. David sinned, and he knew it. However, he chose to pretend that he had done nothing wrong. But God, through His man, Nathan, caused the sins of the king to be uncovered before all Israel. Judge John Sirica, the news media, Senator Sam Ervin, Special Prosecutor Leon Jaworski and many others uncovered our thirty-seventh President and his men in much the same way. They were persistent about our pretensions and prevarications.

David's predecessor, King Saul, had also broken God's law with such desecration that the prophet Samuel had to inform him, "But now your kingdom shall not endure" (1 Samuel 13:14, NASB).

Why did Saul lose his kingdom and David continue to rule even after his grave sins? The answer lies in the difference between confession and repentance as just words. Confession consists of expressing sorrow for sin. Repentance adds change to sorrow. "I am so sorry for my sin that I am going to change so that I will not do that again." This constitutes changing one's mind-set, completely altering his basic motivation and directing his life toward God and His will and away from the person's own selfish will.

What the American people saw as missing in Watergate was the kind of confession and repentance shown by David. This is where President Nixon missed his moment. King Solomon tells us in Proverbs 3 how to "find favor and high esteem in the sight of God and man."

> Let not mercy and truth forsake you; bind them around your neck, write them on the tablet of your heart, and so find favor and high esteem in the sight of God and man.
> Trust in the Lord with all your heart, and lean not on your own understanding; in all your ways acknowledge Him, and He shall direct your paths (Proverbs 3:3-6).

Some of the characters of Watergate have experienced the blessings of these verses. But what about Richard Nixon? Many people believe he could have triumphed over Watergate had he been fully repentant and opened up to the public, asking for forgiveness from God and man. I agree!

This is why we all need to know and understand the Bible. This holy book is packed with practical wisdom and truth. It also includes examples — King David models candor and King Saul remains covered up.

In another example, even Jesus' best men covered up when He needed them most. Nevertheless, when Jesus came back among them in the resurrected state, He forgave them. In John 21, the apostle John set forth the remainder of Peter's repentance. Beside the Sea of Galilee, Jesus led Peter to confess his love for Jesus, giving him three charges: "Feed My lambs," "Tend My sheep," and "Feed My sheep." It is interesting that Jesus questioned Peter as to his love three times, possibly as a reminder of his three denials.

I am convinced that Richard Nixon could become a strong man in the sight of God and man were he openly to repent. He could turn his Watergate ordeal into one of strength, as Peter, "the rock," did. Privately, Nixon may have done this. Yet there is no repentance as solid as overt repentance, especially for public people.

One of the big questions left dangling by the unresolved Watergate affair is whether any or all of the characters involved have become totally uncovered regarding their parts in the tragedy. In reviewing books by the major Watergate defendants, it appears that each is telling his version of the truth. The question is whether each one is telling the whole truth.

Individual Watergate characters comment in books or verbally that there is still more information to come from others involved and that some are still lying. There are yet thousands of hours of taped conversations to be explored, and newsmen, historians and book writers are doing that. Also, sensitive political files, including some of mine, are tied up in court battles. I have refused to become involved in protecting them. The point is that we may never know the whole truth and we may never determine how many people are still covering up. Only God knows.

On September 8, 1985, John Ehrlichman and I discussed the Watergate of his life in his refuge from the world outside of Santa Fe, New Mexico. John has undergone a spiritual experience in his Watergate woes. He feels he has uncovered, with the help of God in prayer, the real John Ehrlichman and the purpose and meaning God intended for his life. He is now a fulfilled and satisfied man although he has no memberships in any organizations. He does not want to be subjected to any more compromises, as he was in the White House.

John now knows how to pray — not for "not guilty" verdicts but for God to use adversity to bless his life. He is convinced God answered his unselfish prayers in Watergate by revealing to him the reality of life. He knows the moment this happened in prayer.

John conjectures where he could be today had he never become involved. It would mean everything he had before and more. But he says he would not exchange the sense of reality and peace he knows today for all he could have had if there had been no Watergate.

John is now using his intellect and writing talents as an author of books and articles. His aim is to help people, especially the kind of people Jesus pointed to — the less fortunate and those caught up in their own Watergates.

John Mitchell is involved in international trade in Washington, D.C. Like John Ehrlichman, he too has no law license. Mitchell is prosperous but still quiet. He knows certain people lied about him in the Watergate hearings and trials. Mitchell is convinced of the validity of *Secret Agenda* and the author's call for more probing by other writers on the subject of a White House and CREEP set-up by the CIA.

The former Attorney General has enjoyed at least one restoration. His portrait now hangs in the halls of the Justice Department with all of the other former Attorneys General. Mitchell disputes any alleged order by him to break into Watergate. And in *Secret Agenda,* Jim Hougan seems to side with Mitchell in this stance. But covering up seemed a vital necessity to Mitchell.

Cover-ups have not just been attempted against God, the Watergate Special Prosecutor and the American people. There are cover-ups in the home, in the church, on the job — wherever man lives, moves and has his being. One of the principal reasons for husband-wife and parent-child difficulties lies in lack of candor and communication.

God created people to have a relationship with Him and with one another. Open and honest communication in the home is essential to unity and development of mature growth. In his book, *The Trauma of Transparency,* Dr. J. Grant Howard points to Jesus' teaching on unity and maturity for His people in His prayer at Gethsemane (John 17:17-23). Dr. Howard says that we "grow in maturity and unity as we share truth between us."[4]

By sharing our thoughts, emotions, needs, concerns, fears and lives, we mature together and are drawn closer and closer to one another. By and large, this is not what is happening in the home, the marketplace or society in general.

In marriage, men tend to repress their thoughts while women are much more expressive. Women often have difficulty really getting to know their husbands. This is a problem in the parsonage too. Ask wives of pastors. Many men can talk openly about sports, business or politics. However, their intimate thoughts are off-limits. They see sharing private thoughts as a sign of weakness and vulnerability. In fact, intimacy is vulnerability, sharing all of oneself — the good and bad, the strong and weak. This means laying bare one's sentimentality, dreams, fears and weaknesses.

Communicating is a major problem between men and women on almost all levels. The lack of communication or the manipulation or misuse of communication is a menace to the survival and well-being of the family and society.

In his book, *The Marriage Builder,* Dr. Larry Crabb says the goal of marriage and all relationships is oneness and togetherness. We need relationships for security and significance. "Nothing reaches into the human personality as relationships," he writes. "The fabric of biblical truth is woven from Genesis to Revelation with the thread of relationship."[5]

Relationship is so highlighted in Scripture because only within the context of relationship can the deepest needs of human personality be met. If we are not open, candid and vulnerable (meaning transparent) with each other, we cannot have significant relationships in the family or in society. We as human beings must find a way to rip off our masks and "deep six" them — a term John Ehrlichman used for suggesting that some Watergate files be thrown in the river. We can find our security and significance — the two top needs cited by Dr. Crabb — in a right relationship with Jesus Christ. When we get honest and open prayer going with Him, we can get honest and open communication going with our fellowman. Jesus opens us up. In Him our fears are removed. Thus, the masks can be discarded.

The biggest obstacles to victory in Christ are pride, peer pressure and the fear of paying a price. It is only when we find ourselves in Genesis 3, see ourselves as we really are, and recognize our number one need — repentance — that we can turn trial and defeat into triumph and strength.

Dr. Larry Crabb cautions in his latest book, *Encouragement,* that we are to be committed as "God's instrument in other people's lives." We are to minister to one another in the home, church, and world and be an encourager and helper to others.[6]

> From childhood on, as soon as we can translate our feelings into ideas, we approach life with fear of exposure and fear of rejection we predict will follow.
> Although our ultimate fear has to do with rejection by God, we learn to attach the fear to someone more tangibly present. We come to fear the rejection of parent and friend and, as we enter adulthood, spouse, children, employer, pastor, and society.[7]

Thus, Dr. Crabb teaches that we must be motivated in all we say and do by the unconditional love of Jesus Christ. We must become more involved in helping people uncover and overcome their fears by the encouragement of love. He writes: "Our words (of encouragement) must come from unfeigned, genuine love for God and people."[8]

Amen!

CHAPTER IX

THE LOG IN MAN'S EYE

The deadliest sins were the consciousness of no sin.

Thomas Carlyle[1]

Hurling the blame at others, tunnel vision, scapegoating, unreality — all of these shine through as a common human frailty in the garden, in Watergate and in the Watergates of our lives. Jesus, in Matthew 7:3-5, talked about being able to discern the sin in others but not in oneself as the height of unreality and hypocrisy.

There was a problem with reality in the Nixon White House before Watergate, but not with the President. Richard Nixon's genius lay in his enormous sense of reality about people, their motives and their prospective actions under a given set of circumstances. I saw the same perception in Lyndon B. Johnson. As United States Senate leader, he used this uncanny ability to sense human character in the cloakrooms, back rooms and on the floor of the Senate to bend powerful senators to "the leader's" will. He could size up their strong and weak points, majoring in their unfailing selfish side to ply them with hidden persuaders.

Under a seige of bunker mentality in Watergate, pragmatic, fearless and realistic Richard Nixon became blind to his faults and those of his close associates as the temple walls were cracking and falling about him. In his book on the Adolph Hitler regime, *Inside the Third Reich,* eyewitness Albert Speer illustrated how power and ego diffuse reality almost to the extent of obliteration. In the garden, God exposed Adam and Eve's fig-leaf phoniness. When He fired His second and third questions at them, He was calling for confession and repentance on their part. Surely they had to know they could not hide from God or fool Him. Yet initially Adam and Eve coughed up only excuses and blamed others rather than themselves. Eve accused the serpent. Adam entered a not-guilty plea by virtue of the blame belonging to Eve and ultimately God. Sin teaches the mind how to defend the sinner by evasion, deceit and passing the buck to others.

Adam responded to the Creator-Judge, "The woman whom You gave to be with me, she gave me of the tree, and I ate." In other words, "God, You caused this. You're the one who said that I needed this helper. So, it was You, Lord, and that woman You insisted that I needed."

This time Eve followed the lead of her husband. She blamed the serpent, who "deceived me."

God was seeking out Adam and Eve in an act of His grace. He had already given them a hiding place in Him. Now He was opening the door for them to return to Him so he could cover their sins. God's grace and hiding place is still available for all of mankind today, as it was for King David in his psalm of deliverance: "You are my hiding place; You shall preserve me from trouble; You shall surround me with songs of deliverance" (Psalm 32:7).

This is the answer to our Watergates: Let God cover our sins and advise us about how to resist the siren songs of Satan in the future.

In Watergate some of the descendants of Adam and Eve implicated in breaking the law followed the scapegoating example of their first mother and father. In my law practice I found this to be the rule rather than the exception.

Dr. Scott Peck addresses this subject of scapegoating in *People of the Lie.* He advances the real proposition that man, by and large, has difficulty accepting criticism, especially self-criti-cism.[2] I know that this is true of me.

John Dean has told me in conversation that he became convinced that he was being set up as the scapegoat of Watergate when President Nixon, Bob Haldeman and John Ehrlichman sent him to Camp David in March, 1973, to write out the story of Watergate as the cover-up coordinator. This is why he ran to the Watergate prosecutors. John Ehrlichman says:

> Dean's time at Camp David from March 23 to 26 was a turning point. Once he'd written out his own vulnerability, he decided to hire a lawyer and try to bargain for leniency or immunity.[3]

Ehrlichman shows how in Watergate the pointing of fingers of blame at one another began to escalate:

Dean's "strategy of containment" was in a shambles. Howard Hunt
was appearing before the grand jury; Magruder was saying Liddy's
break-in had been a White House operation; Paul O'Brien — the
former CIA agent who was the Re-election Committee's lawyer — was
calling for John Mitchell to confess everything to take the heat off
innocent people. Haldeman knew Dean was hiring a criminal lawyer
but he believed Dean was hiring someone to counsel everyone at
the White House; no one realized Dean was hiring a personal
attorney.[4]

The man who broke open the Watergate case was James W.
McCord, Jr. On March 23, 1973, while Dean was thinking over
his report at Camp David, Judge John Sirica unveiled a bombshell
letter from McCord. It caused the judge to postpone sentencing
on all of the burglary team except Liddy, the one he knew would
not talk. Sirica reiterated to them that their sentences would be
very harsh if they did not cooperate with the investigation.

In this letter McCord stated that higher-ups had perjured
themselves in testimony to the grand jury. Later, in interviews
with the Senate committee, he broadened his accusations from
Magruder and Dean to Mitchell and the President. Magruder
credits Judge Sirica's threats with breaking McCord's silence.[5]
Liddy says McCord was bitter. He added:

McCord was also very religious, and I think he experienced a
feeling of estrangement from his God and jumped at the chance
to become once more a "good Christian" back on what the conven-
tional wisdom was telling him through the media was the side of
the angels.[6]

The author of *Secret Agenda* also attests to the religious
side of McCord, though he sees McCord as having had a secret
agenda in Watergate for the CIA.[7] While incarcerated, McCord
was ministered to by some Catholic nuns and by Dr. Richard
Halverson, then a Presbyterian pastor and now U.S. Senate chaplain.

Magruder acknowledged that Hunt's letter was "correct."[8]
As a result of his letter McCord served only two months of a
one-to-five- year term.

McCord turned down a publisher's offer (Holt, Rinehart &
Winston) to have a ghost-writer assist with his memoirs on Water-
gate. Instead, he printed his own book, *A Piece of Tape*.[9] Jim
Hougan describes the book as:

...the strangest (and most difficult to find)....It tells us virtually
nothing about McCord, his work for the CRP or the events leading

to the Watergate arrests....Despite this, *A Piece of Tape* is quite revealing and as psychological evidence of McCord's frame of mind, invaluable. Throughout we are struck by McCord's vindictiveness, by his wrathful piety, by his obsessiveness and by his nearly mystical apprehension of the Watergate affair.[10]

In his book, McCord quotes the Bible. He implies that he was God's agent to bring down the Nixon Administration. McCord gave this ambiguous insight into the taped Watergate door locks and the taped White House conversations:

A piece of masking tape opened a door that shook a nation to its very foundations. A measuring tape that was Watergate plumbed the depths of the most powerful nation in the world. A piece of magnetic tape may impeach the most powerful man in the world. Is a nation's will and character now being measured by yet another piece of tape in the hands of Him who created all that is?[11]

The Bible references in his book have to do with tape as mentioned in the Bible, as in Ezekiel 40:3; 2 Samuel 8:1-6; and Ecclesiastes 5:8. In the Ecclesiastes passage he writes in by interpretation the use of the words "red tape."

His writings have hidden meanings, similar to Jesus' parables. But the message is clear: The Nixon Administration had to fall.

If the Administration could get away with this massive crime of Watergate and its cover up, it would certainly stop at nothing thereafter.[12]

In a secret letter to General Paul Gaynor in January, 1973, McCord explained his concerns in apocalyptic terms:

"When the hundreds of dedicated fine men and women of CIA no longer write intelligence summaries and reports with integrity, without fear of political recrimination — when their fine director [Richard Helms] is being summarily discharged in order to make way for a politician who will write or rewrite intelligence the way the politicians want them [sic] written, instead of the way truth and best judgment dictates, our nation is in the deepest of trouble and freedom itself was never so imperiled."[13]

The mysterious wiretap expert sent a written threat to the White House in another January 1973 letter. It was addressed to a covert Dean investigator, Jack Caulfield.

If Helms goes and the Watergate operation is laid at the CIA's feet, where it does not belong, every tree in the forest will fall. It will be a scorched desert.[14]

Every tree in the forest did fall after McCord began writing and talking. His scorched-earth policy worked. Hougan's revelations have added more credence to the suspicions about the behind-the-scenes struggle and antagonism between Nixon and Richard Helms, then the CIA director. So, whatever the motives of McCord, he hurled a bomb that did indeed shake the foundations of the Nixon temple and Nixon himself.

In his book, *The Powers That Be,* David Halberstam graphically pictures the consequences of McCord's monumental missive to Judge Sirica:

> There was a dynamic to it. Once McCord began to talk, the White House defense began to crumble. It was like a ship on which the rivets of loyalty were more fragile than they seemed and now as the ship began to sink everyone was running for the lifeboats, stopping only long enough to betray his best friends. At the center of it was John Dean, and John Dean was about to become a press industry. He had been right at the center of the cover-up, and if he did not know the details of the original break-in, he was a certifiable authority on how the White House had tried to cover it up ever since. He was smart and cold and very much on the make. Different White Houses had been filled in recent years with the John Deans of the world, selected because they were so hungry, would work such hard hours, and had no real value system or constituencies of their own; instead of values they had what were more useful to superiors — burning ambitions and flexible ethics. Dean was one of the brightest of the young men around Nixon; he even reminded some old-timers there of a young Richard Nixon; he was so eager, so clearly determined to get ahead. The big men of the White House, Haldeman and Ehrlichman, had drafted him to do the dirty work on Watergate and involuntarily he had become privy to the seamy side of the White House. He was so low in rank and the President was so awesomely powerful — a god to pawns like Dean — that it never occurred to them that Dean would not take the fall for Nixon. That had not occurred to Dean either, particularly in the good days, but they had not reckoned with two remarkable qualities that were to surface in him — a highly refined sense of exactly how to survive and a remarkable memory.[15]

Halberstam shows how Dean and his attorney, Bob McCandless, used various news publications to push his strategy for immunity directly or indirectly in return for juicy stories on the now highly competitive Watergate news beat.[16] The Watergate books leave the impression that Dean and Magruder began pointing their fingers for fear of becoming unwilling scapegoats. They both sought immunity and failed. But they did gain leniency. Dean says in *Blind Ambition* that two prosecutors, James Neal and Jill Vollner, complained to him that Jeb had tailored his testimony "to the prosecutors' needs."[17]

Even today the fingers continue to point in blame. Some deliberately lied, others told part of the truth, and others have told the truth the way their thought processes and emotions conditioned the truth to fit their ends.

Unfortunately we do tend to see truth according to our point of philosophical orientation — that is, our bias. What truth we allow to get past our mind's filtering system is often altered by our truth-massaging machine. In their savvy book, *What's Gone Wrong With the Harvest,* James Engle and Wilbert Norton credit this filter with being vital in communications receptivity. The filter lets into our minds that which meets or touches our selfish or felt needs and blocks or dilutes other messages. The authors describe the filter thus:

> God has created the filter to provide a means of protection against unwanted influence. He knew, of course, that this also could be used to screen out His voice, as is documented by frequent biblical reference to unresponsive soil and hardened hearts. Selective attention, miscomprehension, and selective retention, therefore, can result as the individual resists changes in his beliefs.
>
> The filter itself is formed out of the person's attitudes, beliefs, understanding, and personality. The net effect is to create a "map of the world" that profoundly affects both preception and behavior....At the heart of this filter, of course, is the ego....The filter functions to admit those stimuli that are relevant to the self and screens out those that are not.[18]

Even the disciples filtered out Jesus' messages about what was going to happen to Him on the cross. The messages didn't fit their idea of a military messiah who would deliver Judah from Roman rule. After the resurrection they received the message loud and clear. They could see that Jesus had won in death and new life, so their filters flew open. This is how we also are to win — if we appropriate His saving grace.

Looking back at the many sermons I've heard in my lifetime, I can accept the validity of the filter concept. I missed much truth in my lifetime because it didn't fit my interests or presuppositions but was needed, if at all, only by that fellow sitting next to me.

Jesus described this filter system. In His Sermon on the Mount, Jesus said:

> Judge not, that you be not judged. For with what judgment you judge, you will be judged; and with the same measure you use, it

will be measured back to you. And why do you look at the speck
in your brother's eye, but do not consider the plank in your own
eye? Or how can you say to your brother, "Let me remove the
speck out of your eye'; and look, a plank is in your own eye?
Hypocrite! First remove the plank from your own eye, and then
you will see clearly to remove the speck from your brother's eye
(Matthew 7:1-5).

In some Bible versions "plank" is translated as "mote,"
"beam," or "log." Jesus was teaching against the hypocrisy of
condemning in others what we tolerate in ourselves. As a good
teacher, He deliberately drew the ludicrous picture of a person
with a big log (fault) in his eye trying to remove a speck or
splinter (fault) from another person's eye. In fact, this is how we
all behave all too often.

In medical terms, this "loggism" is hyperopia — I can see
the speck in the other fellow's eye at a distance, but I can't see
the big log sticking out of my eye, up close. Another term for
this sight impairment is tunnel vision — we look down a tunnel
to see only that which we want to see. It results in astigmatism
or blurred vision as to personal faults. Jesus said that if we are
going to judge others about a fault, we should first remove the
fault from our own life because God will judge those who arrogate
His judging power for themselves.

In saying this, Jesus touched a sensitive nerve in all of us:
Examine yourself and deal with the reality of your own flaws.
Reality is too much to bear in most cases, especially about our
own shortfalls. The British poet Thomas Stearns Eliot wrote about
it this way in 1935: "Human kind cannot bear very much reality."[19]
Yet the good news about reality is its built-in dependability
because reality just happens to be truth.

That eloquent communicator, Charles Swindoll, defines reality as "the tempered poker that keeps the fires alive...it's the
spark that prompts the engine to keep running...the hard set of
facts that refuses to let feeling overrule logic."[20]

Lack of reality separates the psychotic person from sanity.
So many people are semi-sane because they are semi-realistic.
We live in a world of many myths. We abound with childish Peter
Pans in adult garb and with too many Alices still playing in the
Wonderland of fantasy.

The myths and fantasies especially surface when our self-interest blinds us to the realities of our own sins, weaknesses and
faults. The less clearly we see the realities of this world the more
our minds are befuddled by falsehood, misbeliefs and illusions.
Thus, we are blocked from making sensible, wise and realistic

decisions, as happened in the Watergate fiasco. And change becomes virtually impossible.

Dr. Scott Peck avers that the source of many of the ills of mankind is "the process of making revisions" or changes. Major revisions are painful, he writes, "Sometimes excruciatingly painful."

> Our view of reality is like a map with which to negotiate the terrain of life. If the map is true and accurate, we will generally know where we are.[21]

Dr. Peck points out that we have to revise our maps for life as our world changes. As children we are dependent and powerless. As adults we may become powerful. "When we are poor," he says, "the world looks different from when we are rich." So we must revise our maps to face the realities. Revision and change to confront and conform to reality are tough for man to face.[22]

Rationalizing and pretending are two of our most often used mental tools for avoiding reality. We create shams to cover up reality and truth. To rationalize is to invent plausible explanations for one's acts or beliefs, usually without being aware that these are not the real motives. The criminal uses an alibi. Man often fools himself so he can better deceive or mislead others. He relies only on reason, his own self-interest reason. Pretending is playing make-believe, supposing or doing or saying something for show.

King Saul rationalized his disobedience to God. When caught by the prophet Samuel, Saul first lied, then he rationalized, and then he transferred the blame (1 Samuel 15:13-21).

President Abraham Lincoln had a famous maxim on this subject: "You may fool all the people some of the time; you can even fool some people all of the time; but you cannot fool all of the people all the time."

Misbeliefs are used as much as rationales and pretensions. Misbeliefs are lies which we accept as truth. Myths also feed our attempted escapes from reality. A myth is a fictitious story or belief — one based on fiction, not truth. Too many people live by myths and old wives' tales. We read too many novels, too much fiction.

Time after time, in the Watergate books written by the defendants, as they look at the past they confess reality lapses. John Ehrlichman says his God-given blessing out of Watergate is the revelation of the reality about John Ehrlichman of his White House days..."I didn't like what I saw."[23]

In my practice of the law and in politics I was astounded by the lack of reality I encountered. What surprised me most was the myopic vision I discovered in the White House. The orders I received came down through Bob Haldeman. In my second year there I learned that he was passing on the President's commands in the name of the chief of staff. In a memo dated October 16, 1970, Bob impressed me with the importance of overcoming my reluctance in executing some of his orders: "Any guidance I ever give...comes direct from RN."

About this same time a lady who had been requisitioned from my office to work for Haldeman passed on this account of how our staff orders originated:

> The President would dictate his answers to memos and pending decisions and dictate ideas occurring to him in his own private think sessions in the Lincoln Room late in the evening. When Haldeman would visit the President first thing in the morning, he would pick up the tapes for transcription. Once they were transcribed, Haldeman would prepare action or talking papers. If the President wanted the senior staff or any group to get certain instructions, Haldeman would call a meeting and work from his "talking papers." The talking papers would be Nixon's memos over Haldeman's name and/or from Haldeman's mouth, virtually word for word.

Sometimes I would be told in advance exactly what was to be discussed in the meeting. Sure enough, it would turn out that way. I had the additional benefit of knowing that while it was the voice of Haldeman, it was the mind of Nixon. Of course, we all realized Haldeman spoke for the "Big Man." However, few understood how exactly Haldeman represented the President.

The good side of Nixon radiated with realism; the dark side suffocated reality. The genesis of Watergate was that dark side of the President. That is why Haldeman contends that while Nixon did not order the Watergate break-in, he caused it.

When I ran Senator Strom Thurmond's office, the staff understood that the senator would not countenance any "Mickey Mouse" or "Keystone Kop" capers. If a letter going into the U.S. mail system was not government business, we knew that Thurmond had commanded in writing that we use his own money for the postage. There was to be no cutting of corners on even minor matters of ethics and certainly not on the large ones. Fred Buzhardt and I saw Thurmond fire a former FBI agent for hoodwinking an important political figure in South Carolina. The man likely would never have discovered the deceit the staffer had used to dupe him in the political interest of the senator.

Some people in South Carolina disagree with the senator's conservative philosophy. However, few, if any, question his personal character. This is one of the main factors for his overwhelming election victories as a Republican in a state with far more Democrats than Republicans.

There could not be a Watergate in Thurmond's office. The staff members know their boss and his principles. The senator is as transparent as any political figure I have ever known or studied. He operates "with the bark off." What you see with Thurmond is what you get — like it or not.

There exists in America today a deep sense of cynicism. People have long suspected politicians, lawyers, businessmen, newsmen and government officials of dedication to their own selfish-interests. In 1975, I was shocked to read a Gallup Poll showing the ranking of public confidence in twenty occupations. Listed at the bottom were used car salesmen (20), politicians (19), lawyers (18), government officials (17) and businessmen (16). At the time I had been involved in all five of these occupations in some way, even to an interest in a car dealership that sold new and used cars.

Apparently many of our leaders in the various professions and occupations, Harry Dent included, have not been good role models for their followers, the public. Our society has created an atmosphere of mediocrity and apathy. The goals of truth and reality are fading as people seek to justify their own lifestyles rather than base their behavior on truth. This superficiality in reality, character and commitment has invaded even the churches and synagogues of America. By and large, people in the pews are more spectators than participants, just touching base with God. As Charles Colson has exclaimed: "There is too much of the world in the church and not enough of the church in the world."

What is imperative is a return to truth and reality so that people know who they are and where they stand under God's value system, that system proclaimed in the Sermon on the Mount (Matthew 5-7).

In the Bible the use of the word light equals enlightenment, or bringing reality. The word darkness means illusion, or what I call irreality. The Bible is God's handbook to prepare us to dispel darkness and dispense His light in the world. "This is the message which we have heard from Him and declare to you, that God is light and in Him is no darkness at all" (1 John 1:5).

This passage of Scripture affirms that God is total reality and that there is no illusion in Him. The key to reality is to have the Spirit of Christ ruling in our hearts. We cannot grasp reality by ourselves because of the darkness in our hearts causing illusion here and there in our thinking. Peter tells us that reality and its component parts are to be found in spiritual growth: "His divine power has given us all things that pertain to life and godliness" (2 Peter 1:3).

Peter writes that in Christian growth we can now become "partakers of the divine nature, having escaped the corruption that is in the world through lust" (2 Peter 1:4). Listed as the building blocks of reality are faith, virtue, knowledge, self-control, perseverance, godliness, brotherly kindness and love (verse 7). The foundation of the house of reality is faith; the roof is love. Integrating these building blocks into our lives is how we receive in knowledge and experience God's perspective — the ultimate reality as to life here and now.

The Bible unfolds to us God's world view or perspective, the base point for our world view, what Dr. Larry Richards terms "a patterned perspective on life."[24] We must start from some source of authority and truth. The two major claimants to truth and the correct world view are God and Satan. Adam and Eve were faced with: Whom do you choose to believe? Who has the truth?

Dr. Richards, an author of many books on the Bible, offers these points about the reality of the Bible: its realistic view of man and his problem; its revelation of God's heart as a "lover for loss" while we "love for gain"; the reality of God's total control over the world; and the reality of the working of the gospel into a new way of life by infusing helpless people with Christ, transforming corrupt natures into Christian character.[25]

The standpoints from which we perceive and approach life, our basic presuppositions, comprise our view of the world. From this perspective we arrive at our values, priorities, attitudes, feelings and vision, and thus our conduct and goals in life.

The Holy Bible and all of my experiences with the Lord of the universe have convicted me of the fact that the Bible is the book of reality and truth about the only Reality and Truth, Jesus Christ. This should be our beginning point in life and thus our world view. I am convinced that *the* problem in our world today is that we have moved further and further away in the past 150 years from a biblical understanding of reality. It took me forty-eight years to become focused on God as *the* Reality and thus His Word as *the* reality book. Too many people are caught up in the unreal world of secular humanism, believing that man can make it in the world without the restraints imposed by God and Scripture. Moral relativism, situation ethics, fantasy thinking — these concepts determine how most people live today. Without understanding the facts of reality and truth, we allow Satan to prevail with his appeals to selfism: "You can be as God." "If it feels good, do it."

Many of us are not dealing with the ultimate Reality and His handbook for life. We are playing games with God. However, we all will have to account to the ultimate Reality. We will answer to God for our approach to and conduct in accord with truth and reality as revealed to us in the Holy Bible and in prayer.

CHAPTER X

MAN'S ACCOUNTABILITY

Then He will answer them, saying, "Assuredly, I say to you, inasmuch as you did not do it to one of the least of these, you did not do it to Me."

And these will go away into everlasting punishment, but the righteous into eternal life.

Jesus Christ in Matthew 25:45,46

If you were to be indicted and then called to trial for being a Christian, would there be enough evidence available to convict you? Someone pulled this cute question on me one day, knowing that I was a lawyer. It worked in that it set me to thinking about the burden of proof that would fall on the chief prosecutor: He would have to prove beyond a reasonable doubt that I was a Christian. What a burden of proof! Could I carry that burden successfully if I had to prove that I was a Christian? At the time I thought the best evidence that counted was being good and doing good in the world — salvation by works. Now that I have studied God's law book so much, I understand that works will not get me to heaven.

The questioner indelibly inscribed the question of accountability in my mind. I had operated, like many others, on the principle enunciated by William Ernest Henley in his poem "Invictus": "I am the master of my fate; I am the captain of my soul." I also believed that there was a Scripture passage that said: "God helps them that help themselves." I found this to be a saying of Ben Franklin.[1] Such are the misconceptions, misbeliefs and presuppositions we of today entertain in our race to escape accountability to authority. Yet accountability to God is raised in the beginning of the Bible in God's first question: "Where are you?" (Genesis 3:9). God still is watching our every action, motive and even thought.

In his book to preachers, *Between Two Worlds,* Dr. John Stott addresses the anti-authority mood in today's world:

> Seldom if ever in its long history has the world witnessed such a self-conscious revolt against authority. Not that the phenomenon of protest and rebellion is new. Ever since the fall of man human nature has been rebellious, "hostile to God" and unwilling, even unable, to "submit to God's law" (Rom. 8:7)....It is a basic tenet of the Christian religion that we believe not because human beings have invented it but because God has revealed it. In consequence, there is an authority inherent in Christianity which can never be destroyed.[2]

What is this authority? Who is the Chief Auditor who adds up the balance sheet to determine whether we are solvent or insolvent? Every businessman realizes the importance of that bottom line on the financial statement. In some cases we call it profit or loss, and in the ultimate statement, assets and liabilities that add up to our net worth. There comes a time when our books are audited to determine what we've been doing and where we're going.

This reality never caught my attention until I borrowed $200,000 to purchase an interest in an automobile dealership. This loan put me on the line financially as I never had been before. This was also my first experience in using a certified public accountant to work up a financial statement.

Adam and Eve did not have their eyes fixed on the bottom line when they succumbed to the temptation of the original dirty trickster, Satan, in Genesis 3. They evidently had their minds on the here and now and were rationalizing how understanding God would be if they indulged themselves in countering His will. Besides, they thought they could cover their apostasy. So they decided to put aside love and take on power. Power might bear more clout on the bottom line of life.

God was not as lenient as they had hoped, and He saw the whole sorry spectacle. He moved immediately to call them to accountability. He began with the serpent. In God's world punishment is not so much for reform as for vindicating and satisfying the absolute justice of a Holy God.

Dr. Edward J. Young gives this view of how God dealt with Adam and Eve as against the way He meted out the sentence on the serpent:

> But punishment, according to the Bible, belongs to the moral realm. It is that which God decrees shall be visited upon the sinner. In the questions directed to Adam and Eve we hear God speak as

the absolutely righteous One, and in the curse which He pronounces upon the serpent, we behold His holy justice at work!...The purpose of the curse pronounced upon the serpent is to make clear that there had been a deep-seated wickedness using it, and so the curse of a perpetual degradation was a forerunner of that eternal reproach which was to come upon the one who had used the serpent. The very fact of the pronouncing of a curse in itself makes clear that a higher, spiritual power was involved.[3]

The serpent was judged to crawl on his belly and eat dust all the days, as is the case with the snake today. Then, Satan was to be defeated finally by the Seed of the woman, Jesus Christ (Genesis 3:14,15). The judgment on man and woman amounted to reproof and the offer of restoration through God's grace. The woman became subject to the man and to pain in childbirth. Man had to work hard from then on. Both Adam and Eve were subjected to physical and spiritual death, but they were eligible for spiritual salvation (Genesis 3:16-19). Genesis 3 concludes with Adam and Eve being expelled from the Garden of Eden. By their sin, their nature had changed, and they were separated from God, for God abhors sin.

In the judgments of Watergate, the "Adams" of the Nixon garden of power likewise were separated — from power, prestige, profession and their place. Some lost even more — their families, their savings and their emotions. One, a Republican congressman from Maryland, committed suicide out of despair over possible discovery that he did not report receipt of some campaign contributions. Mo Dean talked about suicide. John Ehrlichman had the thought pass his way. Probably everyone caught up in Watergate likewise flirted with the idea.

Judgment was passed in court on more than seventy individuals or corporations for charges brought by the Special Watergate Prosecution Force. I know what it is to have judgment passed on one by a judge. Fortunately for me and my family, the judgment I received was negligible compared to that of the principal Watergate characters. Yet all the months of agony and uncertainty served as punishment enough. To lose one's own personal honor is bad enough, but to stain and hurt your family is worse.

What will it be like to stand up in court before the Judge of the Bible? In the Bible the subject of accountability runs from Genesis to Revelation. The main word used for accountability is judgment. God is pictured in the Old Testament as the Judge or God of justice. Judgment in the Bible is not merely weighing good and evil, but it also involves God's number-one concern: sin and evil. Thus, the people of God are called to be judges also in waging war against evil.

Evil represents the very opposite of God's character of mercy, lovingkindness, righteousness and truth. But, like the qualities of God's character, God's judgment is personal. In passing judgment, God works out His wrath and His mercy in history and human life and experience.

In the New Testament, God's judgments are for the present and the future, as in the Old Testament. However, it is Jesus Christ who is seen as exercising the Father's function as Judge. We are being judged now, and we will face another final judgment at the return of Jesus Christ. When we physically die our ultimate fate for eternity will have been determined already by our faith or lack thereof in Jesus Christ as Lord and Savior. The final judgment will be either our degrees of reward in heaven or our degrees of punishment in hell.

God's daily judgments come in two forms: final and remedial (or corrective). In the Old Testament, Samuel reports on the immediate judgment of death against Uzzah for touching the holy and untouchable ark of the covenant (2 Samuel 6). Luke reports on the immediate judgment of death on Ananias and Sapphira for lying to God and the church (Acts 5). Fortunately, far more of God's judgments are for purposes of correction and spiritual growth. Watergate was a corrective judgment. For some, there was correction and growth. Chuck Colson is the prime example, but not the only one.

God used this type of judgment on King David in his sin of adultery and the cover-up of his adultery with murder. David also covered up the cover-up with his silence until confronted by God's prophet, Nathan. Then David not only uncovered and confessed his sin, but repented and changed back to the man with a heart for God.

For a time David's high view of God shrank into a low view. His sin nature prevailed until he realized that he had sinned not only against Bathsheba and Uriah but — most importantly — against God. For any sin is a sin against the holy God. The greatest evil in sin is that it strikes at the heart and holiness of God. When we forget or ignore this vital point, our view of God shrinks until it becomes low and blurred.

Under God's judgment, every aspect of our lives is called into accountability — just as with David. Even the secrets of men will be judged (Romans 2:16). The hidden things of darkness will come to light for examination (1 Corinthians 4:5). "For there is nothing hidden which will not be revealed," Jesus said (Mark 4:22). Jesus also warned that "every idle word men may speak, they will give account of it in the day of judgment" (Matthew 12:36).

Again we see that there can be no cover-up from God either now or then. The prophet Nahum writes of God's wrath and judgment in these terms:

> God is jealous, and the LORD avenges; the LORD avenges and is furious. The LORD will take vengeance on His adversaries, and He reserves wrath for His enemies; The LORD is slow to anger and great in power, and will not at all acquit the wicked.
> The LORD has His way in the whirlwind and in the storm, and the clouds are the dust of His feet (Nahum 1:2,3).

Indeed, God did have His way in the whirlwind and storm of the garden. He also has His way in the other whirlwinds and storms of your life and mine. This is why we must stay close to the Judge, know Him, know His ways and fear Him from the standpoint of awe and reverence as well as being concerned about His wrath against sin. Yet, man is not nearly as concerned about the wrath of God as he once was. Charles Swindoll sees accountability as being rarely practiced today because it requires at least four qualities: vulnerability, teachability, honesty and availability.[4]

There exists not only vertical accountability; there is also horizontal accountability. Romans 12 is divided into two parts: our responsibility to God (verses 1-2) and our responsibility to society (verses 3-21).

Even so-called good people are slipping today in their sense of responsibility, in conviction and conduct. The pressures of permissiveness and self-indulgence are great, and criticism of the Bible says of its truth, as the serpent implied in Genesis 3, "It ain't all so." "Good people" are picking and choosing in the Bible, shopping for what they want to fit their lifestyles and whims. Soft sin is so quiet, so slow — but is erosive nonetheless.

C.S. Lewis best phrased the trend toward permissiveness and self-indulgence this way:

> The safest road to hell is the gradual one — the gentle slope, soft underfoot, without sudden turnings, without milestones, without signposts. The long, dull, monotonous years of middle-aged prosperity or adversity are excellent campaigning weather for the devil.[5]

Jesus three times (and more) spoke boldly to good people about His judgment:

For everyone to whom much is given, from him much more will be required; and to whom much has been committed, of him they will ask the more (Luke 12:48).

    *   *   *   *

Every tree that does not bear good fruit is cut down and thrown into the fire. Therefore by their fruits you will know them.

Not every one who says to Me, "Lord, Lord," shall enter the kingdom of heaven, but he who does the will of My Father in heaven. Many will say to Me in that day, "Lord, Lord, have we not prophesied in Your name, cast out demons in Your name, and done many wonders in Your name?" And then I will declare to them, "I never knew you; depart from Me, you who practice lawlessness!" (Matthew 7:19-23).

    *   *   *   *

And to the angel of the church of the Laodiceans write,

"These things says the Amen, the Faithful and True Witness, the Beginning of the creation of God: 'I know your works, that you are neither cold nor hot. I could wish you were cold or hot. So then, because you are lukewarm, and neither cold nor hot, I will spew you out of My mouth' " (Revelation 3:14-16).

These are strong messages from the Master, directed to the good people.

As for man, sin and salvation, nowhere does the Bible explain them more clearly and explicitly than in the first epistle, the letter to the church at Rome by the apostle Paul.

In Romans 1 and 2 Paul proclaims without any compromise the certainty of judgment by God on everyone...that we are all sinners...that we are all without excuse...that we all must be justified by faith and grow in God's grace. In Romans 14:11 and 12 Paul assures us that ' every tongue shall confess to God.' So then each of us shall give account of himself to God."

The key verse in this great doctrinal treatise is Paul's declaration, "For I am not ashamed of the gospel of Christ, for it is the power of God to salvation for everyone who believes, for the Jew first and also for the Greek" (Romans 1:16).

How about you? Are you unashamed of the gospel of Jesus Christ? Have you been made right with God through faith in Jesus Christ and by His grace? Are you becoming more Christ-like or less so? Are you ready to meet your Maker and Judge?

CHAPTER XI

MAN'S SOLUTION: GOD'S GRACE

The recognition of sin is the beginning of salvation.

Martin Luther[1]

The good news emanating from Watergate is the life-changing experience of Nixon's master of dirty tricks being transformed into a modern-day master communicator of the good news of Jesus Christ. The unusual circumstances and timing catapulted Charles W. Colson onto the world scene more than any other of the Watergate characters, except the President. A few of the Watergate people contend that Colson should have earned the spotlight for his evil deeds in Watergate. They remain skeptical about Colson's born-again experience. These people see Colson more as a Jacob of biblical times than as a Paul. Jacob's name means a supplanter, a trickster. He duped his twin brother Esau out of his rightful inheritance. These Colson doubters maintain that this modern "Jacob" has tricked the Christian world in a masterful conversion hoax. Once a trickster, always a trickster, they say. There has to be some envy in this attitude because if one person emerged from Watergate as a winner, this person was Charles Colson.

However, most of the Watergate characters attest to the new Charles Colson. Bob Haldeman told me that he came to hear Colson speak while he, himself, was imprisoned. "I was much impressed with the change I sensed in Chuck," Bob remarked.

Steve Bull's life has a Christian orientation today because of Charles Colson. Steve escaped Watergate without any indictment or trial. As with others in the Nixon White House, he did experience encounters with the Special Prosecutor's office. His travail was over the highly-publicized eighteen and one-half-minute tape gap. There are thousands and thousands of Steve Bulls whose lives have been touched, enriched and changed by the speaking or writing of Charles Colson and his Prison Fellowship ministry in the United States and many foreign countries. Many people compare Chuck to the apostle Paul because of his spiritual conversion and the wide impact of that conversion.

The story of Charles Colson's born-again experience is better known today than that of almost any other Christian. In the midst of the Watergate debacle a bad guy turned good one evening in Lexington, Massachusetts, a town of history where another famous revolution was initiated in 1776. What is not so well known is the story of the "earthen vessel" the Lord used to touch the life of Charles Colson.

Tom Phillips is today the chairman of the board of the largest industry in New England, the Raytheon Corporation, one of the Defense Department's major contractors. In 1973 he was president of Raytheon and a four-year-old Christian convert whose life had been changed in a Billy Graham Crusade. This mover and shaker of industry took his commitment to Jesus Christ seriously.

In addition to studying the Bible, Tom became engaged in some discipleship training programs by Campus Crusade for Christ. Some time before Watergate, he was stretching his spiritual wings and giving his testimony before groups outside of the church, such as the New England Patriots football team. He had known Chuck Colson in Colson's pre-White House days. Here's how Tom told his side of the story to me:

> Before entering the White House, Chuck was practicing law with Raytheon's law firm, Gatsby and Hannah. He handled our work. I lost track of him in the White House. I visited you, Billy Graham, Henry Kissinger, the President and others for a briefing on Nixon's China trip in 1971. I didn't see Chuck then.
>
> When he came out of the White House, Chuck met with Brainerd Holmes, now our president, to talk about providing legal representation for Raytheon through his new law firm. When this word got to our board chairman the question was raised whether to employ an attorney who could have Watergate problems. It caused a schism at the top of Raytheon.
>
> At that time I had been a Christian for about four years, and I prayed every morning. The Colson question was a problem for us. So I prayed that Colson and this problem would just go away. But I had had great discomfort and had a sense of emptiness after the prayer.
>
> I thought, "Maybe this man needs a friend at this time. I could be his friend and tell him what has happened in my life." So I began praying for God's guidance about this thought. These prayers brought an opposite reaction. I felt relief and sensed that God was commanding me to be an Ananias to Chuck.
>
> So on his next visit to our headquarters at Lexington, I asked

Chuck to visit with me. We were not going to be able to retain his services, but I could at least give him the good news about what Christ was doing in my life. I explained how I had gotten to that point in my life where I didn't think my life was worth anything. Then I related the change in attitudes, values, the whole bit.

Finally, I offered to finish the story. Later I did have that opportunity on a Sunday evening, August 12, 1973, with my wife Gert at our home. Chuck came to visit us. The Lord led me into an adventure that night. He worked on me and used me like He sent Ananias to Paul in Damascus. I knew this was what God was directing me to do — to witness to Chuck and help him find how to fill the emptiness in his life with Jesus, the way He had done for me. I felt a real sense of God's will for me to do this. This direction came in my prayers.

The rest of the story is in Chuck's book. There certainly have been many ripples from this book.

I got the impression that Tom Phillips was not too surprised at the outcome of his personal witness to Chuck in March and August, 1973. He knew God was working in and through him in a mighty way. He could feel the spiritual push on his side and the spiritual seeking by Chuck in the questions he was asking.

Tom has been much publicized for meeting his big moment of opportunity for Christian witness. No one has told his story more than I, except Charles Colson. The book *Born Again* has sold more than 20 million copies and has been translated into fifteen languages.

Tom Phillips is another of those good examples for our edification. God used him in the salvation of Charles Colson and the production through that conversion of a tremendous ripple effect around the world for God's glory and the good of man. God also set up Tom to be a teaching aid in the flesh for all Christians who do not witness and fear that they could never do so.

Tom was no expert as a personal witness. This was not his forté. But he was open and obedient to God's will, and God sent him a candidate for salvation. Maybe the candidate for you is another Charles Colson — your mate, your child, or a Billy Graham or Dwight L. Moody. God only asks His people to be faithful, available and teachable to do His work.

This is the way I have seen God working in the Bible and in the world. When we are open and obedient, God is ready to work miracles through our lives. That is how I discovered God's will for my life — when I opened up to Him, got honest and showed Him that I was willing to trust and obey Him.

Chuck Colson's life was uncovered to receive truth and reality that evening at the home of Tom Phillips. The Lord had been preparing him to reach out for help beyond himself through his agonies in damaging Watergate headlines. Tom related his experience to Chuck in a way that touched Chuck's felt needs:

> "The success came, all right but something was missing," he mused...."My life wasn't complete....It may be hard to understand....But I didn't seem to have anything that mattered. It was all on the surface. All the material things in life are meaningless if a man hasn't discovered what's underneath them."[2]

Then Tom turned to Chuck's plight, causing Chuck to raise his guard about Watergate. Speaking gently but firmly, Tom broke through Chuck's defenses.

> "You would have won the election without any of the hanky-panky. Watergate and the dirty tricks were so unnecessary. And it was wrong, just plain wrong....The problem with all of you, including you, Chuck — you simply had to go for the other guy's jugular. You had to destroy your enemies. You had to destroy them because you couldn't trust in yourselves."[3]

Tom had to convince Chuck that he was wrong. He had to put him in Genesis 3 so he could see his need for confession and repentance. He had to steer Chuck to the one who had brought peace and completeness in his own life.

Even though Chuck was admitting to himself that his friend was right on target, he didn't give up easily. His pride was so strong. Yet Chuck privately confessed that his own words "sounded more and more empty to me."

> Tom believed so, anyway....With any other man the notion of relying on God would have seemed to me pure Pollyanna. Yet I had to be impressed with the way this man ran his company...ignoring his enemies, trying to follow God's ways.[4]

Tom then challenged Chuck "to face yourself honestly and squarely," adding, "This is the first step." It is the first step for each one of us. People must know that they need salvation in order to be able to appropriate it. This is the big problem: People do not usually see any need until a Watergate is already overwhelming them.

Tom gave Chuck *Mere Christianity,* C.S. Lewis' classic book. As he did, he read him one chapter, the one on pride and self-conceit. This was precisely what Chuck needed in order to comprehend his problem. C.S. Lewis had experienced the same stumbling block as a brilliant but unbelieving professor. Here is the portion of the chapter that struck Chuck:

> I do not think I have ever heard anyone who was not a Christian accuse himself of this vice....There is no fault...which we are more unconscious of in ourselves. And the more we have it ourselves, the more we dislike it in others.
> The vice I am talking of is Pride or Self-Conceit....Pride leads to every other vice: it is the complete anti-God state of mind....For Pride is spiritual cancer: it eats up the very possibility of love, or contentment, or even common sense.[5]

Tom finished reading the chapter and then asked the penetrating question:

> "How about it, Chuck?" Tom's question jarred me out of my trance....But Tom did not press on. He handed me his copy of *Mere Christianity.* "Once you've read this, you might want to read the Book of John in the Bible."[6]

After referring Chuck to Doug Coe in Washington for fellowship and follow-up, Tom prayed. Chuck writes:

> As Tom prayed, something began to flow into me — a kind of energy. Then came a wave of emotion that nearly brought tears. I fought them back.... When he finished, there was a long silence.[7]

Chuck was still too full of pride to pray. But after leaving Tom's house and getting into his car, the Spirit of God began working in Chuck's life.

> As I drove out of Tom's driveway, the tears were flowing uncontrollably. There were no streetlights, no moonlight. The car headlights were flooding illumination before my eyes, but I was crying so hard it was like trying to swim underwater. I pulled to the side of the road not more than a hundred yards from the entrance to Tom's driveway, the tires sinking into soft mounds of pine needles.
> I remember hoping that Tom and Gert wouldn't hear my sobbing, the only sound other than the chirping of crickets that penetrated the still of the night. With my face cupped in my hands, head leaning forward against the wheel, I forgot about machismo, about pretenses, about fears of being weak. And as I did, I began to experience a wonderful feeling of being released. Then came the strange sensation that water was not only running down my cheeks, but surging through my whole body as well, cleansing and cooling as it went. They weren't tears of sadness and remorse, nor of joy — but somehow, tears of relief.
> And then I prayed my first real prayer. "God, I don't know how to find You, but I'm going to try! I'm not much the way I am now,

but somehow I want to give myself to You." I didn't know how to say more, so I repeated over and over the words: *Take me.*

I had not "accepted" Christ — I still didn't know who He was. My mind told me it was important to find that out first, to be sure that I knew what I was doing, that I meant it and would stay with it. Only, that night, something inside me was urging me to surrender — to what or to whom I did not know.

I stayed there in the car, wet-eyed, praying, thinking, for perhaps half an hour, perhaps longer, alone in the quiet of the dark night. Yet for the first time in my life I was not alone at all.[8]

Another key Watergate character who began reaching out for supernatural help in his tribulation was Jeb Magruder. God answered his prayers through a note from Colleen and Louis Evans. Dr. Evans is the pastor of National Presbyterian Church in Washington, D.C. The letter came in June, 1973, during a very low time for Jeb.

Of all the people we have seen or listened to during this tragic time, we seem to feel a special empathy with you. I think we understand something of where you have been and where you are trying to go — because we have seen God use other painful circumstances to offer His love and show us that He can bring goodness out of disaster.[9]

Jeb and his wife Gail accepted the invitation of the Evanses to let them be encouragers to the Magruders as Barnabas had been to the apostle Paul in his early days as a Christian. Colleen discipled Gail, and Louie worked with Jeb. Louie met Jeb where he was, in pain and in limited Christian understanding. He used "a kind of friendship I had never known," Jeb reveals in his second book, *From Power to Peace*.[10] He introduced Jeb to "a community of Christians I had not known existed," Jeb writes. One of these was Doug Coe of Fellowship House.

All of my life there has been a sort of restlessness inside me....I had to confront my own inner needs....The missing ingredient in my life was Jesus Christ and a personal relationship with him....But the thing I needed most I had never had, and that was the knowledge that God loved me, and would never stop....

From the moment I met Louie Evans I began to experience what unconditional love meant, because he mirrors it in all his relationships....For a long time I wondered how such a love was possible, especially when I began to see it in friends I met through Louie.[11]

Louie began meeting with Jeb in September, 1973. By then it was getting close to the time for Jeb to be sentenced and go to jail. The sentencing came on May 21, 1974, before Judge John

Sirica. When asked if he had any comments to make before sentencing, Jeb responded:

> Somewhere between my ambition and my ideals I lost my ethical compass. I found myself on a path that had not been intended for me by my parents or my principles — or by my own ethical instincts. It has led me to this courtroom....My ambition obscured my judgment.[12]

In prison Jeb underwent emotional difficulties. He had to spend some time at a minimum security institution, some in the horrible District of Columbia jail, and some time at Fort Holabird, Maryland. At Holabird he was incarcerated with some Mafia hit men as well as Charles Colson, John Dean and Herb Kalmbach. The four Watergaters studied the Bible together at Holabird. Louie Evans visited Jeb every Friday, continuing to love and disciple him.

After his release from prison Jeb struggled to put his life together again. The discipleship and growth continued. Soon he was working with Young Life, the youth Christian organization which had indirectly affected my life through my daughters Dolly and Ginny. From there he moved on to Princeton Seminary for a divinity degree and into full-time Christian work as an assistant pastor.

In *From Power to Peace* there is painted a picture of a young man seeking to be loved unconditionally and wrestling with the problems of imperfection even as a Christian. He had to face the Internal Revenue Service, Watergate civil lawsuits, people who doubted the validity of his new Christian life, marital difficulties and discord and rivalry among Christians. Louie explained to Jeb that "None of us is perfect, and we aren't ever going to be, either."[13] As Jeb began to grow in spiritual maturity he came to realize that Christian buzz words such as salvation, forgiveness and personal relationship with Jesus Christ are easier to speak than to fully understand, apply and live out in the world.[14]

The most noted and studied spiritual conversion of all time is that of the persecutor Saul of Tarsus, who was changed into the second-most fruitful personality in the Bible and all of church history, the apostle Paul.

To understand the importance of what happened to Saul on the road to Damascus, we must first grasp the import of Jesus' command, "You must be born again" (John 3:7). Born again equals repentance, which in turn means the core change in one's life from self-will to God's will. The first admonition Jesus gave the world after His baptism and entry into ministry was the command to repent. In Matthew 4:17, His message is recorded this way: "From that time Jesus began to preach and to say, 'Repent, for the Kingdom of heaven is at hand.' "

In Mark 1:14 the record shows Jesus proclaiming, "The time is fulfilled, and the kingdom of God is at hand. Repent, and believe in the gospel."

Then Jesus began calling out His disciples (followers and learners). "Come after Me, and I will make you become fishers of men" (Mark 1:17).

In the oft-cited third chapter of the Gospel of John, Jesus began witnessing about the good news, Himself. Here He boldly explained to Nicodemus, the leading Jewish lawyer of the day and member of the Sanhedrin (ruling Jewish body), what is required of all people to come into a right relationship with God the Father. God's solution to man's Genesis 3 nature is that man be born again of the Spirit of God.

> There was a man of the Pharisees named Nicodemus, a ruler of the Jews. This man came to Jesus by night and said to him, "Rabbi, we know that You are a teacher come from God; for no one can do these signs that You do unless God is with him."
> Jesus answered and said to him, "Most assuredly, I say to you, unless one is born again, he cannot see the kingdom of God."
> Nicodemus said to Him, "How can a man be born when he is old? Can he enter a second time into his mother's womb and be born?"
> Jesus answered, "Most assuredly, I say to you, unless one is born of water and the Spirit, he cannot enter the kingdom of God. That which is born of the flesh is flesh, and that which is born of the Spirit is spirit. Do not marvel that I said to you, 'You must be born again.' The wind blows where it wishes, and you hear the sound of it, but cannot tell where it comes from and where it goes. So is everyone who is born of the Spirit."
> Nicodemus answered and said to Him, "How can these things be?" Jesus answered and said to him, "Are you the teacher of Israel, and do not know these things? Most assuredly, I say to you, We speak what We know and testify what We have seen, and you do not receive Our witness. If I have told you earthly things and you do not believe, how will you believe if I tell you heavenly things? No one has ascended to heaven but He who came down from heaven, that is, the Son of Man who is in heaven. And as Moses lifted up the serpent in the wilderness, even so must the Son of Man be lifted up, that whoever believes in Him should not perish but have eternal life. For God so loved the world that He gave His only begotten Son, that whoever believes in Him should not perish but have everlasting life. For God did not send His Son into the world to condemn the world, but that the world through Him might be saved.
> "He who believes in Him is not condemned; but he who does not believe is condemned already, because he has not believed in

the name of the only begotten Son of God. And this is the condem-
nation, that the light has come into the world, and men loved
darkness rather than light, because their deeds were evil. For
everyone practicing evil hates the light and does not come to the
light, lest his deeds should be exposed. But he who does the truth
comes to the light, that his deeds may be clearly seen, that they
have been done in God" (John 3:1-21).

The word repent comes from the Greek word *metanoia.* This
means an authentic, life-wrenching change from commitment to
self-centeredness to commitment to Christ-centeredness and the
value system as enunciated by Jesus in the Sermon on the Mount
(Matthew 5-7). There is no more repetitive or consistent theme
of the Bible than repentance, both individually and corporately.
The Old Testament prophets called the people of Israel, individually and as a people, to repent of their sins and to come back
to the covenants they had made to obey God and to be His
channel of redemption to the world. As Christians, we need to
repent daily and keep coming back to the vows we made in our
baptism and to all the times we have thanked God for pulling
us out of the Watergate pits of life.

Change is a word that strikes fear into most people's hearts.
Young people are more receptive to change because their rut in
life is not so deep as those of their fathers and mothers. People
are afraid to bolt from their rut for fear of the unknown. They
may not be comfortable in their rut, but it's the only rut they
know. Most times it is only when God permits a Watergate to
flood the rut that a person begins to think about getting out. I
am convinced that nearly every conversion is a product of failure.
God does indeed miraculously command the storms and
whirlwinds of life.

Indeed, every time God changes a life for eternity He is
working a supernatural transformation. The miracle is an authentic
heart transplant being performed by the Spirit of God. He doesn't
deal in artificial transplants. There already is too much artificiality
in man's world. God is in the business of re-creating the real
thing, a heart for God as originally manufactured in the beginning.
All too often man has to be in a state of trauma to be ready to
receive his miracle. Have you missed your miracle?

Charles Colson credits Watergate for resulting in the most
fulfilling event of his life, for it sent him to Tom Phillips and
then to Jesus Christ for a transplant miracle. Watergate launched
me on my search for truth, reality and my new heart. Even Jeb
Magruder, as much as he hurts today in some areas of his life,
thanks God for his Watergate and resultant change. Alexander

Solzhenitsyn, on finding his repentance and salvation in a Russian gulag in the cold of Siberia, thanked God for his Watergate: "And that is why I turn back to the years of my imprisonment and say, sometimes to the astonishment of those about me: 'Bless you, prison!' "[15]

How did Paul view his *metanoia?* In his personal testimony to the church at Philippi, he expressed feelings that are like my own:

> But what things were gain to me, these I have counted loss for Christ. Yet indeed I also count all things loss for the excellence of the knowledge of Christ Jesus my Lord, for whom I have suffered the loss of all things, and count them as rubbish, that I may gain Christ and be found in Him, not having my own righteousness, which is from the law, but that which is through faith in Christ, the righteousness which is from God by faith; that I may know Him and the power of His resurrection, and the fellowship of His sufferings, being conformed to His death, if, by any means, I may attain to the resurrection from the dead.
>
> Not that I have already attained, or am already perfected; but I press on, that I may lay hold of that for which Christ Jesus has also laid hold of me. Brethren, I do not count myself to have apprehended; but one thing I do, forgetting those things which are behind and reaching forward to those things which are ahead, I press toward the goal for the prize of the upward call of God in Christ Jesus (Philippians 3:7-14).

The story of Christ's apprehension of Saul of Tarsus on his way to continue to persecute Jewish Christians is recorded in Acts 9 and is further related by Paul in Acts 22 and 26. The story of Saul's conversion is familiar, but the story of Ananias is much less known. It reminds me so much of God's call of Tom Phillips to come alongside of Charles Colson and of Louie Evans to help Jeb Magruder come to know Jesus Christ.

Saul of Tarsus was the man best prepared by background and education to become a missionary to the Gentile world. The world around Israel was permeated with Greek culture, and Saul was especially trained in the law of God. A Roman citizen and a Hebrew, he was the chief persecutor of Christians for the Sanhedrin and the sect of the Pharisees. This uncomely Jew possessed one of the Bible's greatest intellects, much like the prophet Isaiah in the Old Testament. In changing the heart of Saul, Jesus had a man well fitted for the commission to write thirteen epistles in the New Testament, to save Christianity from being swallowed up by Judaism and to plant churches all over the then-known Gentile world.

In entrusting such a bold mission to this spiritual powerhouse, why would Jesus send only a layman named Ananias to bring Saul to salvation? Evidently for the same reason He sent Charles Colson to the home of Tom Phillips, another layman like Ananias. Many times the layman can relate better to a person of the world. Yet Jesus sent a pastor to Jeb Magruder. This illustrates that God uses the right vessel for each salvation candidate. Chuck needed to hear about pride and self-conceit from a captain of industry, who was a peer and friend. Jeb's felt need was unconditional love, and Louie Evans was an expert in unconditional loving.

Ananias was used to remove the scales of pride from the blinded Saul. And in three days his sight was restored. Now he had spiritual and human vision. This is what I call double vision: being able to discern God's view and will as well as man's. This is one of the great blessings of spiritual regeneration.

In Acts 22:6-10, Paul relates his Damascus Road experience to his Christian brothers in Jerusalem:

> Now it happened, as I journeyed and came near Damascus at about noon, suddenly a great light from heaven shown around me. And I fell to the ground and heard a voice saying to me, "Saul, Saul, why are you persecuting Me?" So I answered, "Who are You, Lord?" And He said to me, "I am Jesus of Nazareth, whom you are persecuting."
>
> And those who were with me indeed saw the light and were afraid, but they did not hear the voice of Him who spoke to me. So I said, "What shall I do, Lord?" And the Lord said to me, "Arise and go into Damascus, and there you will be told all things which are appointed for you to do."

What a change! The man headed to Damascus with orders from the high priest to stamp out this new Nazarene heresy was turned around to carry the good news of the Man from Nazareth to the ends of the earth. Ananias and the other new disciples of Christ in Damascus were to have been targets of Saul's persecution. Instead, Ananias was chosen by God to deliver spiritual sight, baptism and God's mission to Saul.

In writing the book of Ephesians, Paul declared his amazement that he had been selected for such a mighty mission: "To me, who am less than the least of all the saints, this grace was given, that I should preach among the Gentiles the unsearchable riches of Christ" (Ephesians 3:8).

Ananias was likewise astonished at his calling to go and give sight to the chief persecutor of Christians.

> But the Lord said to him, "Go, for he is a chosen vessel of Mine to bear My name before Gentiles, kings, and the children of Israel. For I will show him how many things he must suffer for My name's sake."
>
> And Ananias went his way and entered the house; and laying his hands on him he said, "Brother Saul, the Lord Jesus, who appeared to you on the road as you came, has sent me that you may receive your sight and be filled with the Holy Spirit." Immediately there fell from his eyes something like scales, and he received his sight at once; and he arose and was baptized.
>
> So when he had received food, he was strengthened. Then Saul spent some days with the disciples at Damascus (Acts 9:15- 19).

The Lord had prepared Saul as he stood and held the cloaks of those Pharisees who stoned to death the first Christian martyr, Stephen. One of the first six deacons chosen to help the apostles, Stephen met his death with faith and with forgiveness for those, including young Saul, involved in the conspiracy to kill him. After calling on the Lord Jesus "to receive my spirit," he had cried out, "Lord, do not charge them with this sin." And when he had said this, he fell asleep (Acts 7:59,60).

This heroic stance of Stephen must have initiated an inner working of guilt, shame and reproach in the heart of the young man at whose feet the cloaks of the stone-hurlers had been laid.

God's grace went to work in the heart of even this enemy of Jesus Christ. Through His Spirit, God reached out and used faithful, available and teachable disciples of Christ in that day as He does in this century. This gift was conceived by our creator not just for Saul of Tarsus, Ananias, Charles Colson, Tom Phillips, Jeb Magruder and Louie Evans. It is available to all. No one underscores this teaching more explicitly than does Paul, himself, in Ephesians 2:8-10:

> For by grace you have been saved through faith, and that not of yourselves; it is the gift of God, not of works, lest anyone should boast. For we are His workmanship, created in Christ Jesus for good works, which God prepared beforehand that we should walk in them.

CHAPTER XII

MAN'S NEED TO GROW

As you have therefore received Christ Jesus the Lord, so walk in Him, rooted and built up in Him and established in the faith, as you have been taught, abounding in it with thanksgiving.

Paul in Colossians 2:6,7

Charles Colson is a good example of spritual growth and service in a man. It was appropriate that his second book be written on the process of sanctification. The book is aptly named *Life Sentence,* and that's what salvation is about, a life sentence to grow spiritually in order to serve Jesus Christ. His newest books and more recent speaking engagements illustrate his spiritual growth in more recent years. Today Chuck is a powerful lover and servant. What is the root of this spiritual growth?

God's purpose for man is that all people become lovers and servants for the glory of God and the good of man. God's plan for implementing His purpose is to have people come under His government because of His unlimited love in their hearts, as Chuck did. His instrument to accomplish His will is the body of believers called the Church. The power inside the Church is the Holy Spirit, the executor of the counsel of the Godhead here on earth. He is also known as the "Go-Between God." Where is the Holy Spirit? This third person in the trinity dwells in the Kingdom of God — that is, wherever the Spirit of God is permitted to live and rule in the hearts and lives of those who have accepted Jesus Christ as Lord and Savior.

The Holy Spirit is God at work everywhere in the world, including Chuck's life, mine and many, many more. He is the Spirit of Christ ministering within the individual Christian to convict, counsel, comfort, teach and implement God's will on earth. He does this through faithful, available and teachable people. God the Father wills the salvation of all people, the Son provides the way to salvation, and the Holy Spirit secures the salvation of souls, turning them into lovers and servants.

It is so vital that people inside and outside of the Church comprehend the role and working of the Holy Spirit. Dr. Bill Bright, founder and president of Campus Crusade for Christ, maintains that Campus Crusade surveys show that 95 percent of church members do not understand the role and power of the Holy Spirit. Bright calls the Holy Spirit "the key to supernatural life." Dr. J. Edward Orr names the Spirit "the Commander in Chief of the Army of Christ."

At the moment of spiritual rebirth — which is solely the work of the Holy Spirit — a person enters into an eternal relationship with God through Jesus Christ. The development of this new life "in Christ," as Paul puts it, is accomplished by a joint venture — the spirit of man working in cooperation with the leadership of the Holy Spirit. The aim is simply this: transfiguration of character so that the Christian becomes a change agent for the kingdom.

When any person becomes a new creation in Christ, he makes a three-fold commitment of intellect, emotions and will to the person of the Lord Jesus Christ. The representative of Jesus Christ on earth is His Spirit.

Following regeneration, another process begins. The book of Romans takes us through this life-long process of spiritual growth and development known as sanctification. We are set aside (sanctified) to grow, live, love and serve in obedience to the leadership of the Holy Spirit and the teachings of the Holy Scriptures. Becoming sanctified does not mean being *better than* but rather *different from* the world and the way it dictates we live. We are set aside to be developed into the lovers and servants that God intended in creating us in His image and likeness.

How do we grow spiritually? We become more and more like Christ through the development of the fruit of the Spirit as described by Paul in Galatians 5:22,23: "But the fruit of the Spirit is love, joy, peace, longsuffering, kindness, goodness, faithfulness, gentleness, self-control. Against such there is no law."

The basic fruit is love. Only as we live in love can we grow spiritually and fulfill the will of God for our lives. The believer in Christ must become love-inspired, love-mastered and love-driven (2 Corinthians 5:14,15). Out of the Spirit of love flows the rest of the fruit of the Spirit.

In our inner life we experience patience, kindness, goodness, faithfulness, gentleness and self-control. All of this is generated through the joint venture of the spirit of man and the Spirit of

God for the purpose of men becoming lovers of God and man.

How can we be empowered to do for Christ, to serve Him? The other side of the major work of the Holy Spirit is to help us to discover, develop and use the spiritual gifts He provides for us to serve God and man. Paul gives us the key teachings on spiritual gifts in Romans 12, 1 Corinthians 12, 13, 14 and Ephesians 4. The gifts listed in these chapters can be extrapolated into hundreds and thousands of ministries for service to God and man. The major categories of gifts are preaching, teaching, knowledge, wisdom, exhortation, faith, discernment of spirits, helps, serving, administration, ruling, mercy, giving and love. Again, the key gift, like the key fruit, is love.

Jesus had a special program for developing His disciples. A disciple is a follower who is taught by the discipler. So Christian discipleship is training and equipping the followers of Jesus Christ to become more and more like Him in love and service. Jesus told His followers to focus on Him as the role model — His words and His life. Leroy Eims has written a book on *The Lost Art of Disciple Making*.[1] His point is that, by and large, the church today is shrinking from the art of discipleship training which Jesus illustrated for us in the Gospels. Discipleship is simply "show and tell." Some call it "each one teach one." The aim is not addition in the Kingdom of God but multiplication.

Jesus poured His life into twelve men so that they might be prepared, with others, to build His Church to take the message of salvation to the ends of the earth in accord with His Great Commission (Matthew 28:19,20). The key phrase in the Great Commission is to make (and reproduce) disciples.

Making disciples is what Charles Colson is now doing through his Prison Fellowship ministry. He has taken seriously the Nazareth Manifesto as enunciated by Jesus before He was expelled from His hometown.

> The Spirit of the Lord is upon Me, because He has anointed Me to preach the gospel to the poor; He has sent Me to heal the brokenhearted, To preach liberty to the captives and recovery of sight to the blind, to set at liberty those who are oppressed, to preach the acceptable year of the LORD (Luke 4:18,19).

This manifesto goes beyond those literally economically poor and in prison, for all sinners are poor in spirit, shackled by the chains of sin, blind to the wiles of Satan and oppressed by bondage to Satan's ways. Prison Fellowship is a ministry to the broken people in prisons across America and elsewhere in the

world. It is designed also to influence state and national govern-
ments to improve the administration of criminal justice. Prison
Fellowhsip is not a very welcome ministry to some people, but
it is most fruitful in the lives of prisoners and their families, and
is a way for outsiders to volunteer their time, talents and treasure
to minister to the broken people in the prisons. I have had the
privilege of teaching for Chuck in prisons. I tell prisoners, "You
have plenty of time and nowhere to go, so let's spend this time
to our best advantage." In fact I find more of the authentic love
of Jesus Christ among Chuck's prison disciples than in churches.
Church volunteers for Chuck say the same.

The aim of Prison Fellowship is conversion (making disciples)
of prisoners and development of their spiritual lives toward a
new life of service in Jesus Christ. Chuck is a good role model,
having served time himself. He is equally as fruitful in his personal
ministry around the world in conference centers, seminars, corporate boards and churches. He wrote *Life Sentence* to encourage
Christians in their spiritual growth and walk. The idea came to
him when he read a book with a "fairytale impression that the
Christian life is simple and almost carefree." A Gallup Poll showed
him the paradox that religion was up "but morality down."[2]
Chuck realized that the key to controlling crime lies in changing
lives.

> The paradox was disturbing, even mind-boggling.
> I began making notes of concerns I had about what it takes to
> live the Christian life: commitment, self-denial, Bible study, service —
> what it really means to be born again. There emerged the outline
> of a book, the determination to write it and prayer that God would
> use it to challenge His people to do His work on this earth.[3]

Romans 12 is probably the one chapter in the Bible that best
explains what the Christian life is to be. The essence of the
twenty-one verses of that chapter is wrapped up in verses 1 and 2:

> I beseech you therefore, brethren, by the mercies of God, that
> you present your bodies a living sacrifice, holy, acceptable to God,
> which is your reasonable service. And do not be conformed to this
> world, but be transformed by the renewing of your mind, that you
> may prove what is that good and acceptable and perfect will of God.

Paul writes to us that we are to commit our lives totally to
Jesus Christ because of His mercies and love in our favor — because He first loved us. We are not to permit the world to
squeeze us into its mold. To the contrary, we are to be so
transformed in our hearts and minds through daily renewal that
we become transformers of the world for Christ. We can best

do this by finding God's will and purpose for our lives and putting ourselves to work for Him.

This is what Chuck Colson is doing today. He even calls corporate board chairmen and members to repentance and commitment. He lets them know that they too deserve to be in God's jail until they are redeemed by His grace. No, their successes on earth will never get them to heaven, only their faith will do so. Chuck speaks with the force and conviction of Old Testament prophets such as Amos, Jeremiah, Ezekiel and Hosea. But where would Colson be today had Tom Phillips not sent him for follow-up fellowship and discipleship to a modern-day Barnabas, Doug Coe of Fellowship House in Washington, D.C.? Every new convert must have a Barnabas — an encourager and discipler.

Paul had Barnabas to come alongside him. Timothy had the apostle Paul to lead him, as did Titus. Every Timothy needs a Paul, and every Paul needs a Timothy. An encourager is an enabler. This is what God calls all Christians to be — helpers to others, especially in their spiritual lives. An enabler should be, like Barnabas, available, hospitable, and should radiate full confidence in God's love and power.

Paul needed Barnabas. After being smuggled out of Damascus as a new Christian, Paul was led by God into the wilderness of Arabia for a few years of "post-graduate study" directly with the Lord (Galatians 1:16,17). Some believe he went to the holy mountain of Moses, Mount Sinai or Horeb. The spiritual revolution in his life required time and study to adjust his thinking and perspective to that of Jesus Christ. There he dropped the intolerable burden of Pharisaic law-keeping. He came out of his time of solitude with a new teaching right out of the Old Testament: "Behold the proud, his soul is not upright in him; but the just shall live by his faith" (Habakkuk 2:4).

From this Paul grasped the doctrine of God's free grace and man's faith. Then he returned to Damascus to preach in that area for a few years before returning to his home base of Tarsus, in what is now Turkey. Before leaving for Tarsus, Barnabas came alongside Paul as a friend. Paul needed a good Christian friend — as Colson and Magruder needed Christian friends at first because so few people believed their changes were genuine. The Christian Jews in Jerusalem were even more skeptical and very fearful of Paul, their former persecutor.

If Ananias proved to be a friend to Paul, Barnabas was even more so. He sponsored Paul to the leaders of the Jerusalem church and vouched for his genuineness. After Paul was forgotten in Jerusalem during his several years in Tarsus, Barnabas again sought him out to minister with him in Antioch, the seat of the Gentile church. This outreach to Gentiles had caused the Jerusalem church to send an investigator to Antioch to hold the Gentile Christians in line with Jewish rituals. Fortunately, they sent Barnabas. Instead of being concerned with ritualism, Barnabas was more caught up in features of the outreach movement that called forth his forté — encouragement.

Paul evidently needed encouragement to go to the Gentile world. Thus the Holy Spirit, the church at Antioch and Barnabas launched Paul on what came to be known as his historic first missionary journey.

The Barnabas for Colson, Krogh and Magruder was Doug Coe. He pulled together an encouragement and support team for Colson. It was even bi-partisan, Democrats and Republicans from Congress and the Nixon Administration. The most unlikely team member was liberal Democratic Senator Harold Hughes of Iowa, a fairly recent convert himself. Another member of the group, then a GOP Congressman and later Governor of Minnesota, Al Quie, tried to convince President Jerry Ford to let him serve Chuck's time in prison when a crisis occurred in Chuck's family. This Christian crew rowed along with Chuck when he most needed them — as he was facing the special prosecutor and jail.

Aside from comfort and advice, good Christian friends help in spiritual growth. A number of respected theological people have poured considerable knowledge and growth into Colson. Read his book, *Loving God,* and you'll perceive the growth. In *Loving God,* Chuck gives this definition of real faith: "believing and acting obediently regardless of circumstances or contrary evidence."[4]

Chuck understands real holiness too:

> Holiness must be seen as the opposite of sin....Holiness, then, is..."conformity to the character of God and obedience to the will of God."[5]

Here are the four basic principles Chuck sees as being needed for the Church today:

> 1. The body of believers called the church is to grow from the inside out in response to the Spirit.
> 2. It (the church) must equip the laity to take the church into the world.
> 3. Spiritual discipline — fervent prayer and serious study of God's Word.

4. As one holy nation, we must break free of any provincialism and work for unity in Christ.[6]

Two biblical characters who exemplified growth in their spiritual lives were Peter and Timothy. Peter matured from a raw-boned fisherman with an impetuous personality to one of the greatest and noblest church saints of all time. In his teaching notes on Peter, Rev. Dick Woodward of Williamsburg, a Barnabas for me, pictures not one but three Peters: (1) the impulsive up-and-down Peter of the Gospels; (2) the stable, steady and great leader of the church in Acts, the Peter of Pentecost; and (3) in the epistles, Peter the teacher, sharing out of his heart and experience mature and wise pastoral theology.

Peter grew with every rebuke from the Master, especially following the resurrection. All of the apostles and the other disciples came alive spiritually in witnessing the resurrected Christ. They grew as they moved out to take the good news to the world.

Young Timothy's limitations were a concern to his mentor, Paul. A convert of Paul, Timothy had struggles with issues such as finances, personal purity, commitment to his job, his timidity and the give-and-take of interpersonal relationships. Despite all of this, Paul entrusted to Timothy the Ephesian church, including the training and assignment of pastors. Timothy was assigned the important Ephesian area of ministry only after Paul equipped this loyal young man during his second and third missionary journeys. Paul discipled him by letter and in person, as in a father-and-son relationship. Timothy became a gifted teacher and faithful servant of the great apostle.

Dr. Scott Peck devotes most of his book, *The Road Less Traveled,* to the subject of facing reality (constant self-examination) and growing toward maturity. The problem in psychotherapy, he writes, is that nine of ten come to a psychiatrist or counselor to get a quick fix. When they learn that growth can be painful — looking at the real self and being willing to change — then nine out of ten drop out.

In writing this book, Dr. Peck was led to find Jesus Christ. Then he began equating growth of the inner man with development by the Spirit of God. He discovered God's grace at work, producing healing that he could not as a trained counselor. Thus he concludes that "the ultimate goal of spiritual growth is for the individual to become as one with God."[7] So the road less traveled is the road of spiritual growth, the spirit of man growing with the help of the Spirit of God. Dr. Peck laments that people are not willing enough to submit, to face reality, and to be changed into what God has in store for all of man: "a call out of spiritual childhood into adulthood, a call to be a parent unto mankind." He sees all people as having an obligation because of God's grace "to be the agent of His power and love."[8]

Finally, Dr. Peck really rips at the inner man when he confronts us with this hard truth:

> Most of us are like children or young adolescents; we believe that the freedom and power of adulthood is our due, but we have little taste for adult responsibility and self-discipline.[9]

This is the essence of Christianity: a call to truth, to change, to commitment, to growth, to sacrifice, to responsibility and to self-discipline, all for the purpose of producing lovers and servants for the glory of God and the good of man.

CHAPTER XIII

MAN'S NEED TO PERSEVERE

If you can meet with triumph and disaster, And treat those two imposters just the same; If you can bear to hear the truth you've spoken Twisted by knaves to make a trap for fools, Or watch the things you gave your life to, broken, And stoop and build 'em up with worn out tools, Yours is the earth and everything that's in it, And — which is more — you'll be a man my son.

Rudyard Kipling[1]

Richard Nixon has many strong points in his character. None is stronger than his determination to persevere. In fact, the first book he wrote, *Six Crises*, is on the subject of how he endured through six major crises in his political life. He prevailed against those hard knocks and attained his goal, perhaps the dream of most Americans: the presidency of the United States of America. Then, his fulfilled dream was snatched away from him in his seventh crisis.

What is he doing today? Richard Nixon is on the road to recover his place in history, that place which might have been.

Had he not run for re-election, or had there been no Watergate break-in and cover-up, Nixon would have been in the first tier of great American Presidents. Even today, public opinion polls place him in the top rank among all Presidents in the conduct of foreign policy. However, Watergate keeps him in the bottom tier of overall ratings. But Richard Nixon has not finished persevering yet. *Newsweek* magazine, in its October 28, 1985, issue, featured the former President in an article entitled, "Nixon: The Comeback Kid." The article reported on a political fund-raising dinner sponsored by the Republican National Committee at the New York Hilton Hotel. The star attraction was Nixon.

Newsweek made these comments:

> At 72, his jowls heavier but his drive undiminished, Richard Nixon is back on-stage in a limelight more flattering than any time since he resigned in disgrace in August, 1974....What is Nixon seeking with his reclaimed "visibility"? Not an official position, associates say....what Nixon wants...is less tangible. "He wants to participate," explains (Lyn) Nofziger. "In his world, visibility equals credibility and a sense of being forgiven."[2]

In September, 1985, Nixon was again trekking through Red China as an American hero. In a stop at Peking, he was applauded ten times before he opened his mouth. Knight News Service reported: "Watergate here is some obscure, petty affair that concerns only Americans."[3]

There is a book on this subject, *The Resurrection of Richard Nixon,* by Washington news columnist, Jules Witcover. Witcover opens his 1970 book with a vintage Nixon comment on persevering:

> Anybody in politics must have great competitive instinct. He must want to win. He must not like to lose, but above everything else, he must have the ability to come back, to keep fighting more and more strongly when it seems that the odds are the greatest. That's the world of sports. That's the world of politics. I guess you could say that's life itself. (In a televised campaign interview — Richard M. Nixon, 1968.)[4]

Witcover had witnessed on November 7, 1962, what he, the news media and Nixon's "enemies" had assumed was "the public act of hara-kiri of the century" at the Beverly Hilton Hotel in Los Angeles. This was the famous statement by the twice-defeated Richard Nixon upon losing the governorship of California. He had lashed out at the news media with a number of caustic comments, including this one about his first crisis:

> And as I leave the press, all I can say is this: for sixteen years, ever since the Hiss case, you've had a lot of fun — a lot of fun — that you've had an opportunity to attack me and I think I've given as good as I've taken.[5]

After extemporaneously rambling on for several more minutes, Nixon bid good-bye and good riddance to the news media with this historic quote:

> But as I leave you I want you to know — just think how much you're going to be missing. You won't have Nixon to kick around anymore,

because, gentlemen, this is my last press conference.[6]

Witcover writes that even in this election debacle and political *faux pas,* "Richard Nixon did have that one sustaining strength: his commitment to the political life."[7]

After winning the presidency in 1968, Nixon wrote a new preface to *Six Crises,* which had been published after his 1960 loss to John F. Kennedy. In the new preface Nixon ruled out any design of his own in scoring the remarkable comeback victory of 1968.

> It was not by dint of my own calculation or efforts. No man, not if he combined the wisdom of Lincoln with the connivance of Machiavelli, could have maneuvered or manipulated his way back into the arena.[8]

Did Richard Nixon mean that his rise from the ashes of two major political defeats was an act of God or an act of fate? We may never know, for Nixon is basically silent about his spiritual roots, whatever they may be. Some say he is very private about his faith because of his Quaker up-bringing — Quakers are usually quiet about their faith.

Charles Colson and Billy Graham have visited the former President several times since Watergate. Both have told me that the subject of Nixon's own faith is virtually untouchable. Following Colson's conversion, Chuck talked with President Nixon in early 1974 about the National Prayer Breakfast. This occasion was after Chuck had passed on to Nixon a book by Elton Trueblood on Abraham Lincoln's spiritual life.

Elton Trueblood is a Quaker who is not silent. He has written many books on the importance of getting out the good news of Jesus Christ, particularly through all of the ministers — that is, "all of the people of God." He is a tireless advocate of the ministry of the laity. Tom Phillips had given Trueblood's book to Chuck to read and pass on to the President. Tom wasn't satisfied with just winning Colson. He wanted the man above Colson. On New Year's weekend of 1974 Chuck read a small news item from Nixon's home in San Clemente, California, reporting that Nixon was reading a book about Lincoln. He knew it was Trueblood's book.

On the evening before the 1974 National Prayer Breakfast, Nixon called Chuck to ask questions about the prayer breakfast, as Nixon would be speaking there the next morning. In *Born Again,* Chuck relates this revealing conversation:

"You know, Chuck," he mused, "I've never been able to talk about my beliefs in God in public and I resent people using religion in politics. That's so hypocritical. Not the kind of thing I've ever done." As he talked on, he was as unguarded as I'd ever known him. He spoke of his devout Quaker mother, and how he himself had accepted God when he was a boy and found strength from his faith. I urged him to speak freely at the breakfast.[9]

As President, Nixon spoke at the national breakfast every year, but usually he was reluctant to do so. Because of my friendship with Doug Coe, Doug looked to me to persuade the President to attend and speak. Presidential attendance at these annual breakfasts had started with President Dwight Eisenhower. Nixon had Doug change the name from the Presidential Prayer Breakfast to the National Prayer Breakfast because he saw the name as exerting coercion on a President to speak at the breakfast.

Billy Graham told Chuck that, as he and Nixon rode together to the breakfast, they had enjoyed the most frank discussion ever about Jesus Christ, Nixon's faith and the need for the Lord's hand in guiding an embittered nation. In *Born Again*, Chuck quotes from Nixon's prayer breakfast remarks about Abraham Lincoln's spiritual life:

Although he never belonged to a church, he probably prayed more than any man who has ever been in the White House....He did not have a feeling of arrogance about his side as compared to the other side. He did feel that America was destined to be united....He did believe that America had something to stand for, something to believe in, and something to do in the world bigger than itself. In other words, there was something other than Lincoln, the politician, the President, and the American people, each individual; there was what he called the Almighty, the Universal Being; sometimes he referred to him as God who guided the destiny of this nation.[10]

In concluding Nixon brought the message down to himself:

When I was eight or nine years old, I asked my grandmother, a very saintly woman, a little Quaker lady, who had nine children — I asked her why it was that Quakers believed in silent prayer. When we sat down to the table, we always had silent prayers; and often at church, while we sometimes had a minister or somebody got up when the spirit moved him, we often just went there and just sat, and we prayed. Her answer was very interesting, and perhaps it relates to why Lincoln prayed in silence. My grandmother spoke to me on this occasion, as she always did to her grandchildren and children, with the plain speech. She said, "What thee must understand, Richard, is that the purpose of prayer is to listen to God, not to talk to God. The purpose of prayer is not to tell God what thee wants, but to find out from God what He wants from thee."

Too often we are a little too arrogant [when] we try to talk to God....[Let's] listen to God and find out what He wants for us and then we will do the right thing.[11]

The teaching point in the President's message is a good one: Don't do all the talking in prayer; listen also. This is the teaching that I, like Elton Trueblood, major in today: I try to find God's will and then get about doing it. We are to become "involved in a cause bigger than ourselves." I heard Nixon repeatedly use this Lincoln and Trueblood challenge regarding his own cause.

In the talk, President Nixon had revealed the impact of Trueblood's book on him, and I believe Nixon equated Lincoln's faith with his. Also, Nixon provided a glimpse of the one who is supposed to have had the most effect on his spiritual life, his grandmother, Almira Burdg Milhous. She was the mother of Hannah Milhous Nixon, the lady who gave birth to the thirty-seventh President. On the day of his sad departure from the White House, the disgraced President referred to his mother, Hannah, as a saint.

John Nidecker is an Episcopal priest and former Nixon staffer who was very close to the family for many years. He tells me that it was Hannah's mother who witnessed repeatedly to Nixon as a boy. This is where the Quaker spiritual root emanated. The future President listened at her knee on many occasions as she poured out her Quaker convictions on little Richard. Here is how Nixon tells of his grandmother's influence in *The Memoirs of Richard Nixon:*

She seemed to take a special interest in me, and she wrote me verses on my birthday and on other special occasions. On my thirteenth birthday, in 1926, she gave me a framed picture of Lincoln with the words from Longfellow's "Psalm of Life" in her own hand-writing beneath it: "Lives of great men oft remind us/ We can make our lives sublime/ And departing, leave behind us/ Footprints in the sands of time." I hung the picture above my bed at home, and to this day it is one of my fondest possessions.[12]

This, as much as any other precept in life, has formed Nixon's determination to persevere. His aim today is to resurrect his "footprints in the sands of time."

His memoirs portray a young boy growing up in Whittier, California, with strong Quaker roots and convictions coming out of his family life and the Friends Church.

While at Whittier College he wrote a composition on October 9, 1933, describing his beliefs. He says this is "clearer than anything I could reconstruct today."

> Many of those childhood ideas have been destroyed but there are some which I cannot bring myself to drop. To me, the greatness of the universe is too much for man to explain. I still believe God is the creator, the first cause of all that exists. I still believe that He lives today, in some form, directing the destinies of the cosmos. How can I reconcile this idea with my scientific method? It is of course an unanswerable question. However, for the time being I shall accept the solution offered by Kant: that man can go only so far in his research and explanations; from that point on we must accept God. What is unknown to man, God knows.[13]

After quoting from his composition, Nixon then elucidates further in his memoirs on his view of Jesus and the resurrection:

> I thought that Jesus was the Son of God, but not necessarily in the physical sense of the term: "He reached the highest conception of God and of value that the world has ever seen. He lived a life which radiated those values. He taught a philosophy which revealed those values to men. I even go so far as to say Jesus and God are one, because Jesus set the great example which is forever pulling men upward to the ideal life. His life was so perfect that he 'mingled' his soul with God's."
> I wrote that the literal accuracy of the story of the resurrection was not as important as its profound symbolism: "The important fact is that Jesus lived and taught a life so perfect that he continued to live and grow after his death — in the hearts of men. It may be true that the resurrection story is a myth, but symbolically it teaches the great lesson that men who achieve the highest values in their lives may gain immortality....Orthodox teachers have always insisted that the physical resurrection of Jesus is the most important cornerstone in the Christian religion. I believe that the modern world will find a real resurrection in the life and teachings of Jesus."[14]

One of Richard Nixon's roommates at Duke University in 1934 was Carl Wrenn Haley, now a resident of Norfolk, Virginia. Rev. Haley recalls Nixon "as a very quiet Quaker boy with a sincere faith and a conservative approach to things." Nixon had come to Duke with some fellow graduates of Whittier College. The others came to Duke Divinity School. Not knowing any law students, and operating with meager funds, Nixon and his Whittier friends created a communal housing arrangement with Haley. They shared meals, beds, clothes, and thoughts. Haley reports that Nixon, being the only non-theological member of the group, found himself engaging in many heated discussions of theological and sociological topics.

Thirty-seven years later, on April 18, 1971, Rev. Haley's old roommate invited him to preach for church services in the East Room of the White House. Rev. Haley was impressed with "the inclusion of so many different faiths and his [Nixon's] feeling for those whose sons were given up to the nation in Vietnam." Haley felt this was "indicative of the depth and breadth of his [Nixon's] own faith."

Richard Nixon's *Memoirs* depict a streak of basic pragmatism that personified Nixon the politician and President. It was present in his life as a boy and as a young man.

The beginnings of what came to be known as Nixon's successful "Southern Strategy" in presidential politics are seen in his three years at Duke Law School in Durham, North Carolina.

> My three years at Duke provided an excellent legal background. Despite the fact that we had some intense discussions on the race issue, and while I could not agree with many of my Southern classmates on this subject, I learned in these years to understand and respect them for their patriotism, their pride, and their enormous interest in national issues. After my years at Duke I felt strongly that it was time to bring the South back into the Union.[15]

I turned out to be Nixon's Southern Strategist. This is what gained entry for me into the Nixon White House. The national news media credited Southern Strategy with his victory in gaining the 1968 GOP nomination and in peeling back enough of Alabama Governor George Wallace's Third Party vote to win — barely — the 1968 presidential election. This strategy continued to underpin Nixon's overall plan for the re-election landslide of 1972. Nixon won every Southern state, averaging seventy percent of the South's popular vote. This constituted a historic political feat for a Republican and opened up the South to the reality of a competitive two-party political system. In formulating and implementing his political Southern Strategy, Nixon followed the formula that was born into his mind at Duke: a velvet glove approach to desegregation in order to fulfill the law and "to bring the South back into the Union."

In 1966, the Southern Strategy was germinated at the Columbia, South Carolina, airport following a GOP fund-raiser. The former Vice President had conducted this for me as chairman of the South Carolina Republican Party. He was not sure that he could win the presidency in 1968 because George Wallace would take too many Southern votes from Nixon rather than from the Democratic nominee. I suggested how the Alabama governor could be stiff-armed in enough Southern states so Nixon could win. The key would be to pit Senator Strom Thurmond, the last Third Party candidate in the South, against Wallace. This is what happened in 1968. We had Thurmond all over the South exclaiming that "a vote for George is a vote for Hubert [Humphrey]!" It worked.

Not only did I come into the Nixon Administration out of Southern Strategy, but so did J. Fred Buzhardt, Jr., of McCormick, South Carolina. Both of us worked for Senator Strom Thurmond and in the presidential campaigns for Senator Barry Goldwater in 1964 and for Nixon in 1968. Fred came into the Nixon White House soon after I departed. As General Counsel of the Defense Department, he had impressed many people with his brilliance and his personal integrity.

When Nixon needed a lawyer in 1973 to assist on Watergate problems, Fred was selected to work with Leonard Garment, the resident liberal and a former Nixon law partner. Both attorneys had strong scruples, Fred as a Christian and Len as a Jew. Politically and philosophically poles apart, both were loyal to Richard Nixon and his best interest. Thus, it did not take them long to realize that Nixon should resign.

On November 3, 1973, Fred and Len flew to Nixon's vacation compound at Key Biscayne, Florida, to recommend some very unwelcome advice — resignation from the presidency. The two attorneys had a major problem: Their client was covering up even from them. They were telling Nixon's new chief of staff that they could not marshall the evidence to defend the President because he would not permit them access to any evidence. He provided only excuses. Their quandary is set forth in *The Final Days:*

> In defending himself, the President had planted time bombs, Garment said. Nixon had concealed, he had hedged, he had lied. Some of the bombs had already gone off, and the rest lay ticking. Individually the problems might be manageable, but taken together they were insurmountable. They all interlocked, and the single thread that linked the problems together was the President's tapes. The lawyers represented a President who had bugged himself, who had blurted his secrets into secret microphones. They had not yet heard the tapes, nor seen any transcripts of them. The President would not permit it. They were told to mount a defense, but were not given the information to do so. They could no longer assume their client's innocence, not unless they had evidence to the contrary.[16]

There were many other problems beyond Watergate. The Special Prosecutor was examining almost every White House activity and even Nixon's private matters, such as his taxes, his home and his personal finances. Nixon's Attorney General, Elliot Richardson, had extended the charter of the Special Prosecutor to virtual *carte blanche* investigative powers. One of the facts Haldeman had used to justify the containment strategy was that a Watergate confession by the White House and/or the President would blast open the door in more than a dozen other areas that were under investigation.

My friend Fred was as close to me as a brother. When I would visit him in Washington he was constantly frustrated with what was developing into the "cover-up of the cover-up."

> The President had hidden evidence, first from his lawyers and then from the courts. Then he had proposed to manufacture evidence to take the place of what was missing. He might even have destroyed material that was under subpoena. He had proposed to obstruct justice and had tried to entangle his lawyers in the attempt. The cover-up was continuing and the President was dragging them all into it. Buzhardt himself had now been called to testify publicly in the courtroom of United States District Court Judge John J. Sirica. If the right questions were asked, his testimony would be devastating to the President, Buzhardt warned.[17]

Fred was called to testify repeatedly before Judge Sirica or a grand jury. One of the ironies of the Watergate investigation was that Nixon's lawyers hardly had the time to defend the President because they had to spend so much time responding to the many prosecutors and testifying in court. Had the inquirers raised the right question, the Nixon presidency would have ended months sooner. Fred never did reveal what the dynamite-charged question was.

Len could visualize the new Nixon inner circle on Watergate — Chief of Staff Al Haig, Press Secretary Ron Ziegler and the two lawyers — being prosecuted for obstruction of justice and perjury. The Special Prosecutor's office ultimately gave consideration to indicting Haig, Buzhardt and the third lawyer to join the staff, James St. Clair, after Garment stepped aside from Watergate.

Fred was in a "no-win" situation. Sometimes weeks would pass without Fred's being able to see his client, the President. Reality was not welcomed. Later the President would become miffed with Fred when Fred was transcribing subpoened Watergate audio tapes. If the comments on a tape were barely audible or inaudible — and many were — the President would want the tape to be transcribed his way. This put Fred on his worst spot.

Nixon called Fred a Baptist lawyer, and indeed he was. Fred's mind and morals were among the best I have ever known. His personal integrity was born of his strong faith in Jesus Christ and of his fidelity to the West Point code of honor (class of '46). Fred was grounded and rooted deeply in God's Word. He had applied the Word of God in his life and had taught the Bible in Southern Baptist churches. Also, he had modeled biblical teachings in his workplaces.

The mystique and prestige of the presidency that Nixon felt would save him would not suffice. Fred proffered the same kind of advice that Daniel, as a young Jewish captive, had given to his bosses, King Nebuchadnezzar of Babylon and later King Belshazzar and finally King Darius of Persia. Fred, too, had dared to be a Daniel in the White House "lion's den."

As the consequence of the Watergate pressures, Fred Buzhardt was struck with a massive heart attack in 1974. I, and many others, implored him to resign, but he would not do so. He was loyal to his mission and the President. So he went back to work. He sensed that his work had not been completed, and, indeed, it had not been finished. Upon his return, he came across the "smoking gun" tape of June 23, 1972. This was the tape where Nixon, on suggestion of Haldeman, ordered Haldeman and Ehrlichman to convince the CIA to have the FBI call off the Watergate investigation on the grounds of national security implications. This effort met with failure and ultimate devastation, as did most of the cover-up plans.

The discovery was made on July 24, 1974, as Fred sat in his office with earphones listening to the tape Nixon had described as a problem, usually meaning a disaster. When I would visit Fred in the White House in 1974, usually he would be transcribing tapes for the Special Prosecutor on order of the court. Only Fred did the tedious and dangerous transcription work. This is what made him so vulnerable. Some of the transcripts did not match the actual tapes when they were received by the Congress. The problem was that the President would do his own editing when Fred refused to do so. Then Fred would have to testify before a grand jury, a judge or the prosecutors and do the impossible — defend himself and his client. That's more than a conflict of interest; that's suicide for an attorney. The prosecution force was heavily manned by ex-Kennedy aides. A "cover-up of the cover-up" would be an even bigger prize for prosecution, headlines and fame.

When Fred heard the June 23, 1972, cover-up order by the President, he knew this was the end of the Nixon presidency.

The impeachment proceedings were underway in the House of Representatives, and the outlook for the President's survival was already grim.

I once asked Fred if there was one cause of the Watergate imbroglio. He told me that there was no one event, *per se,* but a series of unrelated acts by different people not knowing what the others were doing. After the Nixon resignation, which was triggered at Fred's insistence, Senator Strom Thurmond and I asked Fred why Nixon had not destroyed his private taped conversations. Fred gave an hour-long explanation. Then Senator Thurmond blurted out in exasperation, "But Fred, why didn't Nixon burn the tapes?"

Fred had recommended that the tapes be destroyed, but Len Garment insisted that this could be another obstruction of justice and a terrible public relations problem. Fred did not see a legal problem if these private tapes were destroyed before being subpoenaed. The President, much to his regret and that of John Mitchell and many others, sided with Len and lost the fight to save his presidency. After the President's resignation on August 9, 1974 — seventeen days after Fred found the "smoking gun" — Leon Jaworski stated publicly that the President could have saved his presidency had he destroyed the tapes, evidently with no legal problems. He repeated his point in his memoir on Watergate: "I believe he would have survived and remained in office."[18]

What did the Special Prosecutor believe about why Nixon refused to eliminate the tapes? Jarworski wrote:

> But Nixon did not destroy the tapes because it never occurred to him that legal action might force him to surrender them. During 1972, and perhaps during the early part of 1973, he thought the tapes possessed extraordinary monetary value. He hoped to realize a fortune from them. And his background showed him to be a man greedy for both money and power. I am confident that he felt secure in his claim of executive privilege. And when that claim was jeopardized by the actions of the Special Prosecutor's office, it was too late.[19]

What did Nixon say about why he kept the tapes? Here is his reasoning in his memoirs:

> Legally the tapes would not actually be evidence until they were subpoenaed. But since we knew that the Ervin Committee or the Special Prosecutor would subpoena them momentarily, it would be a highly controversial move to destroy them. Nonetheless, Buzhardt felt that the tapes were my personal property and he favored destroying them. Garment considered the tapes to be evidence, and while

he did not favor releasing them, he made it clear that he would strongly oppose any move to destroy them. Haig made the telling point that, apart from the legal problems it might create, destruction of the tapes would forever seal an impression of guilt in the public mind. When Ted Agnew came to the hospital to visit, he told me I should destroy them.

We contacted Haldeman to find out what he thought I should do. His advice was to claim executive privilege and not surrender an inch of principle to the witch-hunting of Ervin and his committee staff. Haldeman said that the tapes were still our best defense, and he recommended that they not be destroyed.

*   *   *   *

Many factors bore on my decision not to destroy the tapes. When I listened to them for the first time on June 4, 1973, I recognized that they were a mixed bag as far as I was concerned. There was politically embarrassing talk on them, and they contained many ambiguities, but I recognized that they indisputably disproved Dean's basic charge that I had conspired with him in an obstruction of justice over an eight-month period. I had not listened to the March 21 tape, but Haldeman had, and while I knew it would be difficult to explain in the critical and hostile atmosphere that now existed, he had told me that it could be explained, and I wanted to believe that he was right.

I was also persuaded by Haig's reasoning that destruction of the tapes would create an indelible impression of guilt, and simply did not believe that the revelation of anything I had actually done would be as bad as that impression. On Saturday, July 21, I made a note outlining this rationale: "If I had discussed legal action, I would not have taped. If I had discussed illegal action and had taped I would have destroyed the tapes once the investigation began."

Finally, I decided that the tapes were my best insurance against the unforeseeable future. I was prepared to believe that others, even people close to me, would turn against me just as Dean had done, and in that case the tapes would give me at least some protection.[20]

Fred and Len also played a vital role in another key presidential decision: the selection of Gerald Ford to succeed Spiro Agnew as Vice President after Agnew's 1973 resignation. Nixon wanted to name his future candidate for President, John B. Connally of Houston, Texas. However, Fred and Len convinced Nixon that Connally could not be confirmed by the Congress to be Vice President.

When it became imperative to face the reality of the June 23 tape, Fred initially had to face the President alone. Len had moved to other duties; Watergate frustrations had been too heavy. At first St. Clair did not agree with Fred, and above all, the President refused to accept Fred's view. Nixon listened to two more June 23 tapes. Then he suggested that Fred also review these two tapes, assured they would change Fred's opinion. Fred became convinced that the other two conversations that day between Haldeman and the President only solidified the cover-up scheme, making matters worse. The President emphasized his disagreement and stridently walked out of the room.

Fred then persuaded St. Clair to listen to the tapes in the context of St. Clair's recent testimony to the House Impeachment Committee. St. Clair had flatly asserted that national security was the only motivation for Nixon's orders to the CIA.

> His [St. Clair's] own position was untenable. The tape proved that the President had lied to the nation, to his closest aides and to his own lawyers — for more than two years. Even if the tape did not prove legal guilt, it would certainly mean impeachment and conviction.[21]

After St. Clair joined with Fred, Al Haig's opinion became pivotal. Upon reading the transcripts, Haig told the President:

> Mr. President, I am afraid that I have to agree with Fred and Jim St. Clair. I just don't see how we can survive this one.[22]

The next day, on August 1, Nixon told Haig that he would resign. Over the following several days, the President had to consult with his family and close friends, especially Bebe Rebozo. The talks with the family members were very emotional. Julie, the one most like her father in political instincts, was staunchly opposed. She wanted him to persevere. Tricia's husband, Ed Cox, was also against resignation. Many tears were shed. When he let them know his decision was irrevocable, Nixon recorded the reactions of his three ladies this way:

> My wife and daughters remained an indomitable trio. Each one respected the opportunities public life had given her; and when the blows came, each reacted with dignity, courage, and spirit.[23]

Maybe, but there was much hurting. At this time Julie was involved in being discipled and studying the Bible.

Nixon's version of his prayer time with Kissinger is not as elaborate as that relayed by Kissinger.

> I told Kissinger that I realized that, like me, he was not one to wear his religion on his sleeve. I said we probably had different religious beliefs if we were to examine them in a strictly technical way, but that deep down I knew he had just as strong a belief in God as I did. On an impulse I told him how every night, when I

had finished working in the Lincoln Sitting Room, I would stop and kneel briefly and, following my mother's Quaker custom, pray silently for a few moments before going to bed. I asked him to pray with me now, and we knelt.[24]

The resignation raised two more questions for Nixon. What would happen should he be prosecuted as a private citizen? What would he do now in response to Haldeman's plea for a blanket pardon for Watergate people? Nixon wanted no bargaining with Leon Jaworski. He told Haig and Ziegler, "Some of the best writing in history has been done from prison. Think of Lenin and Gandhi."[25]

As to the question of pardons, Fred Buzhardt had prepared a memo stating that the President's power to pardon was a plenary power with no restrictions. Nixon could even pardon himself. Soon thereafter the U.S. Supreme Court in effect ratified Fred's memo in a separate case.[26] The President elected not to pardon anyone. Subsequently, on September 10, a Sunday morning, the new President, Gerald Ford, ended the Watergate saga for Richard Nixon with an unprecedented act, a pardon for a former President never convicted of a crime.

A year later Betty and I visited the former President at his residence in exile at San Clemente. He had lost the presidential look. He was very humble. His eyes were sallow, and his expression and appearance gave every sign of a fallen leader with no future. I next saw him at a Republican Party fund-raising dinner in Columbia, South Carolina, in January 1982. He was receiving plaudits from every corner of the auditorium, so much so that he was overcome with the joyous reception. The charm of Southern Strategy was still working, even with the leader in exile.

Citizen Nixon was so impressed that he spontaneously arose from his seat at the head table before speaking and proclaimed: "I've never been better received. I only wish Pat was here to experience this joyous occasion. If any of you want to stay after the dinner, I'll be glad to autograph your programs."

Everyone cheered wildly, and everyone stayed. At midnight there was still a line waiting to personally welcome the President back to Dixie and to receive an authentic autograph of the most unusual President in history.

That evening my mind flashed back to Fred Buzhardt who had persevered to serve his President in the best way possible with honor and with the hard reality of truth. He met his Watergate experience with his eye on the present and the hereafter. A little fellow from McCormick, South Carolina, population 2,000, he was called to advise the most embattled and beleaguered President in American history. He suffered many rebuffs for his service. When he left the White House, his own law school, the University of South Carolina, where he had been editor of the *Law Review* and first honor graduate, found no need for his services on the faculty. He was taken into a law firm by a friend, Joab Dowling, at Hilton Head Island in South Carolina. There he died of his second massive heart attack on December 16, 1978. He never wrote what could have been *the* definitive story of Watergate. He believed in the lawyer-client privilege.

The Bible is a book that reports on many who exhorted and exhibited perseverance. John Ehrlichman found these teachings in his search of the Scriptures. He understands Job and his tribulations and Job's persistent trust in God. Job came to realize that we cannot accept all the blessings from God without also expecting to stand tall in the tough times of testing. In Job 14:14, he cried out to God in the midst of his worst agonies, "If a man dies, shall he live again?"

Job evidently understood the answer; we don't just go around once. We go around here, and then, for eternity, there. That's the teaching in the epic book of Job: the sovereignty of God over the here and now and the hereafter.

Ehrlichman told me about his experience with a man who came alongside him in the midst of his two Watergate trials. He said he was going to help John by praying with him. "But," he advised John, "we're not going to pray for not-guilty verdicts." This stunned John. He wondered about the purpose of such praying. The friend said: "We're going to pray instead that God will use your Watergate to lay a blessing on your life such as you've never experienced." John then exclaimed to me, "Harry, now I know how to pray, unselfishly. I also know how to suffer. In suffering we are to look for the message and blessing God has tucked away for us in our trials."

There are all kinds of tests and temptations in life. But these tests enable us to learn and grow by perceiving God's purpose, the silver lining in the dark cloud, as John Ehrlichman experienced. As Paul observes, perseverance produces stronger character and hope (Romans 5:3,4). The temptations by Satan are intended to bend us and break us against God's will with the lure of planning our own lives. Adam and Eve underwent the first testing and failed to prove themselves true to God's will.

The last books in the Bible — Hebrews through Revelation — feature the teaching of perseverance. When they were being written, persecution was raising its head against Christians.

The apostles Peter and James gave particular attention to the need to persevere in the face of testing and temptations:

> Blessed be the God and Father of our Lord Jesus Christ, who according to His abundant mercy has begotten us again to a living hope through the resurrection of Jesus Christ from the dead, to an inheritance incorruptible and undefiled and that does not fade away, reserved in heaven for you, who are kept by the power of God through faith for salvation ready to be revealed in the last time.
>
> In this you greatly rejoice, though now for a little while, if need be, you have been grieved by various trials, that the genuineness of your faith, being much more precious than gold that perishes, though it is tested by fire, may be found to praise, honor, and glory at the revelation of Jesus Christ, whom having not seen you love. Though now you do not see Him, yet believing, you rejoice with joy inexpressible and full of glory, receiving the end of your faith — the salvation of your souls (1 Peter 1:3-9).

Peter, the apostle of hope, encourages us with the assurance that we have been born again into an ever living hope — eternity with Jesus — made possible by Jesus' death and resurrection. That is what Peter defines as being infinitely more precious than even the perishable gold of this world because our salvation begins here and lasts forever and ever.

James also exhorts us to persevere:

> My brethren, count it all joy when you fall into various trials, knowing that the testing of your faith produces patience. But let patience have its perfect work, that you may be perfect and complete, lacking nothing....Blessed is the man who endures temptation; for when he has been approved, he will receive the crown of life which the Lord has promised to those who love Him (James 1:2-4,12).

Paul also stresses joy in any circumstance in Philippians 4:11-13:

> Not that I speak in regard to need, for I have learned in whatever state I am, to be content: I know how to be abased, and I know how to abound. Everywhere and in all things I have learned...both to abound and to suffer need. I can do all things through Christ who strengthens me.

In his valedictory address, Paul bequeathed to us his noblest and most eloquent challenge. We are to run the race of life with endurance.

> For I am already being poured out as a drink offering, and the time of my departure is at hand. I have fought the good fight, I

have finished the race, I have kept the faith. Finally, there is laid up for me the crown of righteousness, which the Lord, the righteous Judge, will give to me on that Day, and not to me only but also to all who have loved His appearing (2 Timothy 4:6-8).

God put Fred Buzhardt on earth to run with a whole heart and to finish the race. God created all of us for a purpose. We are to find that purpose and then run that race with single-minded devotion and integrity, without fear, knowing that a crown of righteousness awaits all who love the Lord and serve Him. Paul declared his single-minded devotion in his letter to the Philippians: "But one thing I do...I press toward the goal for the prize of the upward call of God in Christ Jesus" (Philippians 3:13,14).

Among all of the Presidents of the United States, none endured more election defeats and other setbacks in life before being elected President than Abraham Lincoln. He prevailed in only one election contest out of seven tries prior to being elected President in his eighth political race. The one office he won, after running for it three times, was a seat in Congress. Then he lost his bid for re-election, which resulted in a nervous breakdown. This loser turned out to be one of the greatest Presidents in history. He just kept on keeping on. He persevered, even through family tragedies and personal melancholia and depression. I am sure Nixon has his eye on Lincoln's determination to persevere.

The Bible has many examples of those who persevered. Some who survived major handicaps or miscues were Peter, in his denial of Jesus; Moses, for murdering the Egyptian guard; Rahab, and her harlotry; Thomas, and his doubting of Jesus' resurrection; Jacob, and his life of deceit; Elijah, and depression; Mark, and his desertion of Paul; David, and his major sins; Saul of Tarsus, and his persecution of Christians; all the apostles, and their abandonment of Jesus in his trial; and many others.

All of these people repented of their wrongs. Their lives were changed as a consequence. They persevered, and they were changed.

What about Richard Nixon? Here is the lament of Anthony Lewis of *The New York Times* staff and a concern of many others:

> In watching tragedy the audience finds release — catharsis — for its own fear and pain. So the Greek dramatists taught us. But to meet their definition of tragedy, the hero had to change during the drama. Like Oedipus, he came to understand the destiny imbedded in his character. He accepted reality, and so he expiated the wrongs of the past.

What was so sad about the final moments of Richard Nixon's public life was that he denied his country the empathy and the release it desired. For he made clear that he had not changed. He was still trying to escape reality.

The only reason he gave for his resignation from the Presidency was that he had lost his "political base." The unwary might have thought that, as in a parliamentary system, the legislature had forced him out because of policy or partisan differences. That implication was surely intended.[27]

There is a story about Tom Landry, the popular Christian coach of the Dallas Cowboys football team. In the early years of this top professional team they were losers. Landry commented that "they haven't lost enough games yet to be champs." This is a major teaching of the Bible: Out of death came the resurrection, and out of the resurrection of Jesus Christ came eternal life which is available to everyone.

A Watergate does not have to spell the end; it can and should issue in a new and far better beginning of something that never ends — new life in Jesus Christ.

CHAPTER XIV

MAN'S NEED FOR LEADERSHIP

> The authority by which the Christian leader leads is not power but love, not force but example, not coercion but reasoned persuasion. Leaders have power, but power is safe only in the hands of those who humble themselves to serve.
>
> Dr. John R. W. Stott[1]

In his quest to change the history books about his "footprints in the sands of time," Richard Nixon has produced some excellent writings. He began in 1978 with his voluminous memoirs (more than 1100 pages). To his credit he wrote many pages about Watergate, and with more candor than I had expected.

Then he moved to the area of his forté, foreign policy: *The Real War* (1980), *Leaders* (1982), *Real Peace* (1984) and *No More Vietnams* (1985). These books, his speeches emphasizing foreign policy, and his being consulted by President Ronald Reagan, have all boosted Nixon's public image and respectability. This is causing people to remember his outstanding record in foreign policy and his creditable achievements in domestic policies. So many people remark to me that "I'd vote for him again" or "he's the best President we've ever had for foreign policy." I am grateful for having been permitted to work for a President whose record of service, minus Watergate, may have been the best of all.

In his book on *Leaders,* Nixon limits his subject to "those who lead nations."[2] His views on leadership surface as he assesses key world leaders.

> For the last thirty-five years I have had an exceptional opportunity, during an extraordinary period of history, to study the world's leaders firsthand....Having known both the peaks and valleys of public life, I have learned that you cannot really appreciate the heights unless you have also experienced the depths. Nor can you fully understand what drives a leader if you have only sat on the sidelines, watching.[3]

This is how leadership appears to the man who led America and the Free World for almost six years:

> Great leadership is a unique form of art, requiring both force and vision to an extraordinary degree....Great leadership requires a great vision, one that inspires the leader and enables him to inspire the nation. People both love the great leader and hate him....It is not enough for a leader to *know* the right thing. He must also be able to *do* the right thing....The years ahead will require leadership of the highest order.[4]

Richard Nixon quotes Isaiah Berlin who classifies Winston Churchill as "the largest human being of our time."[5] Churchill once quipped that "We are all worms, but I do think that I am a glowworm."[6]

Nixon writes:

> Shakespeare wrote that "some are born great, some achieve greatness, and some have greatness thrust upon them." During his long life and career Winston Churchill provided examples of all three....Churchill sought power because he honestly felt he could exercise it better than others. He believed that he was the only man who had the ability, the character, and the courage to handle some of the great crises of his time. And he was right.[7]

For every person who seeks to lead there are many more who seek to be led. Some call this the herd instinct. It is easier and safer to follow than to lead. Leadership requires responsibility and, in many ways, more work and more worry. Churchill was convinced that his purpose in life was to be a leader, not only of his country but of the world. He sensed his God-given strengths as a leader.

The problem for leaders is that it is all too easy to fall into the snare of Satan "to become like God," as Adam and Eve did. With leadership and power there come the perquisites and privileges of office and authority, whether given or taken. In politics and in the corporate and union leadership world, this is the rule rather than the exception. This problem even spills over into the Church and into God's work. Have you ever seen a church parking lot with a sign marked, "Reserved, Senior Pastor"?

Seemingly, the bigger the leadership role, the bigger the measure of ego and pride. It is only too easy for any leader to become caught up in himself, looking to himself and his close advisers for answers. Yet man will gain more "followship" from his fellowman if he exhibits in reality and authenticity the kind of leadership Jesus Christ exemplified and commanded in the

Gospels. It is vital that any leader know where he is coming from and where he is going. This awareness means having arrived at a world view. Leaders must discern what is truth, who is the Truth, and how man depends on the unlimited wisdom of this Truth rather than his own limited wisdom.

Today, the first thing I want to know about a leader is what is his belief system? What are his values, his priorities, his world view? Every leader must begin at a base point. I do not give first consideration to a man's political party or to the usual credentials the world expects of its leaders. I want to know his spiritual root and whether it is oriented toward self — as with Adolph Hitler — or toward the love and service of mankind and the creator of all mankind.

When the Lord turned my life around I indeed became a new creature in many ways, even in what previously was my first love, politics. As I look back over my shoulder to politics, law, business, the news media, government and lobby work, I see far more selfishness than service. I see more taking than giving, more love of self than love of others. This is my concern about the leadership I see in America today: too many takers and not enough givers. Not only can individuals turn inward, but nations also can do the same, and they can decay and fall, as history teaches.

By and large, people follow their leaders. In Old Testament days, most of the kings of Israel were selfish and corrupt. The same was true of the priests. The people followed their leaders into the downfall of Israel and Judah through idolatry, injustice, immorality, cold religious ritualism and disunity. All of this combined in rebellion against the lordship of their acknowledged leader, their Lord God Jehovah.

In the Old Testament we are presented with many examples of selfish and improper leadership. But toward the close of the historical books we see the correct role model, for the people then and for us now, in Nehemiah, the governor of Judea 2400 years ago. This man, according to the book of Nehemiah, was selected by God to perform a vital mission under extremely adverse circumstances and at a critical time for his people.

Nehemiah was a Jew in exile in Babylonia, which was then under Persian rule. He was probably born in exile. Despite his status as a Jew, he had become the cupbearer to King Artaxerxes I in approximately 450 B.C. Nehemiah was the equivalent of Bob Haldeman to President Nixon. The last thing he needed to do was to leave his post in "Arty's White House" and become a high commissioner in the small captive state of Judah.

Prior to his call to go to Judah as governor, two Jewish expeditions had traveled across the desert to rebuild the Temple of worship and to renew the spiritual life of the Jewish people. They had met with much opposition from the anti-Jewish pagans who lived across the line in Samaria. To revive and restore Judah and Jerusalem required the reconstruction of the walls of the city. This could not be accomplished without a fight, for the Samaritans and their allies were determined to prevent it. They had destroyed what the first returnees had rebuilt.

Learning of the plight of his fathers' city, Nehemiah prayed to God about the problem. He sensed the call of God to take the leadership role in restoring the walls of Jerusalem. A city without walled security meant a city without any security. Thus Nehemiah petitioned his king and received his permission not only to go to Judah but also to be the political leader of Judah and the restorer of the walls.

A study of Nehemiah's memoirs of restoring the walls in fifty-two days while under constant attack is thrilling, and it is an instructive course in personal leadership characteristics and sound leadership principles. Dr. Cyril J. Barber has printed such a study in his book, *Nehemiah and the Dynamics of Effective Leadership.* The characteristics he found in the leader Nehemiah were personal integrity, loyalty, stability, concern for others, proper discernment for the whole project including the work and the workers, motivation linked with enthusiasm, and tact.[8]

These personal characteristics were rooted in love for and service to God and man. Nehemiah's character was built in the study of God's Word and in worship and prayer. His first duty was obedience to God's mission as a part of God's overall plan for His people. This is what the Bible teaches should also be the first duty of our lives. Yet this is the type of motivation and mission that is missing in so many leaders. Most people want their leaders to be committed to and in contact with God. Public opinion polls reflect concern about selfishness in leaders. When it comes to respect, people tend to look down on instead of up to their leaders.

With regard to sound principles of leadership, Nehemiah developed a thorough knowledge of his task. He knew himself, and he knew his workers. Nehemiah understood what should be done and how to accomplish the mission. He kept his people informed, encouraged and praised. He developed their sense of mission and unity, he set goals, and — most importantly — he set the example for others to emulate.

The miracle of Nehemiah's story lies in the fact that he knew how to handle his enemies without becoming unglued. Nehemiah's problem person was a Samaritan named Sanballat. This shrewd enemy tried to defeat Nehemiah and his workers. He forged an alliance with all of Nehmiah's enemies — with Tobiah the Ammonite and his people, with the Arabs, and with the Ashdodites. Nehemiah's enemies were as determined to thwart his purpose as were the enemies of Richard Nixon to thwart his. But Nehemiah instilled in his people a sense of mission, not just for themselves and their families but for the Lord God Jehovah. So "the people had a mind to work" (Nehemiah 4:6).

Nehemiah's enemies were even bent on murder to achieve their ends. But Nehemiah led his people to be prepared to work and fight — for they knew that "Our God will fight for us" (Nehemiah 4:20).

> And our adversaries said, "They will neither know nor see anything, till we come into their midst and kill them and cause the work to cease."
>
> So it was, when the Jews who dwelt near them came, that they told us ten times, "From whatever place you turn, they will be upon us."
>
> Therefore I positioned men behind the lower parts of the wall, at the openings; and I set the people according to their families, with their swords, their spears, and their bows. And I looked, and arose and said to the nobles, to the leaders, and to the rest of the people, "Do not be afraid of them. Remember the Lord, great and awesome, and fight for your brethren, your sons, your daughters, your wives, and your houses."
>
> And it happened, when our enemies heard that it was known to us, and that God had brought their plot to nothing, that all of us returned to the wall, everyone to his work. So it was, from that time on, that half of my servants worked at construction, while the other half held the spears, the shields, the bows, and wore armor; and the leaders were behind all the house of Judah. Those who built on the wall, and those who carried burdens, loaded themselves so that with one hand they worked at construction, and with the other held a weapon. Every one of the builders had his sword girded at his side as he built. And the one who sounded the trumpet was beside me.
>
> Then I said to the nobles, the rulers, and the rest of the people, "The work is great and extensive, and we are separated far from one another on the wall. Wherever you hear the sound of the trumpet, rally to us there. Our God will fight for us."
>
> So we labored in the work, and half of the men held the spears from daybreak until the stars appeared. At the same time I also said to the people, "Let each man and his servant stay at night in Jerusalem, that they may be our guard by night and a working party by day." So neither I, my brethren, my servants, nor the men of the guard who followed me took off our clothes, except that everyone took them off for washing (Nehemiah 4:11-23).

Nehemiah's unselfish example rallied the Jewish people to persevere and brave the dangers of open warfare as they worked to accomplish God's mission for them.

This was Nehemiah the winner: an unselfish leader dedicated to God and his people and to what he knew was a holy mission. He had vision, and he communicated this vision of God to his people. He did not become distracted by hating his enemies or raising his own image. He was too busy leading, praying and working to become obsessed with his enemies. His only obsession was God's will and purpose for his life and the lives of his people. This gave him and his people the character, confidence and courage necessary to complete the job in fifty-two days despite the many enemies and long odds.

Every public official and leader — believers in Jesus Christ or not — should study Nehemiah's memoirs. God has made a permanent place for them in His handbook for living, for leading and for loving. We ignore these thirteen brief chapters at our peril and that of our nation and our world.

A study of Winston Churchill's life is helpful. However, Winston Churchill, as great a leader as he was, did not seem to know the answer for the future. In a meeting with Billy Graham at Number 10 Downing Street in his final years, the old world leader posed this momentous question to the then relatively young world evangelist:

> "What hope do you have for the world? I am an old man without any hope for the world." Graham instantly rang, "I am filled with hope!" — deftly withdrawing then his small slim black New Testament from his coat pocket, he proposed, "Life is very exciting, even if there's a war. Because I know what is going to happen in the future."[9]

A prime requisite for any leader is that he must know the future as well as the past. This is all set out for us in the Holy Bible. This book overflows with God's wisdom given to help us meet life with victory now and hereafter. Instead of hating our enemies, the Bible commands us to love them, to help them, to win them to the cause of righteousness. This is possible through changed lives and thus the re-creation of new hearts and spirits through Jesus Christ.

In fact, it was Jesus Himself who pronounced the teaching of love of our enemies. In the Sermon on the Mount, Jesus told his disciples:

> You have heard that it was said, "You shall love your neighbor and hate your enemy." But I say to you, love your enemies, bless

those who curse you, do good to those who hate you, and pray
for those who spitefully use you and persecute you (Matthew 5:43,44).

Jesus also presented the golden rule in the same sermon:
"Therefore, whatever you want men to do to you, do also to
them, for this is the Law and the Prophets" (Matthew 7:12).

These teachings work! What Jesus teaches is what people
really want to see in others — love, humility, selflessness, service
to others. These who practice such are the noble saints, and
their influence is all-pervasive. This is walking, not just talking.

Politicians, businessmen, attorneys, labor leaders, even Christians and pastors, should apprehend the meaning of the life of
St. Francis of Assisi. It was so like that of Jesus — dying to live,
losing to win, serving to conquer, loving to lead.

One of the major flaws in politics and other professions lies
in taking credit for the blessings rather than giving the credit to
the Blesser.

In politics the rationale abounds that the leader must have
all the glory so the people will return him to office.

The prophet Jeremiah warned his servant Baruch — and us —
about ambition in Jeremiah 45:5: "'And do you seek great things
for yourself? Do not seek them; for behold, I will bring adversity
on all flesh,' says the LORD. 'But I will give your life to you as
a prize in all places, wherever you go.' "

Baruch was at a crossroads in his life. He was complaining
about the hardships of serving God. He saw the air castles of
his own ambition and advancement come crashing down. So the
Lord told Jeremiah to instruct Baruch to stop putting self at the
center and to give the right of way to God and His purpose.

Baruch followed the advice and stuck with the persecuted
Jeremiah through all of his tribulations. Baruch finished his course,
making an enduring contribution to the plan and purpose of
God. This is what the world needs to comprehend today: Our
lives must be totally committed to the will of God in Christ
regardless of the cost.

If leaders do not show the way, will the people follow? Paul
put it this way: "For if the trumpet makes an uncertain sound,
who will prepare for battle? (1 Corinthians 14:8).

Above all, a leader must have vision. This foresight and
insight must be derived from the one who dispenses vision, truth
and wisdom. The Bible warns that without vision, the people
perish (Proverbs 29:18, KJV).

The best definition of vision I have encountered is found
in a book about the great Baptist leader, George W. Truett:

The man of God must have insight into things spiritual. He must be able to see the mountains filled with the horses and chariots of fire; he must be able to interpret that which is written by the finger of God upon the walls of conscience; he must be able to translate the signs of the times into terms of their spiritual meaning; he must be able to draw aside, now and then, the curtain of things material and let mortals glimpse the spiritual glories which crown the mercy seat of God. The man of God must declare the pattern that was shown him on the mount; he must utter the vision granted to him upon the isle of revelation....None of these things can he do without spiritual insight.[10]

The apostle Paul ranks in the forefront of biblical leaders like Jesus and Nehemiah as an exemplary role model to follow. Paul permitted the Lord to reshape his ambitions after his Damascus Road experience. From a self-centered ambition Paul became motivated by two ambitions: to win the smile of the Lord (2 Corinthians 5:9) and to preach the gospel where it had not been heard (Romans 15:20,21).

Dr. J. Oswald Sanders credits Paul's remarkable singleness of purpose as the key to his fruitful service. He sold out to the vision Jesus Christ had given to him for the remainder of his life. Everything was to be "by Christ," "in Christ," or "for Christ" and His purpose. Nothing would deter or distract him from this holy mission for his life. His vision knew no horizons and no bounds for bringing spiritually lost people face to face with Jesus Christ. That was his driving force.

Previously for Paul, as Saul of Tarsus, the driving force had been pride in his self-righteous life as a moral, successful and law-abiding citizen — a Pharisee among the Pharisees. He saw no need for self-reproach or change. His excessive zeal led him to persecute the early Christian Church. These combined attitudes made Saul a tough candidate to convert. Saul was convinced of his own righteousness and integrity and of his self-sufficiency.

This is the potential trap of leadership. It can breed excessive confidence, the divine-right-of-kings syndrome, self-sufficiency and malignant narcissism. Do you have Saul's problem? Or have you found Paul's solution?

CHAPTER XV

MAN AS GOD'S WATCHMAN

> But if the watchman sees the sword coming and does not blow the trumpet, and the people are not warned, and the sword comes and takes any person from among them, he is taken away in his iniquity; but his blood I will require at the watchman's hand.
>
> Ezekiel 33:6

By now the message of this book should be clear: Man is born into this world as a spiritual cripple and Satan wants to keep him from his place in heaven. The question is this: Who is going to warn man about his condition as a "Watergater" and inform him that supernatural help is available as a gift from God and that it is the answer to all "Watergatism"?

The Scriptures are clear that God's watchmen for the world are the people whom God has redeemed through Jesus Christ. The Bible is written in particular to believers so that they may become prepared to be God's watchmen, witnesses to the unbelieving and spiritually lost world. For what purpose? The apostle John tells us:

> ...that you may believe that Jesus is the Christ, the Son of God, and that believing you may have life in his name (John 20:31).
> These things I have written to you who believe in the name of the Son of God, that you may know that you have eternal life, and that you may continue to believe in the name of the Son of God (I John 5:13).

The passport to life with Christ — having His life in our lives, now and in eternity — is a matter of trusting and obeying. God's grace is free. People need to know this good news so they can choose God.

In the Old Testament the Lord God Jehovah chose the people of Abraham's seed, Israel, to be His watchmen. God delivered them from Egyptian bondage by His miraculous grace. Because of God's unlimited love for them, they were to be Jehovah's agents to push back the darkness of enslavement to sin by being God's light bearers and role models to the world. Exodus 19:5-8 records that as a people, they made a covenant with God through Moses. They committed themselves to be "a kingdom of priests and a holy nation." This is the same commitment we make today in coming to faith in Christ. We accept and commit ourselves to Jesus as Lord and Savior.

God brought the Israelites to Mount Sinai (Horeb) to prepare them to be His watchmen. Having given the Israelites their commission in what is known as the Mosaic or Sinai Covenant, the Lord God Jehovah then pledged them to obedience with the Ten Commandments. They ratified God's Law and their obedience to it with blood (Exodus 20-24). A covenant sealed in blood is never to be abrogated.

At Mount Sinai, God also commanded the people through Moses to "make Me a sanctuary, that I may dwell among them" (Exodus 25:8). The remaining fifteen chapters of Exodus are devoted to the importance God places on worship of and fidelity to Him. He even presented details on the construction and use of the Tabernacle where His presence would be manifested among His chosen people. Here they were to come and worship Him and seek forgiveness for their transgressions against His Law.

This is God's plan for His light bearers of any age: service, obedience and worship. When God entered into the first theocratic covenant with Abraham as recorded in Genesis 12, He established that the seed of Abraham were to "be a blessing" to "all the families of the earth." God elected them to be His chosen people, to be His light bearers, the reflectors of His saving grace (Genesis 12:2,3).

One of the Old Testament books which best portrays the role of Israel, God's chosen people, is Ezekiel. In the time of the prophet Ezekiel, the chosen people were reaping the wrath of God for failing to serve, obey and worship Him in accordance with their commitment as His nation of priests. Corruption and idolatry reigned from kings to priests to people. This is why God called and anointed the Old Testament prophets, to bring the people back to the covenants they had made in blood with their Maker, Deliverer and Lord.

God said to young Ezekiel:

> Son of man, I have made you a watchman for the house of Israel; therefore hear a word from My mouth, and give them warning from

Me: When I say to the wicked, "You shall surely die," and you give him no warning, nor speak to warn the wicked from his wicked way, to save his life, that same wicked man shall die in his iniquity; but his blood I will require at your hand. Yet, if you warn the wicked, and he does not turn from his wickedness, nor from his wicked way, he shall die in his iniquity; but you have delivered your soul.

Again, when a righteous man turns from his righteousness and commits iniquity, and I lay a stumbling block before him, he shall die; because you did not give him warning, he shall die in his sin, and his righteousness which he has done shall not be remembered; but his blood I will require at your hand. Nevertheless if you warn the righteous man that the righteous should not sin, and he does not sin, he shall surely live because he took warning; also you will have delivered your soul (Ezekiel 3:17-21).

In that day, Israel responded briefly to the message on restoration of the Temple, the Law, and the walls of Jerusalem under Zerubbabel, Ezra and Nehemiah. But the revival that came under Ezra's restoration of the Law and Nehemiah's leadership as governor of Judah was short-lived.

Now the channel of good news is the Church founded upon Jesus Christ and built by the apostles. Our charter is the Great Commission, which has it roots in Genesis 1 and 2 and in Genesis 12 and was further stated in Exodus 19, Isaiah, Ezekiel and elsewhere in the Old Testament. In the New Testament the Great Commission was first heard when Jesus signaled the fishermen to "Follow Me" (Matthew 4:19). The Great Commission in full is formally proclaimed in different but similar versions at the end of each of the Gospels and in the first chapter of the Book of Acts.

The charge is the same: Be My light bearers to the lost world. The lost are to be brought to make a commitment to Christ as Lord and Savior. Then they are to be taught to obey all that Jesus has commanded us to be and do. The promise is given that Jesus will be with the new learners always, in His Spirit, to empower and guide through life and into eternity.

This is how the Church has come to be established and planted all over the world. The disciples of Jesus, while startled that this massive mission was commanded of them, nevertheless took their duty seriously and became emboldened when they came to know the resurrected Jesus. They became empowered by His indwelling Spirit in their lives at Pentecost, ten days after the ascension of Jesus. The greatest outreach program for Jesus Christ ensued as ordinary, garden variety Christians fanned out all over the then known world as heralds and watchmen for Jesus Christ. They took the Great Commission to heart because their hearts burned with passion to share the good news they had experienced.

Luke reports in Acts 8:4 that "those who were scattered went everywhere preaching the word." Ray Stedman referred to these first Christians as "ordinary, plain-vanilla Christians."[1] The Great Commission commands us to be witnesses in the home, the church, the marketplace, the world. We are to focus on the early Church in the book of Acts as our role model.

Jesus set up the ministry of the laity for His Church when He called out disciples to be His learners and sent ones. He charged them with the principles and values of the Kingdom of God in His Sermon on the Mount (Matthew 5-7). After presenting them with the beautiful attitudes of life (beatitudes), Jesus led them to their new priorities and then into a discussion of the problems they would encounter in His work.

In the first of the sermon He told them they were to be "salt" and "light" to the world. In Jesus' time, salt was even more vital to life than it is today. It was the primary means of preventing corrosion and decay. Thus the disciples, and we also, are called to prevent sin and corruption from decaying the spiritual lives and usefulness of people. By being "light," all followers of Jesus are to present Him, the light of the world, who came to dispel the darkness of sin in the lives of all people. Of course, the supreme teaching of Jesus was that we are to love God and all of His created human beings wholeheartedly and unconditionally (Matthew 22:37-40). This is the Great Commandment, and it constitutes the basis for the Great Commission. As with the Great Commission, the great Commandment originated in Genesis 1 and 2 when God decided to create man for relationship, harmony and love.

In the epistles, the apostles explain the seed teachings of Jesus and show us how to apply His precepts to our lives. The epistles present doctrine — that is, what we are to believe — and then application — how we are to assimilate these responsibilities into our lives for right conduct. The writers of the epistles were empowered and inspired by the Holy Spirit to continue the work of the risen Christ through His Church. The epistles teach us that God is a holy God commanding holiness (righteous living) in our lives. These letter writers exhort church members to grow to spiritual maturity and completeness in our knowledge of God, our love of God and our work for God. We are to be a manifestation of God's character, love and purpose on earth for all to see and desire. Paul explained in his letter to the Colossian church that God is looking to His Church to do His work: "Christ in you, the hope of glory. Him we preach, warning every man and teaching every man in all wisdom, that we may present every man perfect in Christ Jesus" (Colossians 1:27,28).

The epistles were written to the members of the church to prepare the people of God to be "the hope of glory" as His ministers, evangelists and sent ones — wherever they go in the world. Paul and Peter are very specific on the ministry of all of God's people.

> Therefore, if anyone is in Christ, he is a new creation; old things have passed away; behold, all things have become new. Now all things are of God, who has reconciled us to Himself through Jesus Christ, and has given us the ministry of reconciliation, that is, that God was in Christ reconciling the world to Himself, not imputing their trespasses to them, and has committed to us the word of reconciliation.
>
> Now then, we are ambassadors for Christ, as though God were pleading through us: we implore you on Christ's behalf, be reconciled to God (2 Corinthians 5:17-20).
>
>   *   *   *   *
>
> You also, as living stones, are being built up a spiritual house, a holy priesthood, to offer up spiritual sacrifices acceptable to God through Jesus Christ....But you are a chosen generation, a royal priesthood, a holy nation, His own special people, that you may proclaim the praises of Him who called you out of darkness into His marvelous light; who once were not a people but are now the people of God, who had not obtained mercy but now have obtained mercy (I Peter 2:5,9,10).

The members of the Church have been saved from darkness to be light bearers and ambassadors to represent Jesus Christ in the world while He is constantly interceding for us with the Father in heaven. The teaching all through the Bible is that created men and women are to be lovers and servants. To be the kind of lovers and servants God requires, we must first be restored to a right relationship with Him by the way He has provided — through faith in Jesus Christ as Lord and Savior. Once that faith step is made, we must enter into a spiritual journey of Christian growth and development in our character (our being) and our works (our doing). The apostle James admonishes that we must "be doers of the word, and not hearers only" (James 1:22). In other words, God desires not spectators but participants.

The two principal means for being conformed to God's image and likeness are the study of God's handbook and being in two-way communication with Him. The Bible, from Genesis 3 forward, is a picture of God restoring, reconciling and redeeming fallen man.

The person alienated from God by habitual sin does not know Him, love Him or serve Him because that person is disabled. What he needs is to be enabled. Thanks to God, man's inability can be met and mastered by God's ability through the indwelling rule in man's life by the Spirit of God.

Paul exclaimed in astonishment that he could not believe that God Almighty had turned around his wicked life to be "a light to the Gentiles" by preaching among all peoples in the world "the unsearchable riches of Christ" (Ephesians 3:8).

Charles Colson is still amazed, but pleased, that God tapped him in the midst of his Watergate experience "to preach deliverance to the captives" (Luke 4:18). I still stand in awe of His use of me to become uncovered for the purpose of exhorting "the old Harry Dents" in the pews to come to life in Christ and to get to work for Christ. The end of redemption is the restoration of broken and marred man to the real image and likeness of God so that we might do His will on earth.

Man chose to defile and darken his completeness. Restored man, however, can become complete in Christ. The end of redemption will be that God's original purpose for His created human beings will be realized. We will be as originally designed: lovers and servants for the glory of God and the good of man.

Dr. George Gallup, Jr., as a Christian layman and public opinion expert, is very concerned about the future of America. He has chronicled his concerns and a challenge in his 1984 book, *Forecast 2000*. His ominous words are similar to those of Ezekiel:

> Just beneath the surface of our society, a great historical tidal wave is on the move — a set of monumental political, social, and economic impulses, which are carrying us relentlessly toward a rendezvous with the future....This movement may come to a terrifying culmination during the next two decades....I've come to feel a deep sense of urgency about the Future Forces at work today.[2]

What are these "Future Forces"? Dr. Gallup's forecast reflects: (1) the nuclear threat, wars and terrorism; (2) overpopulation and hunger; (3) economic pressures such as deficits, inflation and the specter of more and more unemployment; (4) the double-edged sword of technological progress; (5) the environmental emergency; (6) the curse of crime and violence; (7) the faltering family; (8) health problems such as drug abuse, alcohol and smoking; and (9) the pressures of apathy and frustration, especially in public affairs. Dr. Gallup appeals to Americans to face up to these holocausts now, not later. He sees as the key a return to individual commitment that leads to action and perseverance in religion, education and public affairs. He deplores superficiality and nominality in commitment and involvement.

> Clearly, it's necessary for us to go beyond nominal involvement in a church, synagogue, or other religious institution if our spiritual orientation is really to have an impact on the world around us. Just becoming a member of a religious body and attending services doesn't necessarily make a person different from those who don't follow these practices.[3]

In concluding, Dr. Gallup moves to a note of extreme urgency in proposing better education and mature commitment. He believes this will issue in stronger moral and spiritual values, broader education and more volunteerism and involvement in dealing with the potential holocausts. Dr. Gallup has put his finger on the prime problem: lack of individual conviction, commitment and concerted action that rises above self-indulgence.

One of the conflicts we face in our dedication to individualism — and no one has been more of an individualist than I — is balancing individualism with responsibility. We are obligated to God for granting our precious freedoms and to our community and country to maintain them. However in too many cases we want our individualism without any duty. Individualism promotes self-interest and self-worship. It can limit public interest and community, or oneness as a people. It can degenerate to self versus society.

Ours is a society that requires people to be strong and independent. This is good except for those who, for various reasons, may not be able to compete or cope. These are the down-and-outers. Here we as a society — and certainly the Church — must mix a big dose of compassion with our insistence on freedom and individualism. We cannot permit individualism to deteriorate into a form of self-interest which fosters the notion of each man for himself or the survival of the fittest.

The founding fathers of the United States had the difficult task of integrating individualism and freedom with what they saw as the main aim — the public good. For this new system to work, it would be necessary to elect and/or appoint public officials whose personal virtue would cause the officials to put the overall public good above self-interest.

Had not religion played such a strong role in American life, I question that this bold American experiment of a republican form of government elected by a democratic society could have survived for these more than 200 years.

A new study by The Brookings Institution exploring the intertwining of religion and politics in American public life, underscored this truth.

> From the standpoint of the public good, the most important service churches offer to secular life in a free society is to nurture moral values that help humanize capitalism and give direction to democracy.[4]

Alexis de Tocqueville, the distinguished Frenchman who toured the United States in the 1830s, recorded his findings on the American character and our country's devotion to individualism in his classic book, *Democracy in America.* He observed religion's vital influence on individual character and action in the new country. He sensed that religion served as a check on self-interest. It gave expression to the benevolence and self-sacrifice that is necessary to counter self-defeating "selfism": If it feels good, do it. In the Book of Judges, selfism was recorded this way: "Everyone did what was right in his own eyes" (Judges 17:6).

The concern of Dr. Gallup and others is my concern too. Dr. Gallup's polling on religion from 1935-1985 reflects the widespread popularity of religion. Yet these polls indicate wide gaps between belief and commitment and between high religiosity and low ethics, as well as a glaring lack of knowledge, a superficial faith and the failure of organized religion, in part, to make a difference in terms of society's morality and ethics. In addition, fewer people are becoming involved in the public good.

Commitment and involvement are the key principles at the core of Communism, the enemy of Christianity and the forces of freedom. Sacrifice and suffering — a reason for living and dying — undergird the commitment to this godless ideology dedicated to a world diametrically opposed to God's plan.

The eminent writer, Harrison Salisbury, paints a picture of just such a commitment in the long march across China fifty years ago by the late Mao Tse-tung and his sixty-mile-long columns of revolutionaries dedicated to change. In this tortuous trek the stage was set for the later Communist conquest of one quarter of the world's population, isolating them from the change God seeks for all men. By the end of the year-long ordeal, only 4,000 Communists survived out of 86,000 who began the 6,000-mile march.

Salisbury reports in his book, *The Long March: The Untold Story,* that men afflicted with dysentery were reduced to eating their belts and harnesses and even to plucking undigested grains from their companions' feces. Salisbury asserts that "no event in this century has so captured the world's imagination and so profoundly affected its future."[5]

Richard Nixon brilliantly perceived the vital necessity to uncover Communist China and to restore relations with Red China in order to defuse a potentially grave threat to the Western world and Christendom. No foreign policy initiative has been as bold and successful as Nixon's trip to China in 1971.

Nixon's friend Whittaker Chambers wrote his two powerful books, *Witness* and *Cold Friday,* to awaken the Western world and Christendom to a new awareness of the growing menace of world Communism, particularly the Soviet brand which he had served as a covert espionage agent. Chambers embarked on his college studies in 1920 "as a conservative in my view of life and politics, and I was undergoing a religious experience." By the time he left college, he writes: "I was no longer a conservative and I had no religion."[6] This has happened to so many of our young people who are idealists looking for meaning and purpose. They find that the attractive type of all-out commitment offers only a very liberal cause, professing idealistically to help people but without a commitment to God. And young people tell me that they want to help people.

The appeal that caught the heart of young Whittaker Chambers was the Communist cry "to change the world" to help people.

> Their power...is the power to hold convictions and to act on them. It is the same power that moves mountains; it is also an unfailing power to move men. Communists are that part of mankind which has recovered the power to live or die — to bear witness — for its faith. And it is a simple, rational faith that inspires men to live or die for it.[7]

Chambers then points to the teachings of Genesis 3 to warn the world about the real danger posed by this Communist faith:

> It is not new. It is, in fact, man's second oldest faith. Its promise was whispered in the first days of the Creation under the Tree of the Knowledge of Good and Evil. "Ye shall be as gods." It is the great alternative faith of mankind. Like all great faiths, its force derives from a simple vision. Other ages have had great visions. They have always been different versions of the same vision: the vision of God and man's relationship to God. The Communist vision is the vision of Man without God.
>
> It is the vision of man's mind displacing God as the creative intelligence of the world. It is the vision of man's liberated mind, by the sole force of its rational intelligence, redirecting man's destiny and reorganizing man's life and the world. It is the vision of man, once more the central figure of the Creation, not because God

made man in His image, but because man's mind makes him the most intelligent of the animals. Copernicus and his successors displaced man as the central fact of the universe by proving that the earth was not the central star of the universe. Communism restores man to his sovereignty by the simple method of denying God.

The vision is a challenge and implies a threat. It challenges man to prove by his acts that he is the masterwork of the Creation — by making thought and act one. It challenges him to prove it by using the force of his rational mind to end the bloody meaninglessness of man's history — by giving it purpose and a plan. It challenges him to prove it by reducing the meaningless chaos of nature, by imposing on it his rational will to order, abundance, security, peace. It is the vision of materialism.[8]

Chambers declares that every man can find in this vision "the two certainties for which the mind of man tirelessly seeks: a reason to live and a reason to die." He avers that "no other faith of our time presents...the same practical intensity."[9]

I also have been impressed with the eloquent and alarmed writing and speaking of Dr. Os Guinness of Oxford, England. Here is a man who Dr. John Stott told me is a "prophet in our day." I agree! Os Guinness is concerned with the steady dilution of commitment and conviction in the Church today. Dr. Guinness articulates his views in his book, *The Gravedigger File.* He states:

Christianity contributed to the rise of the modern world; Christianity has been molded and undermined by the modern world to which it contributed; Christianity has become, in effect, its own gravedigger. As a European it's amazingly interesting to see that you've never had more money, more positions of influence. Yet the gospel in America is not making the impact it has in the past. The main reason is not because of the philosophical infiltration, although that obviously has played a part. The main answer is the extraordinary cultural subversion of the American Church. In committing herself to American culture the Church in America has become brashly worldly to an extraordinary degree."[10]

His prime challenge to American churches is this: "Don't miss your moment, America!"

Dr. Guinness attributes the cultural subversion of the Church to three factors: (1) Our faith is private, not public — what he calls privatization; (2) our faith is weakened by the increase in choice and change which make us less committed and more superficial — pluralization; and (3) our faith is being subjected to rationalization so that it is being ignored as irrelevant — secularization.

These messages to America and Christendom are the same warnings against the prevailing powers and passions of their day that the Old Testament prophets proclaimed to God's people in Israel and again in exile. Like Ezekiel, all of the prophets were directed to be the watchmen of their day. Their mission was to alert their people, calling them to return to their faith, their promises and their commitment to their nation, to their God, and to their holy mission to be evangelists — all of them. They were to be the "light to the Gentiles" (the other nations) in rolling back the darkness engulfing the souls and hearts of people who had been duped by the original dirty trickster of Genesis 3.

History books testify repeatedly to the basic causes that eventually sound the death knell of powerful and prosperous nations. Invariably the signs are the same that we see in our land today: the disintegration of the family; the mad craze for worldly pleasures and power, leading to sexual promiscuity, more materialism and the escalation of crime and irresponsibility; and a decline in commitment to spiritual authority and values.

People must be challenged and convicted to return, as was the prodigal son, to our Father. We all have the same creator. He has title to us all. For:

> The earth is the LORD's, and all its fullness, the world and those who dwell therein. For He has founded it upon the seas, and established it upon the waters.
> Who may ascend into the hill of the LORD? Or who may stand in His holy place? He who has clean hands and a pure heart, who has not lifted up his soul to an idol, nor sworn deceitfully. He shall receive blessing from the LORD, and righteousness from the God of his salvation (Psalm 24:1-5).

America and Christianity both foster the cherished concept of freedom but in what I now understand to be different ways. I once had my country and my faith wrapped together in a flag — a civil religion. Individualism was one of the principal lords of my life. Now I know the difference in the two proffered freedoms.

In America we virtually have the freedom to do as we wish. This is wonderful, provided that our freedom is balanced by submission to a spiritual governor who controls our lives. I have come to realize that the most vital and fulfilling freedom to come into my life has been the freedom from bondage to the darkness of habitual selfishness and sin. Now, thanks to the grace of God, I have the spiritual vision to discern the true from the false, reality from illusion, light from darkness and good from evil. As I study God's Word more and more, as I talk to God and listen more and more, as I submit to the Spirit of Jesus to change my life more and more, I find that I am just beginning to become an educated man.

The better news is that I know that I can anticipate even more light and understanding in the future. There is no bottom to God's wellspring of wisdom, truth and reality that is available to me and my posterity — and to you and yours. We must live close to God, His Word and His will and purpose for our lives if we are to move the Church from maintenance to mission and ourselves from artificial watchers to authentic watchmen.

You may say, "But being a watchman is too difficult and complex for a person like me. That's for the Billy Grahams of the world." It is true that most people would consider Billy Graham to be a super watchman for God. Yet he is really quite simple in his background, lifestyle, message and approach to his mission. At Amsterdam '83 he shared with thousands of itinerant evangelists his conclusions about certain psychological and spiritual factors that exist in everyone. They are: (1) People have needs beyond the material; (2) there is an essential emptiness in every life without Christ; (3) there is a cosmic loneliness in man; (4) people have a sense of guilt; and (5) people have a common fear of death.

Billy Graham knows from his vast experience that all people are standing in need of the good news. So, he recommends that this theme be presented by all of us with authority, simplicity, repetition and urgency. He says this good news is best communicated by a holy life, by our love of our fellowman, by a compassionate social concern, and by our unity in the Spirit.[11]

Billy Graham is a watchman who gets supernatural results because he lets the Spirit of God work through him to communicate God's provision for man's profound problem.

What about you? Are you interested in being a part of the solution to man's problem rather than being a part of the problem? You can work for God right where you are, beginning in your own home.

CONCLUSION

MAN'S NEED TO LOVE

What the world needs now is love, sweet love; No — not just for some, but for everyone. It's the only thing that there's just too little of.

Hal David and Burt Bacharach[1]

Man has but one hope: the love of God as exemplified in Jesus Christ. A person's biggest need is to be loved; equally as vital is that every person needs to love. The only love that fulfills and sticks to the heart is Jesus' kind of love. It is what Dr. James Dobson calls "tough love." What the world needs today is more "tough love."

God created man and woman to be relational, that is, to have fellowship and live in harmony and peace with Him and with one another. God Himself wants fellowship with each one of us. He initiates this relationship with the very being and essence of Himself — His unconditional and unlimited love.

God is the source of this love, and Jesus on the cross is the proof of God's love. Nowhere in the world is God's love more precisely and beautifully articulated than in the lines penned by Paul in 1 Corinthians 13.

> Though I speak with the tongues of men and angels, but have not love, I have become as sounding brass or a clanging cymbal. And though I have the gift of prophecy, and understand all mysteries and all knowledge, and though I have all faith, so that I could remove mountains, but have not love, I am nothing. And though I bestow all my goods to feed the poor, and though I give my body to be burned, but have not love, it profits me nothing.
>
> Love suffers long and is kind; love does not envy; love does not parade itself, is not puffed up; does not behave rudely, does not seek its own, is not provoked, thinks no evil; does not rejoice in iniquity, but rejoices in the truth; bears all things, believes all things, hopes all things, endures all things.

> Love never fails. But whether there are prophecies, they will fail;
> whether there are tongues, they will cease; whether there is knowl-
> edge, it will vanish away. For we know in part and we prophesy in
> part. But when that which is perfect has come, then that which is
> in part will be done away.
>
> When I was a child, I spoke as a child, I understood as a child,
> I thought as a child; but when I became a man, I put away childish
> things. For now we see in a mirror, dimly, but then face to face.
> Now I know in part, but then I shall know just as I also am known.
>
> And now abide faith, hope, love, these three; but the greatest
> of these is love.

The late Henry Drummond is credited with providing one of the best commentaries on Paul's love masterpiece. He wrote in *The Greatest Thing in the World* that in verses 4-7 Paul "passes this thing, love, through the magnificent prism of his inspired intellect, and it comes out on the other side [like light] broken up into its elements."[2] These elements Drummond called the spectrum of love, the analysis of love. They are patience, kindness, generosity, humility, courtesy, unselfishness, good temper, guiless-ness and sincerity. They amount to the fruit of the Spirit.

We are to pass the hard questions of life through the prism of God's love and then look for the answers in the spectrum or perspective of this unique love that comprises the very being of God. What a difference this approach would have made during Watergate! What a difference this approach can make in your life!

Paul tells us in his letter to the Galatians that love is the core fruit of the Holy Spirit in building Christian character. All the other types of fruit grow out of "the greatest of these" — "love" (Galatians 5:22,23).

As with Paul, Peter also stresses love, "above all things" as the *summum bonum,* the supreme good, "for love will cover a multitude of sins" (1 Peter 4:8). The apostle John has written the most verses in the Bible on God's love. One explanation is in 1 John 4:7- 20.

> Beloved, let us love one another, for love is of God; and everyone
> who loves is born of God and knows God. He who does not love
> does not know God, for God is love. In this the love of God was
> manifested toward us, that God has sent His only begotten Son
> into the world, that we might live through Him. In this is love, not
> that we loved God, but that He loved us and sent His Son to be
> the propitiation for our sins. Beloved, if God so loved us, we also
> ought to love one another.
>
> No one has seen God at any time. If we love one another, God
> abides in us, and His love has been perfected in us. By this we
> know that we abide in Him, and He in us, because He has given

us of His Spirit. And we have seen and testify that the Father has sent the Son as Savior of the world. Whoever confesses that Jesus is the Son of God, God abides in him, and he in God. And we have known and believed the love that God has for us. God is love, and he who abides in love abides in God, and God in him.

Love has been perfected among us in this: that we may have boldness in the day of judgment; because as He is, so are we in this world. There is no fear in love; but perfect love casts out fear, because fear involves torment. But he who fears has not been made perfect in love. We love Him because He first loved us.

If someone says, "I love God," and hates his brother, he is a liar; for he who does not love his brother whom he has seen, how can he love God whom he has not seen?

John emphasizes that we ought to love God and one another "because He first loved us." How? In creating us, in sacrificing His Son for our sins, in giving us the comfort and power of His Spirit and so many more blessings.

Jesus is our role model for love, not just in giving His life on the cross, but also in all of His teachings. One of the most meaningful and instructive prayers in the Bible is Jesus' final petition to the Father in the Garden of Gethsemane. There He prayed for love and unity among His people. He prayed for Himself, His disciples and finally for all of us today with these words:

I do not pray for these alone, but also for those who will believe in Me through their word; that they all may be one, as You, Father, are in Me, and I in You; that they also may be one in Us, that the world may believe that You sent Me. And the glory which You gave Me I have given them, that they may be one just as We are one: I in them, and You in Me; that they may be made perfect in one, and that the world may know that You have sent Me, and have loved them as You have loved Me.

Father, I desire that they also whom You gave Me may be with Me where I am, that they may behold My glory which You have given Me; for You loved Me before the foundation of the world. O righteous Father! The world has not known You, but I have known You; and these have known that You sent Me. And I have declared to them Your name, and will declare it, that the love with which You loved Me may be in them, and I in them (John 17:20-26).

If there is one basic credential for Christians, it is love. Jesus commanded that this be the mark of every follower as He was announcing His departure at the Last Supper (see John 13:34,35). Jesus knew that only God's love can produce the peace, unity and harmony that God intends as a remedy for the brokenness of this world. What is the essence of this love of God? The love of God is selflessness. It is nothing less than the very life and character of God, for, as John tells us, "God is love." God's love is the brick and mortar for repairing and building bridges of relationship between people, races and nations. We are called to build where there is no relationship, no understanding, no compassion, no selflessness, no love, no hope.

We can get only so far in healing and restoring the many broken relationships in the world through the use of government handouts, diplomacy, conciliation, politics and man's kind of love. The problem with all of these approaches is that they are not pure, transparent, unlimited or eternal. Man's kind of love — the philial and erotic types — is limited and must be earned in some way. Also, it can fade, or it can be feigned. It can be turned on and off, and it can turn into love's opposite, hate. In diplomacy and politics there is hardly a move without some hidden agenda. I found in my experiences that the end all too often is, "What's in it for me and my side?"

With God's love, there is no secret agenda, no injustice, no *quid pro quo,* no temporalness. Love is all up front and out in the open and forever. For all of us on earth "love is the greatest of these" because love is the best way we can demonstrate what and why we believe. It is the only grace that can be understood by anyone and communicated to any person anywhere in the world. The secret to knowing how to love lies in being possessed by God's love in a new two-way relationship — vertically with God and then horizontally with our families, friends, neighbors, business associates — even with our enemies.

One of today's greatest illustrations of God's kind of love is focused in the 1979 Nobel Laureate winner Mother Teresa. Her life is one of selfless devotion to the needy people in the filthy and disease-ridden streets of Calcutta, India. It was the experience of seeing this godly little saint at work binding up the wounds and hurts of helpless humanity that God used to transform the life of noted writer and non-believer, Malcolm Muggeridge of London, into a great apologist for Christianity. In his book, *Something Beautiful for God,* Muggeridge tells of the difference he saw between his life and values and those of Mother Teresa:

> It was a scene of inconceivable confusion and horror, with patients stretched out on the floor, in the corridors, everywhere. While I was waiting, a man was brought in who had just cut his throat from ear to ear. It was too much; I made off, back to my comfortable flat and a stiff whiskey and soda, to expatiate through the years to come on Bengal's wretched social conditions, and what a scandal it was, and how it was greatly to be hoped that the competent

authorities would...and so on.

I ran away and stayed away; Mother Teresa moved in and stayed. That was the difference....

I never experienced so perfect a sense of human equality as with Mother Teresa among her poor. Her love for them, reflecting God's love, makes them equal, as brothers and sisters within a family are equal, however widely they differ in intellectual and other attainments, in physical beauty and grace.[3]

Dr. Earl Palmer cites Muggeridge's comment to show the difference between God's love and man's love.

Agape love moves into tough situations and stays. Agape love has justice, righteousness, and truth in it. It is not frightened off by the worst kind of human sin or need; it is not afraid of the deepest of human crises.[4]

One of the grand side benefits of God's love (called *agape* in the New Testament Greek language) is that instead of ruling out all other loves, *agape* enriches and re-directs the love of man to the source of all love, God the Father. It is also the basis of our good works for the glory of God and the good of man.

The concerns I have expressed in this book can be lessened and substantially resolved if we heed and appropriate the answer God has provided in the love of Jesus Christ. In love the Father created us. In love He pursues us. In love He saves us. In love He will restore the hearts, hurts and brokenness of humanity in the Watergates of life. For, the greatest solution for running the race of life is *L-O-V-E*, Jesus' kind of love.

In current literature I have found no better definition of this special love of God than in *Concentric Circles of Concern* by the late Professor W. Oscar Thompson, Jr.

Love is
NOT a word of emotion,
NOT a word of feeling.

Rather, love is
A word of reason,
A word of volition or will,
A word of action,
Love is doing!

Love *builds* relationships;
Love *maintains* relationships;
Love *fulfills* relationships;
Love *initiates* relationships.

Love is meeting needs![5]

In concluding his memoirs on his time in the White House and in suffering through his Watergate experience, John Ehrlichman confessed to committing marital infidelity. The transgression came during his second trial.

> I was telling myself I had no marriage in terms that I couldn't blink away. I was also responding to someone who was willing to say, "Regardless of what they are saying about you in the papers or in court or behind your back, I will take you into my arms." I needed that.[6]

When I visited John in 1985, I referred to this notation in his book. I likened the incident to a desire for unconditional love. He agreed.

I believe that today John knows where this kind of love can best be found — in Jesus Christ.

Are you prepared to meet the Watergates of your life, or do you need, as did John Ehrlichman, to burn down to ground zero to find the answer?

The choice is yours; God designed you to be able to make choices in this life and to be accountable for your choices. We have the privilege of choosing what "footprints we will make in the sands of time." We can choose to make these footprints by ourselves or with the help of Almighty God. I heard President Ronald Reagan proclaim at the 1982 National Prayer Breakfast that it is better to make the footprints with God's help. He said he learned this for certain in 1981 when the assassin's bullet caused him to realize that "God was carrying me on His shoulders." Because of his brush with eternity, the President promised, to the top leadership of Washington and to God, "the rest of my life belongs to Him."

If you will permit Him, our Lord would like to help you make the right choices and to love unconditionally. He will do this not only because we must choose to love, but also because God made that choice to be love for our sakes "before the foundation of the world" (Ephesians 1:4).

Serving and loving are the only ways man can find true meaning and fulfillment in this life. God created us for this purpose as He fashioned us in His own image and likeness — to be with Him in right relationship and like Him in character. For most of my life I lived with a gnawing sense of emptiness and incompleteness despite successes. Why? Because I did not have a "wide open" heart as Paul commands us to have in 2 Corinthians 6:13. Today I know the difference between incompleteness and completeness. I am uncovered and open for Christ and thus loving and serving Him because of His work in me. This same gift is available to you.

> For in Him dwells all the fullness of the Godhead bodily; and you are complete in Him, who is the head of all principality and power (Colossians 2:9,10).

GOD MOVES IN A MYSTERIOUS WAY

God moves in a mysterious way
   His wonders to perform;
He plants His footsteps in the sea,
   And rides upon the storm.

Deep in unfathomable mines
   Of never-failing skill,
He treasures up His bright design,
   And works His sovereign will.

Ye fearful saints, fresh courage take
   The clouds ye so much dread
Are big with mercy, and will break
   In blessings on your head.

Judge not the Lord by feeble sense,
   But trust Him for His grace;
Behind a frowning providence
   He hides a smiling face.

His purposes will ripen fast,
   Unfolding every hour;
The bud may have a bitter taste,
   But sweet will be the flower.

Blind unbelief is sure to err,
   And scan His work in vain;
God is His own interpreter,
   And He will make it plain.

— William Cowper[7]

NOTES

Preface:
1. George Bernard Shaw, *Heartbreak House* (New York, Penguin Books, Inc., 1965), preface (quoting Hegel).

Chapter I:
1. Henry Wadsworth Longfellow, "Retribution."
2. Richard M. Nixon, *RN: The Memoirs of Richard Nixon* (New York, Grossett & Dunlap, Inc., 1978), p. 872.
3. Jeb Stuart Magruder, *An American Life: One Man's Road to Watergate* (New York, Atheneum, 1974), pp. 195-97.
4. G. Gordon Liddy, *Will: the Autobiography of G. Gordon Liddy* (New York, St. Martin's Press, 1980).
5. Ibid., pp. 219-20.
6. Michael Drosnin, *Citizen Hughes,* (New York, Holt, Rinehart & Winston, Inc., A Bantam Book, 1985), p. 45.
7. Liddy, *Will,* pp. 236-37.
8. Ibid., p. 237.
9. Ibid., p. 244.
10. Ibid., pp. 244-45.
11. Charles W. Colson, *Who Speaks for God,* (Westchester, IL, Crossway Books, Good News Publishers, 1985), p. 48.

Chapter II:
1. A. W. Tozer, *The Pursuit of God* (Harrisburg, PA, Christian Publications, Inc., 1948), p. 11.
2. Ibid., p. 47.
3. Ibid., p. 46.
4. Ibid., p. 52.
5. Earl Jabay, *The God Players* (Grand Rapids, Zondervan Publishing House, 1970), p. 17.

Chapter III
1. Viktor E. Frankl, *Man's Search for Meaning* (New York, Simon & Schuster, Pocket Books Division, 1984), p. 191.
2. Theodore H. Epp, *The God of Creation,* (Lincoln, NE, Back to the Bible Broadcast, 1972), p. 98.
3. John Ehrlichman, *Witness to Power: The Nixon Years* (New York, Simon & Schuster, 1982), pp. 412, 414, 416-17.
4. Bob Woodward and Carl Bernstein, *The Final Days* (New York, Simon & Schuster, Inc., 1976), pp. 422-23.
5. Ibid., p. 424.
6. Ibid.
7. Jeb Stuart Magruder, *An American Life: One Man's Road to Watergate* (New York, Atheneum, 1974), pp. 286-87.

Chapter IV:
1. Ray Stedman, *Understanding Man* (Waco, TX, Word Books, 1975), p. 32.
2. From a talk given by Richard Halverson at Asheville, North Carolina, in July, 1984.
3. Hannah Whitall Smith, *Everyday Religion* (originally published in 1893 by Fleming H. Revell), p. 72.
4. Edward J. Young, *Genesis 3* (London, The Banner of Truth Trust, 1966), p. 108.
5. Ibid., pp. 109-10.

Chapter V:
1. C. S. Lewis, *The Screwtape Letters* (New York, Macmillan Publishing Co., 1961), p. 3.
2. M. Scott Peck, *People of the Lie* (New York, Simon & Schuster, 1983), pp. 182-84).
3. Richard Lovelace, *Dynamics of Spiritual Life* (Downers Grove, IL, InterVarsity Press, 1979), p. 18.
4. Jeb Stuart Magruder, *An American Life: One Man's Road to Watergate* (New York, Atheneum, 1974), p. 220.
5. Sissela Bok, *Lying* (New York, Pantheon Books, 1978), p. 242.
6. Ray Stedman, *Understanding Man* (Waco, TX, Word Books, 1975), p. 71.
Chapter VI:
1. Theodore Epp, *The God of Creation* (Lincoln, NE, Back to the Bible Broadcast, 1972), p. 101.
2. Ibid., pp. 102-03.
3. G. Gordon Liddy, *Will: the Autobiography of G. Gordon Liddy* (New York, St. Martin's Press, 1980), p. 246.
4. Gordon Liddy as quoted in *The Columbia* (South Carolina) *Record* (November 6, 1985).
5. Madeleine Edmondsun, *The Women of Watergate* (New York, Stein & Day, 1975), pp. 30-31.
6. Winzola McClendon, *Martha: The Life of Martha Mitchell* (New York, Random House, 1979), pp. 204-5.
7. Ibid., p. 232.
8. Ibid., pp. 30-37, 63.
9. Ibid, p. 177.
10. John Dean, *Blind Ambition: The Whitehouse Years* (New York, Simon & Schuster, 1976), pp. 216-17.
11. Charles W. Colson, *Life Sentence* (Lincoln, VA, Chosen Books, 1979), p. 206.
12. Jim Hougan, *Secret Agenda: Watergate, Deep Throat and the CIA* (New York, Random House, 1984), p. 59.
13. Julie Nixon Eisenhower, *Special People* (New York, Simon & Schuster, 1977), p. 11.
14. Ibid., p. 69.
15. Ibid., p. 148.
16. Ibid., pp. 77, 79.
Chapter VII:
1. Sam Ervin, *The Whole Truth: The Watergate Conspiracy* (New York, Random House, 1980), p. 310.
2. Jeb Stuart Magruder, *An American Life: One Man's Road to Watergate* (New York, Atheneum, 1974), pp. 316-17.
3. Anthony Campolo, Jr., *The Power of Delusion* (Wheaton, IL, Victor Books, 1983), p. 11.
4. Thomas J. Peters and Robert H. Waterman, *In Search of Excellence* (New York, Harper & Row Publishers, Inc., 1982), pp. 156-99.
5. Richard J. Foster, *Money, Sex and Power: The Challenge of the Disciplined Life* (New York, Harper & Row Publishers, Inc., 1985), pp. 196, 201.
6. Esther Milner, *The Failure of Success: The Middle Class Crisis* (St. Louis, Warren, Green, Inc., 1968), p. 23.
7. Anthony Campolo, Jr., *The Success Fantasy* (Wheaton, IL, Victor Books, 1980), p. 9.
8. Ibid., p. 15.
9. Ibid., p. 17.
10. Albert Speer, *Inside the Third Reich: Memoirs of Albert Speer,* translated by Richard and Clara Winston (New York, Macmillian Publishing Company, 1970).

11. Ibid., p. 127.
12. Ibid., pp. 92-93.
13. Ibid., p. 644.
14. Nixon, quoted by John Ehrlichman in *Witness to Power: The Nixon Years* (New York, Simon & Schuster, 1982), p. 267.
15. Ibid., p. 411.

Chapter VIII:
1. J. Grant Howard, *The Trauma of Transparency: A Biblical Approach to Inter-Personal Communication* (Portland, OR, Multnomah Press, 1979), p. 27.
2. Gordon MacDonald, *Ordering Your Private World* (Nashville, Thomas Nelson, 1985), pp. 8-9.
3. Charles R. Swindoll, *Dropping Your Guard* (Waco, TX, Word Books, 1983), pp. 9-10.
4. Howard, *Transparency,* p. 198.
5. Larry Crabb, *The Marriage Builder: A Blueprint for Couples and Counselors* (Grand Rapids, Zondervan Publishing House, 1982), pp. 19-20.
6. Larry Crabb, *Encouragement: The Key to Caring* (Grand Rapids, Zondervan Publishing House, 1984), pp. 39-45.
7. Ibid., p. 32.
8. Ibid., pp. 71-73.

Chapter IX:
1. Thomas Carlyle, quoted in *The Encyclopedia of Religious Quotations,* ed. Frank S. Mead (New York, Pillar Books for Revell, 1976) p. 605.
2. M. Scott Peck, *People of the Lie* (New York, Simon & Schuster, 1983), pp. 73-77.
3. John Ehrlichman, *Witness to Power: The Nixon Years* (New York, Simon & Schuster, 1982), pp. 371-72.
4. Ibid., p. 372.
5. Jeb Stuart Magruder, *An American Life: One Man's Road to Watergate* (New York, Atheneum, 1974), p. 284.
6. G. Gordon Liddy, *Will: the Autobiography of G. Gordon Liddy* (New York, St. Martin's Press, 1980), p. 293.
7. Jim Hougan, *Secret Agenda: Watergate, Deep Throat and the CIA* (New York, Random House, 1984), pp. 22-26.
8. Magruder, *American Life,* p. 284.
9. James W. McCord, Jr., *A Piece of Tape* (Rockville, MD, Washington Media Services, Ltd., 1974).
10. Hougan, *Agenda,* p. 24.
11. Ibid., pp. 24-25 (quoting McCord).
12. McCord, *Tape,* p. 60.
13. Hougan, *Agenda,* pp. 22-23.
14. John Dean, *Blind Amibition: The Whitehouse Years* (New York, Simon & Schuster, 1976), p. 177.
15. David Halberstam, *The Powers That Be* (New York, Alfred A. Knopf, 1979), p. 689.
16. Ibid., pp. 690-92.
17. Dean, *Ambition,* p. 359.
18. James Engle and H. Wilbert Norton, *What's Gone Wrong With the Harvest?* (Grand Rapids, Zondervan Publishing House, 1975), pp. 27, 36.
19. T. S. Eliot quoted in *Growing Strong in the Seasons of Life* by Charles Swindoll (Portland, OR, Multnomah Press, 1983), p. 350.
20. Ibid.
21. M. Scott Peck, *The Road Less Traveled* (New York, Touchstone Books, Simon & Schuster, 1979), pp. 44-45.
22. Ibid., p. 45.

23. Ehrlichman, *Witness,* p. 416.
24. Lawrence O. Richards, *Creative Bible Study* (Grand Rapids, Zondervan Publishing House, 1979), p. 127.
25. Ibid., pp. 98-99.

Chapter X:
1. Benjamin Franklin, "Sayings of Poor Richard" from *Poor Richard's Almanack.*
2. John R. W. Stott, *Between Two Worlds: The Art of Preaching in the Twentieth-Century* (Grand Rapids, Wm. B. Eerdmans Publishing Co., 1982), pp. 51,57.
3. Edward J. Young, *Genesis 3* (London, The Banner of Truth Trust, 1966), p. 95.
4. Charles R. Swindoll, *Dropping Your Guard* (Waco, TX, Word Books, 1983), p. 172.
5. C. S. Lewis quoted in *Growing Strong in the Seasons of Life* by Charles Swindoll (Portland, OR, Multnomah Press, 1983), p. 353.

Chapter XI:
1. Martin Luther, quoted in The Encyclopedia of Religious Quotations, ed. Frank S. Mead (New York, Pillar Books for Revell, 1976), p. 607.
2. Charles W. Colson, *Born Again* (Old Tappan, NJ, Chosen Books, Inc., dist. by Fleming H. Revell Co., 1976), pp. 109-10.
3. Ibid., p. 111.
4. Ibid., p. 112.
5. C. S. Lewis, *Mere Christianity* (New York, The Macmillan Company, 1960), pp. 94,97.
6. Colson, *Born Again,* pp. 114-15.
7. Ibid., pp. 115-16.
8. Ibid., pp. 116-17.
9. Jeb Stuart Magruder, *From Power to Peace* (Waco, TX, Word Books, 1978), p. 66.
10. Ibid., pp. 64-78.
11. Ibid., pp. 69-71.
12. Ibid., p. 88.
13. Ibid., p. 208.
14. Ibid., pp. 211-12.
15. Alexander Solzhenitsyn quoted by Kitty Muggeridge in *Gazing on Truth* (First published in 1975 by Triangle, SPCC, London. U. S. Edition by Wm. B. Eerdmands Publishing Co., Grand Rapids, 1985), p. 61.

Chapter XII:
1. Leroy Eims, *The Lost Art of Disciple Making* (Colorado Springs, Nav Press, 1978).
2. Charles W. Colson, *Life Sentence* (Lincoln, VA, Chosen Books, 1979), p. 9.
3. Ibid., p. 10.
4. Charles W. Colson, *Loving God* (Grand Rapids, Zondervan Publishing House, 1983), pp. 37-38.
5. Ibid., p. 127.
6. Ibid., pp. 178-80.
7. M. Scott Peck, *The Road Less Traveled* (New York, Touchstone Books, Simon & Schuster, 1979), p. 283.
8. Ibid., p. 302.
9. Ibid., pp. 304-5.

Chapter XIII:
1. Rudyard Kippling, from "If," *The Best Loved Poems of the American People,* selected by Hazel Felleman (Garden City, N.Y., Garden City Books, © 1936 by Doubleday & Co., Inc.), p. 65.
2. Howard Fineman, "Nixon: The Comeback Kid," *Newsweek* (October 28, 1985), p. 45.
3. Charleston, South Carolina, *News and Courier* (September 5, 1985), p. 6-C.

4. Jules Witcover, *The Resurrection of Richard Nixon* (New York, G. T. Putnam's Sons, 1962), p. 11.
5. Ibid., p. 20.
6. Ibid., p. 22.
7. Ibid., p. 32.
8. Ibid., p. 33.
9. Charles W. Colson, *Born Again* (Chosen Books, Inc., dist. by Fleming H. Revell Co., Old Tappan, NJ, 1976), p. 183.
10. Ibid., p. 183.
11. Ibid., pp. 183-84.
12. Richard M. Nixon, *RN: The Memoirs of Richard Nixon* (New York, Grossett & Dunlap, Inc., 1978), p. 13.
13. Ibid., pp. 13-14.
14. Ibid., p. 16.
15. Ibid., p. 21.
16. Bob Woodward and Carl Bernstein, *The Final Days* (New York, Simon & Schuster, 1976), p. 23.
17. Ibid., p. 25.
18. Leon Jaworski, *The Right and the Power: The Prosecution of Watergate* (Reader's Digest Press, Houston: Gulf Publishing Company, 1976), p. 272.
19. Ibid., p. 272.
20. Nixon, *Memoirs,* pp. 901-3
21. Woodward and Bernstein, *Final Days,* p. 309
22. Nixon, *Memoirs,* p. 1057
23. Ibid., p. 1074
24. Ibid., p. 1077
25. Ibid., p 1080.
26. Jaworoski, *Right,* p. 248.
27. Anthony Lewis, *End of a Presidency* (New York, Holt, Rinehart & Winston, 1973), p. 87.

Chapter XIV:
1. John R. W. Scott, "What Makes Leadership Christian?" *Christianity Today* (August 9, 1985, p. 26.
2. Richard M. Nixon, *Leaders* (New York, Warner Books, 1982), p. 3.
3. Ibid., p. 2.
4. Ibid., pp. 4-5.
5. Ibid., p. 39.
6. Ibid., p. 7.
7. Ibid., pp. 38-39.
8. Cyril J. Barber, *Nehemiah and the Dynamics of Effective Leadership* (Neptune, NJ, Loizeaux Brothers, 1980), pp. 179-81.
9. Marshall Frady, *Billy Graham: A Parable of American Righteousness* (Boston/Toronto, Little, Brown & Co., 1979, p. 322.
10. *George W. Truett Library,* four volumes (Nashville, Broadman, 1980), p. 266.

Chapter XV:
1. Ray Stedman, *Birth of the Body* (Santa Ana, CA, Vision House Publishers, 1974), p. 132.
2. George Gallup, Jr., *Forecast 2000* (New York, William Morrow & Co., Inc., 1984), pp. 11-12.
3. Ibid., pp. 153-54.
4. A. James Reichley, *Religion in American Public Life* (Washington, D.C., The Brookings Institution, 1985), p. 359.
5. Harrison Salisbury, *The Long march: The Untold Story* (New York, Harper & Row, 1985), quoted in "Step by Bloody Step," *Newsweek* (October 14, 1985), p. 87.

6. Whittaker Chambers, *Witness* (New York, Random House, 1952), p. 164.
7. Ibid., p. 9.
8. Ibid., pp. 9-10.
9. Ibid., p. 11.
10. Os Guiness, from a talk at Columbia Bible College in 1984.
11. Billy Graham quoted in article on Amsterdam '83 in *Christianity Today* (September 2, l983), pp. 28-31.

Conclusion:
1. Hal David and Burt Bacharach, "What the World Needs Now" (Los Angeles, CA, Blue Seas Music Publishers & Jac Music, Inc., 1965). Lyric by Hal David; music by Burt Bacharach. Copyright © 1965 Blue Seas Music, Inc. and Jac Music Company, Inc. International copyright secured. Made in USA. All rights reserved.
2. Henry Drummond, *The Greatest Thing in the World* (Westwood, NJ, Fleming H. Revell Company, 1968), p. 26.
3. Malcolm Muggeridge, *Something Beautiful for God* (New York and London, Harper & Row Publishers, 1971), pp. 22-23.
4. Earl Palmer, *Love Has Its Reasons* (Waco, TX, Word Books, 1977), pp. 91-92.
5. Oscar W. Thompson, Jr., poem in *Concentric Circles of Love* (Nashville, Broadman, 1981), p. 101.
6. John Ehrlichman, *Witness to Power: The Nixon Years* (New York, Simon & Schuster, 1982), p. 413.
7. William Cowper, "God Moves in a Mysterious Way," quoted by Robert Foster in *A Challenge to Men From Ecclesiastes* (Colorado Springs, CO, Challenge Books, LTD., n.d.), p. 28.